MAZZINI AND THE SECRET SOCIETIES

By the same Author

PIO NONO

Giuseppe Mazzini, Triumvir of the Roman Republic, 1849.
From an engraving at the Museo Centrale del Risorgimento
at Rome, made from a portrait by Mazzini's friend, Emily
Ashurst Venturi.

MAZZINI
AND THE SECRET SOCIETIES

The Making of a Myth

by

E. E. Y. HALES

P. J. KENEDY & SONS
New York

THE AUTHOR

E. E. Y. Hales was born at Nottingham, England, in 1908. At the age of 21 he gained first class honors in the school of modern history at Oxford, and the following year was appointed an instructor in the history department of Yale University. At Yale's Sterling Library he continued his researches into the Italian Risorgimento begun at the British Museum in London. In 1939 he was appointed to a post as H.M. Inspector of Schools in England, and in 1945, was made Staff Inspector of History there. Receiving a Carnegie International Fellowship in 1949, he returned for three months to the United States to study education for international understanding in American colleges and schools. Throughout these years Mr. Hales' study of Italian history continued at intervals in Rome, in Florence, and in Genoa, as well as in London.

To the Memory of G. F.-H. Berkeley
and to Mrs. Berkeley
historians of the Italian Risorgimento
in gratitude and affection

ACKNOWLEDGEMENT

I would like to express my thanks to Mr. D. Mack Smith, of Peterhouse, Cambridge, whose generous help on any aspect of the Italian Risorgimento has always been forthcoming and is always illuminating; to Mr. Derek Beales, of Sidney Sussex College, Cambridge, and to Mr. Charles Baty, for helpful criticism of the text; and to Mr. G. O. Griffith who patiently discussed Mazzinian theology with me. Amongst the many Italian scholars who have shown me kindness and given me help I would like to thank in particular Professor A. M. Ghisalberti and Dr. Emilia Morelli, of the *Istituto per la storia del Risorgimento* in Rome, Professor A. Codignola of the *Istituto Mazziniano* at Genoa, and the Avvocato A. G. Garrone at Turin; also Professor Gaetano Salvemini who, many years ago, assisted my studies at Yale University. The responsibility for what I have said remains, of course, my own.

E.E.Y.H.

CONTENTS

ILLUSTRATIONS

Giuseppe Mazzini, Triumvir of the Roman Republic, 1849. From an engraving at the Museo Centrale del Risorgimento at Rome, made from a portrait by Mazzini's friend, Emily Ashurst Venturi.   *Frontispiece*

The drawings by G. Mantegazza
are taken from *La Vita di Giuseppe
Mazzini* by Jessie White Mario by
permission of the publishers, Casa
Editrice Sonzogno of Milan.

MAPS

INTRODUCTION

Only one serious study of Mazzini in English (that by Bolton King) has appeared without any attempt by the author to explain, in a descriptive clause, within the title, what he regarded as the significance of his hero. To glance at these titles is thus one way to appreciate the impact of the Italian upon the English-speaking world. From it we discover that Mazzini was "A Great Italian", "Patriot and Prophet", "The Greatest Prophet of Modern Democracy", and "Prophet of Modern Europe".[1]

If we turn to Italian studies another and a longer list can, of course, be made. But it will suffice to notice what is most characteristic about Italian descriptions of Mazzini, namely the repetition of the epithets *Il Profeta, Il Santo, Il Grande, Il Nostro*. Of these the first is the commonest, and, since it is also the word which occurs most frequently in the English clauses, we may fairly conclude that Italy, Britain and the United States are agreed in regarding Mazzini first and foremost as a prophet. It is true that some of Mazzini's greatest Italian critics have had their doubts, de Sanctis insisting upon rejecting the title of prophet and calling him rather a precursor, and Professor Gaetano Salvemini emphasizing the grave limitations to Mazzini's understanding of the Italian genius and destiny. But there can be no doubt what has been the popular verdict, and it was one which found wide echo when President Wilson and Lloyd George redrew the map of Europe in 1919 in accordance with principles which bore a more than passing resemblance to those Mazzini had taught.

It is, however, a danger with prophets of established reputation, like Mazzini, that everything is seen as originating in their fertile minds; one has only to compare the conflicting movements and ideas which have been fathered upon Jean-Jacques Rousseau. At each turn in the fortunes of their country Italians have looked back to *Il Nostro* and have sought to reassure themselves in what they proposed to do by finding his approval; and

[1] These words were written before the announcement of the English edition of Professor Gaetano Salvemini's *Mazzini* (Catania, 1915) promised by Jonathan Cape.

since he wrote so much, and taught so many things, this approval has not generally been found to be lacking. There was much, for instance, that he had said which seemed to justify the violent anti-clerical policies of Nicotera or Depretis after the victory of the Left in Italian politics in 1876; nor was it altogether surprising that Mussolini, with his emphasis upon national mission, sacrifice, duty and the rest, should insist upon placing Mazzini amongst the forerunners of Fascism. But today, in a special sense, Mazzini emerges in Italy as the true prophet because, outwardly at least, the very ideal for which he suffered for so long seems to have been attained, the voice of the people having rejected the monarchy he so detested and having established in its place the republic which he preached.

The serious work of Mazzinian criticism in Italy may be said to have been begun around the turn of the century by Alessandro Luzio, Gaetano Salvemini and F. L. Mannucci, and it has been carried forward more recently by a host of writers, amongst them Arturo Codignola, Luigi Salvatorelli and Emilia Morelli. But even more important has been the work of the Italian National Commission which, since the year 1905, has been editing his collected writings. It has now published its hundredth quarto-size volume, and there are more to come. It would be hard to find a parallel, in any country, to the scholarship and industry which, inspired first by the zeal of M. Menghini, have now for fifty years been lavished upon this vast undertaking. Yet no less an effort was needed if a comprehensive edition was to be made, for Mazzini probably wrote some fifty thousand letters, of which some ten thousand have been found; he wrote in a microscopic hand; he generally did not date his letters; and he was seldom in a position to give his address. Moreover many of his published writings were anonymous, and cannot always be identified with certainty, and they often appeared in ephemeral journals which enjoyed only a hidden existence before being suppressed by the police, and are difficult, today, to trace. When the edition was undertaken, in the year 1905, the centenary of Mazzini's birth, it was known that the task of the editors would be formidable; the undertaking of it and the way in which it has been carried out are one testimony to the way in which Italians feel about their prophet.

This National Edition, by collecting together so large a quantity of Mazzini's letters, has made it possible to reconstruct his life, in some degree of detail, even though he spent much of it in hiding. But I have here confined myself to trying to portray the earlier part of it, the part before his exile in England. It is the part least known to English readers, but it was the creative, and in that sense the decisive part, the part in which he was actively engaged, day and night, in the work of the secret societies, when he served the Carbonari, made Young Italy and tried to launch Young Europe. It was also the period of his life when he evolved the faith from which he never departed. It ended in January 1837, when Mazzini, still only thirty-one years old, went into exile in England and so for a decade was cut off from continuing, in any direct way, his labours as a revolutionary. But, before it ended, the myth of him had been made, he had become a legend in Italy and in Europe, so that, when the conflagration broke out eleven years later, in 1848–49, it was Mazzini, the Roman revolutionaries instinctively felt, who must replace the Pope at Rome. This single fact is the most remarkable testimony to what he had been and what he had done before the year 1837. We have his own bitter word for it that his association, Young Italy, was dead, as an active society, after that year. We know too that, after reaching distant and indifferent London, he was reduced to writing literary criticism, for pitiful payments, to keep body and soul together. Yet he had only to reappear in Italy, in 1848, to be hailed at Milan and at Florence and to be summoned to Rome and appointed Chief Triumvir there.

It is important, then, to try to see him as closely as we can in this early period, which is called his apostolate. And the only way to do this is to meet him in his letters and amongst his friends and to see what he was trying to do as well as what he was teaching. Italian scholarship has now made this possible, and the proportions which Mazzini has come to assume in our historical thinking have made it necessary. And if this closer view suggests that Mazzini was human, even very human, that will be disillusioning only to those who have sought to make an idol of him. His peculiar fascination is only enhanced by closer acquaintance with his reckless generosity, his wild impatience, his sympathy, his rigid, doctrinaire constancy, his affections, his furies, his chimerical plots, his despairs, his obstinacy, and even his rare but terrifying doubts. It was thus that his fellow revolutionaries knew him and it was from this knowledge that they made his myth.

I have tried not to separate too sharply Mazzini's teaching and his life – what he called *pensiero ed azione* – because he himself did not do so. But I have given preference to his life because I think it was more important, being sacrificial, and so giving power to what he had to say. I have also 'separated off' his dogmatic teaching, what may reasonably be called his theology, and have discussed it at the end, in a separate chapter. To many it will be wearisome, and they can thus conveniently avoid it; to others it will seem, as it seemed to Mazzini, the heart of the matter, and they will thus have an opportunity to consider it as a whole. The range of his vision and imagination far transcended the practical problems of the Italy of his day. He was probably happiest when comparing Beethoven and Rossini, Victor Hugo and Lamartine, Byron and Goethe, Christianity and his Religion of Humanity. He was most effective when attacking other revolutionary systems, such as those of Saint-Simon, Fourier, Bentham or the Carbonari. He was remarkably ignorant of Italy. Before 1848 he had never been to Milan, Venice, Bologna, Rome, Naples, or Sicily; he depended for his knowledge of the peninsula upon fellow exiles who, like himself, had fallen foul of their governments. Nor was he much interested in contemporary Italian life. Nurtured in classical and Italian medieval history, in Jansenist religious principles, in the French revolutionary philosophers, and in the romantic poets, he was obsessed with two visions: one, learnt from history, was a vision of Italy's past greatness, the other, learnt from romanticism, was a vision of the infinite possibilities of a regenerated nation.

But although his inner eye was always upon his visions, he devoted the whole of his life to the practical task of upsetting the

existing political order in Italy, this being the necessary pre-
liminary to the emergence of the Italy he dreamed. In this, the
destructive part of his task, he had more in common with the
other revolutionaries of his time than he had in his visions.

It should be recognized that the numbers of the exiled and
the discontented, and of the disturbances which they created,
argue, at the least, some *malaise* in the peninsula. What, then,
was wrong with the political order in Italy in the time of Mazzini's youth?

The fairest verdict to pass upon it is to say that it was out of
date. It was an eighteenth century order of petty despotisms,
enlightened or unenlightened according to the tendencies of the
individual rulers, an order which had been broken up by the
irruption of Napoleon between the years 1796 and 1814 but
which those assembled at the Congress of Vienna in 1815 had
done their best to restore. In Sicily and Naples, which constituted a separate kingdom (the largest in Italy), the Spanish
Bourbons, who had ruled there in the eighteenth century, were
reinstated in the rather weak person of King Ferdinand. Further
north, Pope Pius VII, who had won the sympathy of the
world in his courageous stand against Napoleon, but who
had become the Emperor's prisoner at Fontainebleau, found
himself restored to rule over the fullest extent of the Papacy's
past temporal dominions, including Bologna, Ferrara, and
Ravenna in the north. This he owed to the skill of his Secretary
of State Consalvi, who proved a match for the best of the
diplomats assembled at Vienna. But the need for the Pope
to possess an extensive temporal domain had, in reality,
passed, and much harm to the Church in the nineteenth
century might have been avoided had it been realised that,
whatever the need for it in earlier ages to help preserve Rome
from wanton attack, in an era of great powers and better com-
munications the same purpose could be better achieved by
international guarantee. There was, however, still much popular
support for Papal rule at Rome; it was at Bologna and in the
surrounding district of the Romagna that jealousy of Rome and
a strong anti-clerical tradition made the reimposing of the tem-

poral power unwise. A government of clerics was natural enough
at Rome, where they numbered the majority of the educated part
of the population; it was less natural at Bologna and it was
resented there. The year 1831 saw a revolution in the Romagna
on the accession of Pope Gregory XVI; when it had failed many
of those who had taken part, together with others from the two
small duchies to the north, Parma and Modena, joined themselves
to Mazzini.

Small in territory, these two duchies were not without significance in the story of the Italian Risorgimento. Parma was ruled
by Napoleon's widow, Marie-Louise, who was popular, Modena
by Duke Francis IV, who was not. Both rulers were Hapsburgs,
and Modena was a veritable nursery for revolutionaries. Yet so
mixed were the motives of the conspirators that Francis IV, who
was perhaps the least enlightened ruler in the whole peninsula,
was for long a favoured candidate for an hypothetical Italian
throne. To the south and west lay tolerant Tuscany, a "refugium
peccatorum" whither some of those who fell foul of the police
escaped across the Apennines. Under its Hapsburg Grand Dukes
Tuscany boasted a relatively free press and a coterie of considerable intellectuals who debated, in their enlightened societies,
science and agriculture, trade and politics.

Across the river Po lay the might of Austria, now firmly established at Venice (the ancient and glorious republic of the Doges
had been suppressed by Napoleon) and at Milan, where Vienna
had already been accustomed to rule in the eighteenth century.
Thus Lombardy and Venetia, though entirely Italian, were both
provinces of the Austrian Empire, and although this state of
affairs was in harmony with the ancient Hapsburg, Holy
Roman, and classical tradition, which stood above language and
above race, it ignored that nationalist sentiment which had
already been kindled in northern Italy, as in Germany, by the
exactions of Napoleon's armies. And the presence of Austrian
armies in Lombardy-Venetia, ever ready to cross the Po to
support the authority of the other princes of the peninsula,
provided a potent stimulus to the awakening everywhere of that
pan-Italian sentiment which Mazzini was so concerned to foster.

Outside the Hapsburg sphere of influence, a buffer state

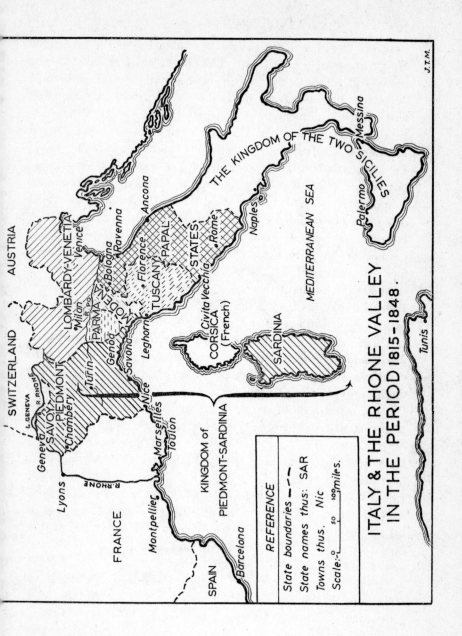

ITALY & THE RHONE VALLEY
IN THE PERIOD 1815-1848.

REFERENCE

State boundaries — ·—·—

State names thus: SAR

Towns thus. Nic

Scale:- 0   50   100 miles.

AUSTRIA

SWITZERLAND

LOMBARDY-VENETIA

Milan

Venice

R. PO

PARMA

Bologna

Ravenna

Ancona

Florence

TUSCANY

PAPAL

STATES

Rome

Civita Vecchia

Leghorn

Savona

Genoa

Turin

PIEDMONT

SAVOY

Chambery

GENEVA

Geneva

R. RHONE

SWITZERLAND

SAVOY

Nice

THE KINGDOM OF THE TWO SICILIES

Messina

Palermo

Naples

MEDITERRANEAN SEA

CORSICA
(French)

SARDINIA

KINGDOM of
PIEDMONT-SARDINIA

Marseilles

Toulon

R. RHONE

Lyons

Montpellier

FRANCE

Barcelona

SPAIN

Tunis

J.I.M.

19

between Vienna and Paris, lay the dominions of the ambitious
House of Savoy whose Dukes, like the Electors of Prussia, had
managed, through the centuries, not only to extend their
dominions but also to get themselves recognized as Kings. They
had suffered submersion, with their territories, in Napoleon's
French Empire, but had surfaced again in 1815 when Victor
Emmanuel I succeeded in securing absolute rule over Savoy,
Piedmont, Genoa, and the island of Sardinia. This remarkable
outcome of years of disaster he owed to Metternich's determination to create a state strong enough – with Austrian support – to
provide a bulwark against the aggressive tendencies of France.
However, it was later made apparent that the powerful Austrian
Chancellor, who was the architect of Italy's restoration, had in
fact paradoxically created a state strong enough, in alliance
with France, to drive the Austrians themselves out of northern
Italy and take the lead in uniting the whole peninsula under her
own Savoyard ruling house.

There were those at Genoa – and Mazzini's father was one –
who could appreciate that the extensive territories which were
combined to form the Kingdom of Piedmont-Sardinia in 1815
might provide the nucleus for a wider union of Italians even
though, as citizens of the once proud Republic of Genoa, they
might resent being placed under a king in Turin. But for Giuseppe
Mazzini himself freedom was one; the union and regeneration of
Italy must proceed from the liberation of Italians, and this
liberation could only be accomplished by revolutions which
would sweep away all the rulers (including the House of Savoy)
as well as drive out the Austrians. And certainly, in the period of
his Young Italy, the period with which we are concerned in this
book, the ruling monarch at Turin, Charles Albert, showed little
sign of leading a crusade against Vienna.

The most serious criticism of this restoration settlement in
Italy was that it ignored what had occurred in the previous
generation. A case could certainly be made for striving to prevent
a recurrence of some of the things that had happened under the
French, but it was not enough simply to ignore the political
transformation which had then taken place. Milan, Venice,
Modena, the Romagna, Bologna, and the Papal State down to

South of Ancona had been made by Napoleon into a Kingdom of Italy. Most of the western side of the peninsula, down to some distance south of Rome, had been incorporated into the French Empire. Trade barriers had been removed, new administrative and legal provisions had been made, new hopes and dreams had been stimulated, new nationalist angers had been aroused when the hopes had been disappointed. Though the life of the peasants might go on as before, amongst the politically minded classes no part of Italy was the same after 1815 as it had been in 1796, when Napoleon had first invaded. From the fashionable salons of Milan down to the caves of Apulia political change was discussed. The French occupation had shown that every sort of change was, in fact, possible, and in the Lodges of Freemasons or Carbonari (themselves often of French origin), in secret meetings on ships, in woods, or in upper rooms overhanging the narrow alleys conspiracies were hatched. And all the time the mood of a wider public was being prepared by writers who, in their impatience with existing authority, used literature, as Alfieri or Manzoni used it, or history, as Foscolo or Sismondi interpreted it, to challenge complacency about the existing Italian way of life.

No doubt we should be careful – much more careful than we generally have been – in eulogizing the changes made by the French, in criticizing the Vienna restoration as "blind", or in condemning the restored régimes as oppressive. No doubt it was very natural, and even laudable, that the Austrian Chancellor, after the upheavals of the previous generation, should seek to secure, for Italy and for Europe, "le plus grand des bien-faits – le repos". But we must also recognize that something more than a mere restoration was needed and that, so long as a strict political censorship was maintained in most parts of Italy, so long as democratic institutions were denied even to those states like Piedmont, Tuscany, Milan or Venice, which had a sufficient educated class to attempt to work them, so long as trade barriers remained high and complicated, and so long as Austrian military power obtruded itself, for so long there would be liberals working, underground if need be, for change. It was not so much a matter of brutality – by many more modern standards these rulers were not cruel – it was a matter of new ideas and aspirations which sought in vain for means of expression.

This Italy Mazzini despised. Not for him to contrive constitutional compromises or work out patient reforms. The very existence of independent states with hereditary rulers was anathema to him. Castigating alike those who sought salvation through reforming princes and those who sought it through French intervention he called upon Italians to have faith in themselves. Going into voluntary exile he culled new concepts from foreign revolutionaries, from contemplation of the sea or the sky, or from the aspiring Alps. His function, in the rather mixed metaphors of one of Metternich's spies, was to impart to Italians "an indelible impression, an electric shock, a magnetic attraction".

Chapter 1

GENOA: "FANTASIO" AND HIS FRIENDS

Giuseppe Mazzini's parents lived at the house now numbered eleven in the *via Lomellini*, at Genoa, a narrow, respectable street above the port. It is a dignified house, now made into a museum and a place of pious pilgrimage where the visitor may see the room in which Maria brought her infant boy to birth and the crib in which the baby revolutionary was rocked.

In a humbler quarter, some streets away, another genius had been born some years earlier; the parents were the Paganinis. When Maria Mazzini first laid her infant son in the wooden crib in the year 1805, the Paganini boy, twenty-two years old, was already a famous violinist; another thirty years and the violinist was unveiling a bust of himself outside his old home at Genoa while Maria's boy was an exile in Switzerland with a sentence of death hanging over his head. This, to Maria – good Jansenist that she was – most evidently was not Justice. Her own boy, as she was wont to tell him in her letters, was the Elect of God. The other boy was only a fiddler. "I am unable to conceive", she wrote to Giuseppe, "how even a great player can be worthy of a a statue while he is still alive. What in the world has he ever done for the good of humanity?"

That, at least, was a question which nobody needed to ask about her son. In the intervening years he had made himself feared by rulers everywhere and was the prime object of the hostility of the custodian of Europe's peace the Austrian Chancellor, Prince Metternich. Church, State and Society – he had tilted against them all. Prelates, Princes and Aristocracies he had ridiculed with his pen and menaced with revolution – unsuccessfully as yet but full of hope for the future. It seemed clear enough to his mother that no right-minded person could doubt what her son was doing and what he was suffering for humanity.

Yet one who did doubt, by the year 1835, was her husband, Dr. Giacomo Mazzini, the boy's father.

In 1797, eight years before his son's birth, Dr. Mazzini had supported the revolution at Genoa caused by the invasion of General Bonaparte and the French revolutionaries, and he had held positions of responsibility in the Ligurian Republic which was its outcome. He had contributed to the *Censore Italiano*, which was demanding the uniting of the Italian peninsula, and he was known for a republican and an anti-clerical. He was therefore quite well rooted in those ideas which his son was later to popularize. But experience of life amongst revolutionaries had disillusioned him. He had found them deluded and unreliable and he had come to prefer, for company, the *Filippini* fathers of the nearby monastic church where he attended daily Mass. He was, by profession, a doctor, and, after 1816, a professor at the University of Genoa; he pursued his vocation with skill, zeal, and charity towards the poor. No doubt, as his son's biographers love to say, he disliked parting with his money.[1] But experience had led him to believe that men should earn their own livelihood, and, if his son later insisted upon living in exile, as a revolutionary, he saw no reason why he should support him indefinitely in that occupation. But such views were unfashionable amongst the youth of Genoa. The era of romanticism had dawned in Italy, and with it the notion that a man's duty, now that the French revolution had emancipated him from the past, was to refashion society. Moreover, since Napoleon had been banished to Saint Helena, proud Genoa had been placed under the rule of the House of Savoy, at Turin. It was uncongenial to the more virile spirits of the ancient port, with its distinguished history, that their city should be no more than a part of an artificial kingdom of Piedmont-Sardinia even though (as the Mazzini parents both hoped) this union might prove a useful step towards a wider union of Italians. And it seemed retrogressive that, after Napoleon had created a Kingdom of Italy, the Pope should be confirmed in his rule over Bologna as well as over Rome and the

---

[1] It would seem he had been brought up to be careful of it, for his father had earned the nick-name *buasso* ("stupid") from a priest hissing the word at him when, to economize, he had blown out the altar candles before the liturgically permissible moment at Mass.

Austrians in theirs over Milan and Venice. Nor did there seem much virtue, to republican eyes, in the Bourbon régime at Naples, or in the Hapsburgs Ferdinand at Florence, Francis IV at Modena, or Marie-Louise at Parma. Maria Mazzini, as a Jansenist (and in northern Italy this often meant a republican), was clear that all this was wrong and was supported in her hopes for change by ardent friends who preserved their enthusiasm after her husband had lost his.

The Mazzinis had four children, and they were all religious, in one way or another. Rosa, the eldest, was born in 1797 and entered a convent at San Pier d'Arena, just outside Genoa, at the age of 23. Young Giuseppe was only 16 when she left home; he never forgot her going:

"I remember her smallest gestures, her last words, and her strange smile, mingling her sorrow at leaving us and her religious determination, as she kissed me for the last time before stepping into the carriage for San Pier d'Arena".

She was not to be there for long. In the words of her Superior,

"caught up in God, and often, in rapture, raising herself to heavenly contemplations, she besought her Spouse unceasingly that He would not let her escape from His pure embrace and that, pitying her for the burning flame that consumed her, He would call her to the cool calm of the ecstasies of divine love. And God granted her exalted prayer; after some years passed in the exercise of mortification, purified and worthy of the crown, she was called by the Lord, in the early spring of her life, to be with Him in Paradise".

She had died less than three years after entering the convent.

The second child was Antonietta, who was born in 1800. She was the favourite of her father, but became somewhat estranged from her mother when, in 1829, she married a banker, Francesco Massuccone. Maria Mazzini disliked the Massuccones and disliked still more letting Antonietta have any of the dowry which her son could so well have used. Nevertheless the Massuccones were not rich and Antonietta, who was religious and attended daily Mass, lived simply. She always remained on good terms with her brilliant brother and, after 1854, when their mother died, she corresponded with him frequently and he would stay at her house on the visits which he paid, in disguise, to Genoa.

Giuseppe was the third child, born on June 22nd 1805, and generally called Pippo.

The fourth and last was Francesca, called Cichina, who was born in 1808. She idolized Pippo and was the comfort and joy of both her parents. Her brother later loved to write to her, and she to him; he often teased her and she knew how to respond. Her death from consumption at the age of only 30 was a blow which struck the whole family cruelly.

Giuseppe was a precocious boy, reading easily by the time he was four but slow in learning to walk. His mother made it her business to supervise his early studies and she did so with the care which was proper to one who was convinced that her boy was a "divine emanation" destined to raise mankind to a higher level. This inner faith in her son's religious destiny was her own secret; but others could see the boy's exceptional gifts. One who was profoundly impressed was Maria's cousin, Colonel Giuseppe Patroni, who, when Pippo was only 8, wrote his mother a letter which afterwards seemed so apt that it was wrongly supposed to be apocryphal:

"Believe me, Signora Cousin, this dear boy is a star of the first magnitude, destined to shine with a true light and to be admired by the culture of Europe. . . . Supreme geniuses who, in past epochs, were the glory of their ages, generally showed, in their infancy, just those powers which can be seen in him . . .".[1]

"Amen", said Maria, adding "prophetic letter", in her own hand, under the good colonel's signature. Patroni's advice was that the boy should be taught Italian history, world history, French, English, German, music, and dancing; but he also thought that his mother should see to it that he ran about, jumped, and played boyish games, every day, so as to keep himself fit.

But Patroni was only a Colonel of Artillery, and Maria soon felt she needed the advice of somebody with a profounder understanding of the times. So she wrote to one of the foremost of the Italian liberals, Giacomo Breganze, friend of the patriot and poet Ugo Foscolo. She had known him at Genoa fifteen years earlier, and she now started a correspondence with him about Pippo.

[1] The letter is printed in Cod. *Giovinezza* . . . 191.

Breganze had served the Napoleonic Cisalpine Republic, in 1798, at Milan, with distinction and courage. When the Russians and the Austrians occupied Milan in 1799 he and Foscolo had removed, with other Italian liberals, to Genoa. It was then that he had known the Mazzinis (six years before Pippo's birth) and had suffered with them the siege imposed by the Russian general Suvorov and by the British navy upon the city. During the year that it lasted (1799–1800) the city was the last stronghold of liberalism in Italy, and it has been said, not altogether without reason, that during that year of hardship at Genoa the Italian Risorgimento was born. For it was then that the liberals, disillusioned by the many new-fangled republics into which Napoleon, for his own purposes, had divided Italy, discussed together the idea of Italian unity and freedom, and publicised it in their paper, the *Redattore Italiano*. And it was of this year that the grown-ups, during Pippo's boyhood, would always be talking, so that one of his earliest recollections was a hero-worship for Foscolo, which impelled him, much later, to try to edit the poet's writings, and also for Breganze, in whose fate we find him, a generation later, interesting himself from England. Breganze had disappeared from Genoa in 1800 to serve Napoleon's new "Republic of Italy", only to abandon public life in disgust in 1806 when the Republic had turned into a Kingdom. With the return of the Austrians in 1814 he had settled to the pursuit of his vocation as a lawyer. And it was in this year that he wrote the first of his surviving letters to Maria Mazzini about the education of her son.

Breganze's advice did not differ very radically from that already given by Colonel Patroni. Poor Pippo, it seems, whether he wanted to or not, was to "walk a lot, run, and jump"; when he should attain to the age of twelve this informal exercise was to yield place to regular instruction in fencing and dancing from which he would gain "pleasure and comfort amidst the tempests of life". Tempests his life would assuredly bring; but it is hard to imagine the grown Mazzini, hidden in the Alps or beggared in Bloomsbury, comforting himself by fencing or dancing. Breganze was nearer the mark when he recommended music for the same purpose; the grown Mazzini would comfort himself very often

with his guitar. And Breganze may well have been wise to elimin-
ate German from the list of foreign languages previously recommended, although the pupil's inability to read Goethe in the
original or to converse, in his exile, with the German-Swiss
inhabitants of the Canton of Solothurn would later be a grief to
him.

Maria's detailed letters to Breganze, reporting progress and
requesting further advice, have disappeared; but from Breganze's
replies something can be learned of the young Mazzini's progress.
When he was still only ten the mentor was advising that he be
given not merely Cicero's letters but his treatises *De Senectute*,
De Amicitia, and *De Officiis*. He was eleven when a letter came
expressing pleasure that the boy's health was surviving his
studies, but urging that his mother should watch his digestion
carefully, and, whenever she found it was irregular or weak,
should be sure to see that he rested his brain so that the blood
could return to his stomach. By the time he was fifteen his
mother was worrying about his satirical turn of mind and
Breganze was saying that this tendency should be checked, that
it was probably due to pride, arising from his being so much
praised.

Maria's husband, it would seem, although he had become a
professor at the university, was not much consulted in the matter
of their boy's education. And the ideological gulf between
husband and wife was always growing wider. Yet, if the professor
had changed, there still clung around him remnants of the soil in
which he had been rooted. Thus, when the family moved in 1811
to a larger house near the Acquaverde at Genoa, he failed to take
the opportunity to destroy his collection of newspapers of the
great days of the French revolution, with the result that one day
his precocious son found them and feasted himself upon the deeds
and words of Lafayette, Mirabeau, Danton, and Robespierre.
And another contact with his father's past presented itself in the
shape of the Ruffini family, for Bernardo Ruffini had been a
favourite companion of the doctor's exciting days. Ruffini, like
the doctor, had, in the meantime, rather grown out of that sort of
thing. But not so his wife, Eleanora. She had enough of the
revolutionary instinct in her blood for two – indeed for a whole

family. Already she outshone the reserved Maria as the lodestar of the younger Genoese liberals, and she educated her numerous offspring to be apostles of Italian liberty with a zeal which recked little of convention. As their children grew up she and Maria fed each other's enthusiasm; but Maria acknowledged Eleanora's leadership and even allowed Pippo to call her his "other mother". She could afford to be generous, for, although Eleanora's son, Jacopo, had a spirit as daring, there was never any question but that the leadership belonged to Pippo. Jacopo and Pippo were bosom friends, but, from the start, Jacopo was a disciple; we may meet him in his younger brother Giovanni's autobiographical novel, *Lorenzo Benoni*, written in 1853.

It is from that novel that we learn something about the Royal College of Genoa, which was where, for a short time at least, the young Mazzini went to school.

It was a place where boys were principally preoccupied with the problem of how to overthrow authority. Both inside and outside the classroom they learnt how they could do this if only they were bold enough. Inside they were taught to worship Brutus – Brutus, whom Dante had placed in the very centre of Hell, but whom the Romantics had lifted up into Heaven. In their classical studies they learnt that Rome had been great in the days of the Gracchi and of Cicero; that the rot had set in under the Emperors. In their historical studies they learnt that Italy had been great in the days of her virile medieval republics – Genoa, Venice, Florence and Pisa. But what happened outside the classroom taught them still more. There they learnt that if you wanted to achieve any purpose, if you wanted to "down" an arrogant bully amongst the boys, you formed a secret society to do it. You might be thrown into a dungeon for it (the rather vivid term used by Italians for a confinement little more onerous than detention at English Public Schools of the time). But even if that happened you could always scratch Odes to Liberty, or to Despair, upon the walls; you could organize sensational rescues by tapping, in code; or, at worst, you could gladly resign your liberty as your sacred sacrifice for your Eternal Principles. The great thing was to belong to a secret society. That, alone, enabled you to act effectively. Secret passwords, secret gestures, handshakes with the fingers in peculiar positions – these were the means of mutual identification, passports to a hidden world where great deeds were planned.

Such was life at the Royal College of Genoa, and the only difference when a boy left, and went to the University of Genoa (which Mazzini did in 1819, at the age of 15), was that his cabalistic excitements acquired an added note of realism. Instead of being shut up by the school authorities, if he led a riot, he was arrested by the police – a much more exhilarating sensation. This happened quite early to Giuseppe Mazzini. On June 21st 1820, the day before his sixteenth birthday, he was arrested for helping to lead a tumult in the University Church. The next day he was released – perhaps because he was young, and it was his birthday, and because the University protested on his behalf. The tumult had arisen because boys from the Royal College of Genoa were occupying seats in the Church which the University students reckoned were reserved for them.

Mazzini was still only 16 when he had his first chance to demonstrate his sympathy with real revolutionaries. Armed with sticks, he and fellow students demonstrated, in March of 1821, in support of the Carbonaro revolt of the spring of that year, in Piedmont. By this time the Prefect of the Schools was noting that "although a young man of exceptional talent he is nevertheless very dissipated and often goes out of the building to linger in the courtyard and confer with his companions".

Later, Raimondo Doria, Grand Master of the Spanish Lodge of the Carbonari, would say of Mazzini: "he was born a Carbonaro". And, in saying so, that liar of genius for once told the simple truth.

If this spirit of rebellion, this hatred of authority, had been all that the young Mazzini had to offer it would explain his joining the Carbonari but it would not explain the affection he already inspired. That affection was the human response to his own human sympathy, to his exquisite sensitivity. There is a much told story of him, still a little boy, clasping and kissing a beggar in the street. He was afflicted by the sight of suffering and impelled to relieve it, whether with his own money or with his

devoted mother's. And he had the true romantic's horror (un-
common amongst his compatriots) of unkindness to animals. For
this spirit of sympathy, so genuine in him, his university friends
were ready to forgive him his aloofness, his insistence upon
solitude, his long monologues on duty, mission, dedication of
one's life. And more than to forgive him, to listen to him, with
respect and devotion, to become, already, his disciples. We learn
as much from *Lorenzo Benoni*. Giovanni Ruffini wrote the novel
much later, when he was inclined to laugh at his earlier behaviour,
and when it suited him to 'play up' what would appeal to his
English public, such as pictures of priestly corruption. But no
reader of those vivid pages can doubt that the book gives a true
picture of the author's youth; and we have the word of one of the
little band of friends that it presents a good portrait of Mazzini,
whom it calls "Fantasio"[1]. When the author first meets Fantasio,
in the novel, they have both just been involved in a characteristic
contretemps with the police:

". . . within a month after this circumstance, which had brought
Fantasio and me together, we had sworn a mutual friendship in life
and death, and, somehow or other, an intimacy had sprung up
between the two families. Every morning, without fail, I went to
Fantasio's house, and every evening, in like manner, Fantasio came
to ours. My mother and my brothers, especially Caesar [Jacopo],
were captivated by him. He was certainly the most fascinating little
fellow I ever knew.

"Fantasio was my elder by one year. He had a finely-shaped head,
the forehead spacious and prominent, and eyes black as jet, at times
darting lightning. His complexion was a pale olive, and his features,
remarkably striking altogether, were set, so to speak, in a profusion
of flowing black hair, which he wore rather long. The expression of his
countenance, grave and almost severe, was softened by a smile of
great sweetness, mingled with a certain shrewdness, betraying a rich
comic vein. He spoke well and fluently, and, when he warmed upon a
subject, there was a fascinating power in his eyes, his gestures, his
voice, his whole bearing, that was quite irresistible. His life was one
of retirement and study; the amusements common with young men
of his age had no attraction for him. His library, his cigar, his coffee;
some occasional walks, rarely in the daytime, and always in solitary
places, more frequently in the evening and by moonlight -- such were
his only pleasures. His morals were irreproachable, his conversation

---

[1] Federico Campanella, in the *Italia e Popolo*, June 17 and 18, 1855. See the
article by Camillo Guerrieri *Per la Storia e la Fortuna del 'Lorenzo Benoni'* in
Giovanni Ruffini e i suoi tempi, Genoa, 1931.

was always chaste. If any of the young companions he gathered round him occasionally indulged in some wanton jests or expression of double meaning, Fantasio -- God bless him! -- would put an immediate stop to it by some word which never failed of its effect. Such was the influence that the purity of his life, and his incontestable superiority, gave to him.

"Fantasio was well versed in history, and in the literature, not only of his own but of foreign countries. Shakespeare, Byron, Goethe, Schiller, were as familiar to him as Dante and Alfieri. Spare and thin in body, he had an indefatigably active mind; he wrote much and well both in prose and verse, and there was hardly a subject he had not attempted -- historical essays, literary criticisms, tragedies, etc. A passionate lover of liberty under every shape, there breathed in his fiery soul an indomitable spirit of revolt against tyranny and oppression of every sort. Kind, feeling, generous, never did he refuse advice or service, and his library, amply furnished, as well as his well-filled purse, were always at the command of his friends. Perhaps he was rather fond of displaying the brilliancy of his dialectic powers at the expense of good sense, by maintaining occasionally strange paradoxes. Perhaps there was a slight touch of affectation in his invariably black dress; and his horror of apparent shirt-collars was certainly somewhat exaggerated; but, take him all in all, he was a noble lad".[1]

Giovanni Ruffini goes on to give a vivid account of the war then raging in Italy between the Classicists and the Romantics.

"Unable to find vent on the forbidden ground of politics [because of the strict political censorship] passions ran counter in the lists of literature. The Classicists were the Conservatives in letters, the champions of authority, swearing by Aristotle and Horace, out of whose Church there was no salvation to be found. The imitation of the ancients was their creed. The romantic school was that of the Liberals in literature, the enemies of authority. They would not hear of Aristotle and his unities. According to them genius knew no lawgiver but itself, imitation was mere impotence, nature was the sole and eternal spring of the living and the beautiful . . . Manzoni, the avowed chief of the romantic school in literature, had just published his *Promessi Sposi.* . . . According to the former Manzoni was a demi-god, if you gave ear to the latter he was scarcely a man.

"There could be no doubt as to Fantasio's choice in this matter. He espoused the cause of the romantic school with all the ardour and devotedness belonging to his nature. He published in a Florentine periodical, attached to the romantic party, a series of articles full of spirit, in which he laid down the most revolutionary theories with respect to art. We gave him our enthusiastic applause . . . Fantasio, with his characteristic feverish activity, immediately conceived the plan of a literary paper, of which he was to be the conductor and I one of the contributors. But some difficulty, which I do not well

[1] p. 188, etc., of Edinburgh edition of 1853.

remember, came across the project, the realization of which was deferred".

Giovanni's memory had served him well, and his account of the romantic furore amongst the Genoese friends is authentic. The Florentine journal was the great *Antologia*, and the critical review of consequence in Italy after the Austrians had suppressed the Milanese *Conciliatore* in 1819. To it Mazzini had contributed his first serious essay, *On a European Literature*, in 1829. But Giovanni fails to tell how Fantasio did succeed in acquiring control over a Genoese commercial paper, the *Indicatore Genovese*, in 1828, and in turning it into a literary paper with a thinly veiled political intent. In this ingenious adventure he was aided by the two Ruffini brothers, but more importantly by a fellow student at the university, Elia Benza. Benza's home was at Porto Maurizio, on the Ligurian coast west of Genoa, but while they were all fellow students at the university he would join Mazzini and the Ruffinis for long colloquies, in the warm evenings, strolling on the *Acquasola*, or sitting smoking on Mazzini's little balcony. Benza was a romantic moral philosopher, who later claimed the credit for lifting Mazzini out of the sceptical phase through which he passed as a student, even though the God Mazzini came to worship was so different from Benza's God of Christian orthodoxy. If, however, it is true that it was from Benza that Mazzini acquired his peculiar notions concerning the prophetic office of literature, Benza's own contributions to the *Indicatore Genovese* are cool and precise where Mazzini's are ardent and often violent – a difference which is in harmony with the subsequent careers of the two men, for, when Mazzini was in exile with Giovanni Ruffini, and Jacopo had been driven to commit suicide, Benza, though as deeply implicated in their plots as any of them, was quietly making a good living practising as a lawyer on the Ligurian coast.

The particular enemy of these young romantics was the rather distinguished historian Carlo Botta who did not hesitate, in the Roman *Arcadia*, to call the innovators of the *Indicatore* "rascally boys" "degraded slaves of foreign (French) ideas' or to accuse them of sowing a pest (romanticism) in Italian letters, and thus being "betrayers of their country".

"Betrayers of Italy!", exclaimed Mazzini in the *Indicatore*, "no -- the betrayers of Italy are those who sell their intellect and soul to force, which compels, or to wealth, which pays; they are those who, with ludicrous municipal pride, and with their eternal arguments about language, perpetuate division between brothers -- they are those who make Italy wretched with their absurd grammatical arguments and their learned tomfoolery or else induce her to sleep, soothed by the laurels won by her ancestors; they are those who, in the nineteenth century, insist upon trying to bind the teeming minds of the Italians in the swaddling bands of their own infantilism and who fight, as best they can, against the universal onrush of the human intellect, damning it to everlasting immobility and to nourishing itself upon fairy tales, alien to the nation, to her traditions, to her needs . . .".[1]

The fairy tales were the "Hymns to the Virgin or the Saints", and the "ludicrous municipal pride" was the pride of the Florentines or of the Milanese in their local linguistic traditions and usage. But these things, whatever might be thought about them, were, in fact, very Italian, even though they might be unworthy; and Botta, actually, had some reason to call Mazzini and his friends foreign. Their inspiration was foreign; it was French.

Behind the literary argument in the *Indicatore* lurked the more dangerous political argument, the implied invitation to Italians to rise and throw out their oppressors. In fact the paper was, as the Piedmontese government slowly began to realise, "subversive". As Mazzini later explained,

"the literary controversy turned itself into political controversy; it was only necessary to change a few words to be aware of it . . . the government ended by perceiving and being irritated by this tendency. And when, at the end of the first year, we announced cheerfully to the readers that the journal would be enlarged, a governmental veto extinguished it".

This was at the end of 1828. Fortunately for the little group another outlet for their energies immediately offered itself, for Domenico Guerrazzi, the polemical romantic playwright of Leghorn, down the coast, in Tuscany, wrote imploring Mazzini and Benza to send him copy for his own somewhat similar *Indicatore Livornese*. They jumped at the opportunity, and were soon writing articles invoking compassion for the poet Silvio Pellico (by then languishing in the Austrian prison of the Spielberg), or

[1] From his article *Carlo Botta e i Romantici*, I, 63–66.

Maria Mazzini, mother of Giuseppe. From an oil painting in the
Museo del Risorgimento at Genoa.

Mazzini, aged 15, encounters the "man of stern and fierce countenance, dark, bearded", at the port of Genoa.

Drawing by G. Mantegazza.

drawing a significant moral from the story of the French *Jacquerie* – that the remedy for oppression always rests with the people themselves. Finally Mazzini, goaded by a champion of the Classicists (Spotorno of the Genoese *Ligustico*) to say what he meant by Romanticism, wrote his *Essay on some tendencies of European Literature in the Nineteenth Century*. If anybody wanted to know what Romanticism might be, Mazzini ironically suggested, "the authority [Austria] which struck down in Italy the *Conciliatore* and persecuted the young writers of that journal understood better than anybody else the true meaning of that word". Published in the *Indicatore Livornese* in December 1829 this was defiance which even the tolerant and easy-going government of Tuscany, under the Grand-Duke Leopold at Florence, could not tolerate, and by February 1830 Guerrazzi's journal at Leghorn in its turn was suppressed. For Mazzini had pointed his accusing finger straight at Vienna, and Leopold, for all his benevolence, was a Hapsburg. Three years later the Grand-Duke felt it prudent to meet the wishes of his august relative, the Emperor Francis, by suppressing the *Antologia* itself. The voice of independent criticism was thus, for more than a decade, virtually silenced in Italy, a fact which goes further than any other to justify the desperate remedies in which Mazzini and his friends were to indulge.

Mazzini was already an effective writer, in the romantic vein, and sometimes a deeply moving one; but he often became wearisome through falling into the prophet's habit of declamation and reiteration. He said, later, that his abandonment of a literary for a political career was his "first great sacrifice", but one is driven to protest, in the words of an Italian critic, that "he was born to be the apostle that he was, certainly not the man of letters which he believed he should have become."[1] Nor, in the correct sense of the word, was he a scholar. He was only interested in scholarship in so far as it would tend towards giving intellectual corroboration to his intuitions. His friend Benza was a scholar; and it is

---

[1] F. L. Mannucci *Giuseppe Mazzini e la prima fase del suo pensiero letterario*, Milan, 1919, p. 84. But really, as U. Limentani has observed (*L'attività letteraria di Giuseppe Mazzini*, Turin, 1950, p. 9), Mazzini's sighing after the life of letters was nostalgic and sentimental rather than real.

B

characteristic of Mazzini's attitude that, when Benza's scholarship led him gradually away from the mazzinian *credo*, the prophet regarded him as "sterilized by excessive analysis". Mazzini had a more powerful and penetrating intelligence than had any of his friends, but he was too obsessed for scholarship, too preoccupied with one idea, so that he misunderstood or simply ignored what was opposed to it.

And this idea was, as yet, quite simply to "liberate Italy". From what? From the Austrian occupation of Venice and Milan, and from Vienna's indirect control over the rest of the peninsula. From the despotism of the princes in the other states; from the hold of the Church; from the privileges of the aristocracy. It was still uncertain what was to emerge in the place of these, Italy's traditional guides. Like most born revolutionaries he was preoccupied with the need to level the ground, and with the means of doing that, rather than with the new structure which should ultimately be built. His was Rousseau's optimistic view that, once released, the General Will, by virtue of what it was, would provide for what was needed. The important point was that "Italy" was to be "freed". Not long after he left school a chance incident, as he was walking with his mother and a friend, had served to focus his aspirations to that extent, and to imprint them upon his mind as Duty. For as they went along the street

"a man of stern and fierce countenance, dark, bearded, and with a piercing look which I have never forgotten, hailed and stopped us from a distance. He held out in his hands a little white handkerchief, and uttered simply the words: for the exiles of Italy. My mother and her friend put some money into the handkerchief; and he went off to repeat his gesture with the others. . . . That day was the first on which there took shape confusedly in my mind I will not say the thought of Fatherland and Liberty, but the thought that one could and therefore one should struggle for the liberty of the Fatherland".

The man with the stern and fierce countenance was one of those who had fought, the month before, in the revolt organized by the Carbonari. He wanted money to help his fellow revolutionaries make the voyage to Spain where the Carbonari had been more successful. "With a piercing look which I have never forgotten". That was how, writing forty years after the event, Mazzini remembered him. Probably it was his first meeting, face to face, with a proscribed political revolutionary, escaping from one defeat to join in another battle. When, in the person of that man, he met the Carbonaro movement in action he was still in his first year at the university. By his last year (1827) he had found out enough about the secret society to enable him, through a university friend, Pietro Torre, to be initiated into it.

Chapter 2

GENOA: THE CARBONARI

Historians have often seen fit to laugh gently at the Carbonari; and, indeed, the complexity of the ritual which this secret society inherited from the charcoal burners of Franche Comté lends itself rather readily to mirth. Yet what the Carbonari achieved in Italy, in the shape of revolution in 1820–21, and again in 1831, was remarkable.

The Neapolitans had caught the Carbonaro infection from the soldiers of the French revolution in southern Italy. In their hands it had become a secret society dedicated, in rather general terms, to the cause of freedom, against tyranny, and as such it had been made use of by Bentinck and King Ferdinand in the anti-Bonapartist cause. The paradoxical result of this ill-assorted alliance was that Ferdinand, a Bourbon, who mistrusted constitutional liberty rather more strongly than did his opponents, Murat or Joseph Bonaparte, was put back in 1815 upon the throne of the Kingdom of the Two Sicilies. This unfortunate outcome of their earlier endeavours the Carbonari later prepared to remedy, and they were so far successful, in the uprising which they planned in 1820, that by July of that year their leader, Guglielmo Pepe, was in the new government, and King Ferdinand was swearing loyalty to the constitution which they had imposed upon him. Following, as it did, upon the success of the revolution in Spain in the same year, in which the Spanish Carbonari had played their part, the success was striking and, from the point of view of Metternich and of the Holy Alliance of the legitimate rulers of Europe, menacing. The Austrian Chancellor had to lecture the puzzled and frightened Ferdinand, who was summoned to the Congress of Laybach in December 1820, explaining to him that his acceptance of the revolution was not in accordance with that principle of legitimacy upon which the tranquillity of European society rested and that it would be necessary for him to put the matter right by accepting an Austrian army to restore him to his rightful position. By the beginning of March 1821 this army had marched down through Italy and was not far from the Neapolitan frontier. Guglielmo Pepe bravely advanced with his revolutionary force to meet the Austrians at Rieti, in the Papal State. His defeat there on March 7th was the end of effective revolution in Naples until the year 1848; but it is worth noting that Pepe's adventure had, in fact, lasted since the previous July, and that had it not been for the abysmal failure of his associates to come to sensible terms with the Sicilians (who, as always, were trying to secure independence for their island) the Austrian army might have had a hard task, fighting at the end of such long lines of communication.

This rising in the south of Italy provided the opportunity for Genoa and Turin in the north, and the revolution of 1821 in Piedmont, in favour of which the fifteen-year-old Mazzini demonstrated at Genoa with his stick, broke out three days after the defeat at Rieti. In theory the Carbonari were a cosmopolitan society, with a Supreme Lodge at Paris and members active the whole way from Ireland to the Aegean and even across the Atlantic. In practice their operation was local, and the Lodge at Naples would seem to have failed to co-ordinate its efforts with the Lodges at Turin or at Milan. In northern Italy the Carbonaro leaders belonged to the aristocracy, they counted upon support from the army, and they hoped and intended to have Charles Albert, nephew of King Victor Emmanuel of Sardinia-Piedmont, as their leader, and to persuade Victor Emmanuel himself to accept their programme. The king, however, like Ferdinand, had been lectured by Metternich at Laybach, and he preferred to abdicate. Charles Albert, too, thought better of the whole affair and cut himself loose from his revolutionary friends, while Charles Felix, Victor Emmanuel's brother, ascended the throne and crushed the revolution, with the help of the Austrians, near Novara, on April 8th 1821. One of those who escaped from that disaster was Mazzini's "man with the stern and fierce countenance"; he and his companions set sail for Spain and the Austrians entered the city of Genoa.

The Carbonari were curiously compounded of cut-throats and of cultured aristocrats of liberal outlook. At Milan, for instance, where they generally went under the name of *Italici Puri*, or *Federali* (distinct societies, of French origin, which became affiliated to the Carbonari), the leading light was Count Federico Confalonieri, a cultured Voltairean sceptic who enjoyed meeting the literary liberal visitors from France and England. But there was also within the society at Milan the religious poet, Silvio Pellico, who edited the "enlightened" Milanese *Conciliatore*. In Tuscany and Piedmont, similarly, there were *Guelfi* and *Adelfi*, affiliated to the Carbonari, and embracing on the one hand bandits and poisoners, and on the other high-minded political liberals like Santorre di Santarosa, who led the Piedmontese revolution of 1821, or the cultured contributors to the Florentine *Antologia*. We should picture the position as one in which anybody, noble or humble, idealist or opportunist, cultured or boorish, who sought a change in the existing social and political order, and who was prepared to share in the hazards of a revolution, would almost automatically join one of the affiliated societies. Yet, despite their lack of common purpose, or doctrine, or centralized planning, these Carbonari managed somehow, for months at a time, in Naples in 1820, in Piedmont in 1821, and in the Papal State in 1831, to take over effective control of the government in important areas.

To act, then, in any revolutionary capacity, in the 1820s, the first step was to join the Carbonari; so in 1827 Mazzini paid his entrance fee of twenty-five francs, and thereafter his five francs monthly. "A heavy contribution for me, a student", he wrote later. But by then he had experienced the agonizing difficulty of raising the money needed to run a secret and voluntary revolutionary society, and he does not blame the Carbonari for being extortionate.

"It is a serious fault to receive money from others and make a bad use of it; it is a more serious fault to hesitate before a financial sacrifice when there is a probability that it will help a good cause".

The serious blame, he came to believe, attached not to the Carbonari, for being extortionate, but to the Italians for being

ever readier to sacrifice their lives than their money in the cause
of Italy.

There was a local Lodge of the Carbonari at Genoa, called the
Speranza, and it soon found plenty of work for its gifted and
energetic recruit. He was initiated into the second grade, which
enabled him to enrol new recruits, and he was active in this
capacity amongst the university students. Soon he was made
secretary of the Lodge. All the same, he remained rather puzzled
as to what it was all about.

"In my own mind I reflected with surprise and suspicion that the
oath [of allegiance to the society] contained nothing but a formula of
obedience and not a word of the purpose. My initiator had not uttered
a syllable which gave a hint as to federalism or unity, as to republic
or monarchy. Just war against the government, no more".

Nor was his first major task reassuring. Raimondo Doria, the
same who styled himself Grand Master of the Spanish Lodge, was
then living at Genoa, and was not averse to holding forth about
his acquaintance with Spanish and French Carbonarism and
even with the London Lodge. But compared with Mazzini he was
a man of no education at all, and he was delighted to find somebody who could write fluently in French and translate from
English. So he set the new recruit to work to write a lengthy and
indignant commentary (in the form of a letter to King Charles X
of France) upon the French intervention of 1823 which had
crushed the Spanish revolution. Mazzini had not been in Spain,
but Doria and plenty of others on the Ligurian coast around
Genoa had taken part in the Spanish revolution and could give
him the facts. The document was intended for the Supreme
Lodge at Paris, and was something of a *tour de force* extending
over more than sixty pages. But Mazzini never discovered that it
was sent to Paris, or, if it was, that anybody there ever bothered
with it.

When he was not doing jobs for the Carbonari Mazzini was
reading the French romantic poets, or the lectures of Guizot and
Cousin, or articles in the *Monde*, from which he gained a notion
of the German philosphers Lessing, Herder and Kant. He read
Goethe and Schiller in French translations. He became wildly
excited about Byron and taught himself English, so he said, to be

able to appreciate *Manfred* better. He wept at the sorrows of Werther and was driven "almost to madness" by the suicide of Foscolo's *Jacopo Ortis*. Interpreting the whole romantic revolt as a political and religious revolt against authority he continued, in his literary articles, to sail as close to the wind of the police as he dared. But all the time he was searching for action; thought without action, he told his friends, sitting on his balcony, was useless in the sleepy Italy around them; they must act, sacrifice themselves, suffer martyrdom if need be, at all costs raise the revolution!

Yet the Carbonari, whom he had joined in such high hopes, seemed strangely slow to move. In July 1830 King Charles X had been driven from Paris and Louis Philippe had ascended the throne, accompanied by much talk of liberty and some carefully contrived free institutions. This had been a serious set-back for Metternich's system, and it seemed to provide an admirable opportunity for revolutionaries everywhere. Then why were the Carbonari in Italy not acting? They talked of awaiting instructions from the Supreme Lodge in Paris but, Mazzini pointed out, they should not wait upon Paris. Carbonarism was something Italy had given to France, not France to Italy; it was an Italian initiative that was now wanted.

To Raimondo Doria, the local celebrity of the society, the eyes of the revolutionaries turned, and he saw that he must do something, if only to quiet Mazzini. That young secretary, despite his small stature, was imposing himself upon everybody with his sombre, penetrating eyes, his tireless eloquence and his reiterated appeal to duty and the spirit of sacrifice. Doria found him rather tiresome and decided at one and the same time to make some show of action and to get rid of him for a spell by sending him on a mission to Tuscany to make contact there with that turbulent prophet F. D. Guerrazzi. But before his departure Doria determined that the young man should be taught that the watchword of the society was Obedience, that there was no place – only death – for anybody who tried to challenge the leadership. He chose the night before Mazzini's departure to issue his warning, and arranged the occasion with an eye characteristically fastened upon dramatic effect. Mazzini found himself summoned to a meeting, at midnight, on the *Ponte della Mercanzia*, outside Genoa.

"I found", he says, "some of the young men I had enrolled in the society themselves, likewise, summoned there without their knowing why. After a long wait Doria appeared and there followed him two unknown men muffled in coats up to the eyes and as silent as ghosts. Our hearts leapt within us in our hope and our longing for action. We made a circle and Doria, after a brief talk, directed at me, on the blameworthy errors, indiscretions and unguarded behaviour of inexperienced and rash youths, turned to the two cloaked figures and declared that they would depart the next day for Barcelona, there to slay a Carbonaro guilty of having dared to criticize his Chiefs; *for the Order, when it found rebels, crushed them.* It was a reply to my own criticisms, repeated by some talkative member. I remember still the spasm of fury which seized me at this foolish threat. I determined, on that first impulse, to say that I was no longer going to Tuscany, and the Order could crush as it pleased. Then, as I cooled down, and was warned by my friends that, without being aware of it, I was sacrificing the cause of the country to my resentment as an individual, I changed my mind and departed, leaving a letter to reassure my family".

His family may well have required some reassuring, for his parents had flatly refused to approve of his going to Tuscany for such purposes, and in order to obtain from his mother the necessary money for the journey he had been obliged to tell her that he was going on a short visit to a friend at Arenzano.

At Leghorn Mazzini found a truly kindred spirit in Carlo Bini, who was destined to be his disciple. With him he founded a Carbonaro Lodge there. Then the two went on together to Montepulciano, where Guerrazzi was then under preventive detention.

The interview with the great man was revealing.

"We saw Guerrazzi. He was writing the *Siege of Florence* and he read us the introductory chapter. The blood mounted to his head as he read, and he bathed his forehead to calm himself. He thought highly of himself, and that petty persecution, which should have made him smile, inflamed his whole spirit with rage. . . . He lacked that inner peace which comes only from a strong religious belief or from the overpowering impulses of the heart. He had little respect and little love. I could not find in him one spark of that immense love which poured from the eyes of Carlo Bini while, stirred by the reading of those magnificent pages which the youth of Italy now know by heart, he gazed at him with the look of a mother thinking only of his suffering".

At last the great man stopped his recital and it was Mazzini's turn. The rôles were now reversed and, to the young secretary's prophecies about Progress, and Faith, and the Future, Guerrazzi replied with a smile

"half sad, half quizzical. And that smile", Mazzini continues, "frightened me, as if I had caught a glimpse of all the dangers confronting that gifted mind; it frightened me so much that I left without speaking to him openly of the chief purport of my visit, leaving Bini to do it".

In due course Guerrazzi would join Mazzini's Young Italy, but he would never accept the Mazzinian religion, he much preferred Machiavelli. In this early encounter between the future dictator of Tuscany and the future dictator of Rome may be seen the forerunner of many a temperamental clash at secret meetings on the waterfronts of Genoa or Marseilles, of Geneva or Lausanne, between the young visionary and older revolutionary hands.

By the time he returned to Genoa from this brief visit Mazzini had been for three years in the Carbonari. He was beginning to build up an inner group of his own friends, along the Ligurian coast, many of whom he had himself initiated and who might be expected to follow his lead. He intended these intimate associates to act as a leaven in the Carbonari, to be more worthy than the others, in their zeal and their devotion, of the model he was always holding up to them, that Greek Hetairia, which had already achieved victory in the struggle for the independence of Greece. He returned from Leghorn announcing an Italian Hetairia.

"Taking advantage of the faculties which had been given me I gave myself up to enrolling recruits amongst the students. I foresaw the time when, growing in numbers and forming amongst ourselves a compact nucleus, we should be able to infuse a little young life into that old body".

But he had, as yet, no idea of separating his own followers from the main body.

"I was powerless at that time to attempt anything of my own, and I was confronted by a society of men who, unequal probably to the purpose, at least embraced thought and action in one, and, despising excommunications and death sentences, persisted, when one weapon had been shattered, in making another out of it. And that was sufficient for me to feel bound to give them my name and my service. Even today, in my old age, I believe that, after the virtue of guiding the highest is knowing how to follow; to follow, I mean, one who is leading towards the Good".

This is an argument to be respected. The difficult thing is to understand how a man of Mazzini's sensibility could have felt that either Raimondo Doria or his own immediate Chief, Francesco Passano, was at all likely to be "leading towards the Good".

Francesco Antonio Passano, Grand Master of the Ligurian Lodge of the *Speranza*, at Genoa, had enjoyed a singular career. Corsican by birth, and a Freemason of the Napoleonic days, he had had some dealings with Napoleon when the Emperor was on Elba. It was his hobby to dabble in all the Italian secret societies, learning their signs and passwords, and cheating their members. Caught out by the Papal police, when he was settled at Ancona in 1817, he had suffered a mild "preventive detention" from which he was released in 1824. He had pursued a number of occupations, including that of French Consul at Ancona; when he finally returned in 1825 to Genoa, where he had lived in his youth, he gathered into his hands all the threads of Carbonarism in the Peninsula. Meanwhile, for his livelihood, he carried on a successful business in precious stones; both in this and in his revolutionary activities he enjoyed the help of his brother, Antonio, at Corfu, who ran the Greek Carbonari and enjoyed a reputation for piracy on a considerable scale. Francesco Passano must have been a man of some capacity; but whether we should believe his favourite story that, during his imprisonment at Rome, he had succeeded in converting a priest to Carbonarism while making his confession to him, may fairly be doubted. Passano said that the priest was at Turin, but an attempt to hold a dinner there in his honour, at which he was to relate this remarkable episode, broke down because the guest of honour had disappeared.

If Passano was the Chief at Genoa, and had some influence in Italy and in Greece, Raimondo Doria regarded himself and was generally regarded as an international figure on a much wider scale. With him Mazzini, at least before the episode of his mission to Tuscany, was on the closest terms, *amicissimo* he said later;

he lent Doria money, and he visited him constantly, to make reports and to receive orders. This sinister Grand Master was part-Corsican and enjoyed the title of *Marchese di S. Colombano e Capo Corso;* he came from a younger branch of the famous old Genoese family. Born in 1794, he had been enrolled in the Carbonari at the age of 18, and had seen service in the Napoleonic armies in Spain, where he had been a party to much intrigue, treachery, and Carbonaro vendetta. But he had later been remarkably well treated by the Kings of the House of Savoy, for Victor Emmanuel I gave him a captaincy in the Sardinian Cavalry in 1815 and later allowed him to go and fight again in Spain, giving him some money for his immediate purposes and a pension when he finally returned to Turin in 1826. It was soon after his return that he met Passano, at Genoa, where his imposing title of "Grand Master of the Spanish Lodge", his aristocratic name, and the belief that he was a key member of the Supreme Lodge in Paris lent him an air of great distinction. In his strange way Doria was, indeed, a not inconsiderable figure. He was a true cosmopolitan. He knew the Carbonaro Lodge in London, which he visited in 1825, and he was one of those who, during the revolutionary wars in Spain and in the Spanish American Colonies, kept in touch with the English support given to the rebels, particularly at Gibraltar, where the secret society was strong. He certainly knew the members of the Supreme Lodge in Paris, and of the international committee there which was supposed to try to co-ordinate Carbonaro movements everywhere. He knew who were the leading members in Germany, in Switzerland, in all the Italian States, and in Austria, and he claimed also to be in touch with the activities of the society across the Atlantic.

Doria had met Mazzini in 1828 and had soon recognized the worth of the young apostle. Here was a man who could be used not merely locally, as Passano was using him, to initiate new members, to arrange meetings, or to fulfil any of the numerous petty duties which a devoted secretary will patiently perform, but rather for the wider purposes of cosmopolitan Carbonarism. A secretary who had a wide knowledge of European politics and who could write both in French and in English was much too valuable to be used merely to enrol local seamen or even university students. He should be used to compose manifestos to English sea-captains at Gibraltar, to French members of the Paris committee, or even to Ireland. So we find "Strozzi" (Mazzini's Carbonaro pseudonym) writing even to O'Connell, assuring him that his fight against England is only part of the general European war of the peoples against the oppression of their governments.

It is interesting to see what Doria thought about Mazzini. He was at least trying to tell the truth when he said, a little later:

"I knew him in 1828 and if, to do him justice, I say, on the one hand, that his moral character is without stain, I should make it clear, on the other, that, as a member of the Sect, he is one of the most dangerous and the most influential who exist within it; when his political passions are aroused there is no longer anything that he will refuse to do, as is apparent from his project for killing His Majesty the Emperor of Austria and Prince Metternich.

"Since he is also a very distinguished writer, his connections with the men of letters of the various countries of Europe are very extensive, and his energy is such that all those that meet him feel the effect of it".

With Doria's opinion we may compare that given by Pietro Svegliati, a spy in Austrian pay, who wrote:

"The character of this young enthusiast is most dangerous because, being free from any semblance of any personal interest, he lives only for the regeneration of Italy, being ready, in order to gain that, to meet every danger, to sacrifice everything, even life itself, adopting even, when necessary, the role of the assassin where this may redound to the advantage of Italy. Voltaire, in his Mahomet, has given us Seide driven to crime by religious fanaticism: this man is ready to become another Seide in the fanaticism of a misconceived love of country".

It is impossible to be sure whether Doria was justified in claiming that Mazzini was party to a project for killing the Austrian Emperor and Chancellor. He said that Mazzini was ready with such a scheme as early as the year 1825 on the occasion of the Emperor's visit to Genoa; but the future conspirator was only a student then, a youth of 20, and there is no evidence that what he was planning was at all likely to take place. A more serious matter was the plot, hatched in the summer of 1830, in which Mazzini was supposed to have been involved. Its author was a certain Argenti, a Lombard whom the Austrian government had refused to recognize as Argentinian Consul at Milan, and who attributed his disappointment in this matter to Metternich. Consumed with desire to assassinate the Chancellor Argenti tried to interest the Carbonari at Genoa in the idea. At a meeting in Genoa harbour, on an American frigate, with Passano, Doria and Mazzini present, he urged support for his plan, saying that he was assured of an organization ready for the purpose at Milan and of abettors in Vienna. He himself was ready to carry it out. But the members of the Genoese Lodge opposed him, at least for the time being. Some of them pointed out that the constitutions of the Carbonari required assassination of traitors within their ranks but not of open enemies; others thought the assassination would come better as a sort of *coup de grâce* after a general uprising in Italy. Mazzini, we are told, "was silent". According to one witness the organizer of the plot at Milan was the Marchese Camillo D'Adda and his contact in the Genoa group was Mazzini; the same witness says that Elia Benza, Mazzini's closest associate at this time, was declaring that Metternich must be killed if he could not be removed in any other way – his removal would complete the downfall of the three great conservative governments, Wellington having already fallen in England, and Polignac in France. But there is nothing which definitely connects Mazzini with any initiative in the matter.

The plot which Argenti and his friends were hatching for the assassination of Metternich was one of many repercussions in Italy of the revolution of July 1830 in Paris. But, in Mazzini's view, assassination, whatever its value, on occasion, might be, should never be regarded as constituting in itself a sufficient revolutionary policy. The opportunity opened up by the Paris revolution should be grasped, he was urging, in a more positive way, and we need not doubt that he was pressing his views upon Passano and Doria. "Mazzini was known to be the best educated, and Passano and Doria, although more powerful, followed his suggestions". So said Albinola, one of the Carbonari who later gave evidence against his friends at the inquiry held at Milan into the activities of the secret societies.

If Passano and Doria were following Mazzini's suggestions at this date they were certainly also finding him and his friends an increasing embarrassment. Besides the Ruffini brothers and Elia Benza there were already other young men of intelligence and zeal in Mazzini's little circle such as Carlo Cattaneo, a future leader in the Risorgimento, and Frederico Campanella whose mother was a friend of the Ruffinis' mother. They were a more cultured group than were those near-gangsters, product of the era of the Napoleonic wars, Passano and Doria. Indeed one wonders what Doria and some of his friends can have made of meetings at which Mazzini's lofty and visionary essays were read aloud, as we are told his lengthy article *On a European Literature* was read at Doria's house. But one wonders still more to find Mazzini walking hand in hand with Doria, and with his friend the murderous Sgarzaro, and the would-be assassin Argenti, to go on board Sgarzaro's ship, the *Spartano*, in Genoa harbour, "almost every day". What did they talk about when they were not plotting? Not, we may guess, about Goethe and Schiller. We know that Sgarzaro's conversation ran along rather different lines. He was once heard boasting that

"when he was serving the Constitutionalists in Spain he had the task of disposing of fifty-three friars whom he took out to sea and dropped into the waves, tied together in twos, apart from the last whom, Sgarzaro added smiling, he was obliged to let drop alone".

This is not the sort of joke that was calculated to appeal to Mazzini. Still, if they were coarse and cruel, these men, he recognized, had at least been willing to act. They had been imprisoned, they had fought, and they had built a society which was willing to fight. The brutality of the old guard amongst the Carbonari assuredly bothered Mazzini less than did his growing fear, as the summer of 1830 wore on, that his masters were not going to seize the opportunity provided by the revolution in Paris. Why had not Doria gone to Paris, after that revolution, to concert action with the Italian committee there?

The answer was simpler than Mazzini thought. He was not merely up against Doria's inertia. He was up against his treachery. He had been wholly deceived in Doria. That "Grand Master of the Spanish Lodge" was planning something further than mere restraint of the zeal of the precocious secretary of the *Speranza;* he was planning to betray him.

For how long Doria had been playing a double game is uncertain. We have to visualize in him a man of aristocratic connections, who had seen the seamy side of Carbonaro revolution in Spain and had become disgusted by it. No doubt his kindly treatment by the Kings of Sardinia, and the commission he received in their army, had something to do with softening his antipathy towards reigning princes. No doubt, too, he had for long been an unreliable revolutionary. At all events it is clear that by the time he met Mazzini at Genoa, in 1828, he had already determined to bring about the ruin of the sect, not merely in Sardinia-Piedmont but, if possible, in the whole of Europe. And however much we may deplore his double-dealing we are bound to recognize, with the Italian historian Luzio, that it is inconceivable that he was motivated merely by the hope of some reward from the parsimonious Piedmontese government. The very dangerous game which he had decided to play meant, as he well knew, that he would have to spend the rest of his life dodging the daggers of the enraged "Cousins", and that was something he was unlikely to be agile enough to do for long. The fact was that he had come to hate them, and to feel ashamed of having to serve and obey them; he had come round to the view that the legitimate governments of Church and State were a better source of authority after all. So all the time when Mazzini knew him and served him he was really waiting and watching till he had as many as possible of the revolutionary strings in Italy and Europe in his hands, at which time he would hand over the leaders to their governments. He even envisaged a dinner, *à la Caesar Borgia*, in Paris, with all his guest-victims present and then suddenly arrested. The French revolution of July 1830, however, and Mazzini's increased activity in Italy made matters more urgent for him, and by the time Mazzini returned from Leghorn, in the autumn of that year, he had decided that he must strike at once, and that the leaders of the Lodge of the *Speranza* should be the first to go. So he got into touch with the Governor of Genoa, Venanson, who was profoundly impressed by his revelations, and the two hatched a little plot to trap both

Mazzini (centre) listens to Guerrazzi reading the manuscript of his *Assedio de Firenze*.

Drawing by G. Mantegazza.

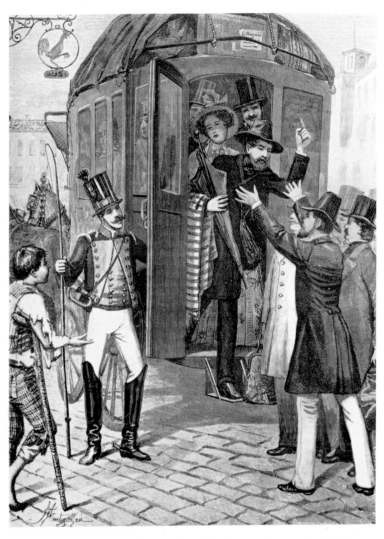

Mazzini returns to Genoa from Leghorn, announcing he has
founded an "Italian Hetairia".

Drawing by G. Mantegazza.

Grand Master Passano and Secretary Mazzini. A willing café keeper called Vallé was bribed to adopt the pseudonym "Major Cottin" and to have himself initiated by Mazzini into the second grade of the Carbonari at a hotel called the "Red Lion". A policeman, dressed up as a waiter, was introduced into the hotel in order that he might later be able to identify Passano and Mazzini. In Mazzini's words:

"I was introduced into his [Major Cottin's] bedroom. When the door was closed he went down on one knee and I, as was the custom, drew a sword from my sword-stick and began to administer the oath to him, when suddenly there opened a little shutter let into the wall beside the bed and there appeared the face of an unknown man. He took a look at me and closed it. Cottin begged me to take no notice, saying that it was his faithful servant and excusing himself for having forgotten to lock the shutter".

This little theatricality occurred on October 21st. Doria himself was away at Leghorn. He had urged Governor Venanson to delay making an arrest, saying that he hoped to extend the net more widely. However, when he returned to Genoa on November 6th he recommended that the Genoese group should be arrested forthwith. Venanson agreed; so, on November 13th, Mazzini, returning from an initiation, was arrested at his father's door, the police having been at the house since six o'clock in the morning. His pretence that he was a patient calling upon the doctor, his father, failed; but he succeeded in concealing the incriminating evidence which he had upon his person, and in the house the police found nothing of interest except a pistol and a little gunpowder. He was led away to the Sarzano barracks where, after seven days, he was interrogated, but denied the entire episode at the Red Lion, or, indeed, that he had been in Genoa at all during the past month. Since Vallé had been bribed to play his part as Major Cottin on the understanding that he would not be brought personally into the prosecution, the interrogators could make no progress. Nevertheless Mazzini was trundled off at dawn, with Passano (they were careful not to recognize each other), to the fortress of Savona, while his poor father called after him to keep up his spirits. Five others were arrested and imprisoned elsewhere.

At Turin an enquiry was forthwith conducted into the circumstances of the arrest. The evidence of Mazzini and the others, of Vallé, of the policeman turned waiter, of Governor Venanson and of Doria was all carefully considered by the president of the appropriate Senate committee and one other. They also had before them a police statement that, on the night of November the 6th, at ten o'clock, Passano, Mazzini and three others, armed with daggers, had taken an oath, their hands between Passano's, while the latter uttered the words: *the hour for vengeance is come*.

The two commissioners finally made their report on January 9th 1831 to Lescarène, Sardinian Minister of the Interior. They found, first, that the story of the oath taken at night was valueless, because the police had not stated who saw it taking place; that accusation therefore collapsed. On the other charges they found that the accounts given by the different defendants were so clear, concise and uniform that they rang true; that there was no evidence that the accused were in the habit of meeting together; that when they did meet it was only in a bookshop, open to the public; that it did not seem likely that there was a High Lodge of the Carbonari at Genoa, at all, or that Passano was at all a likely person to be a Grand Master; that there was no reliable evidence that any of the accused were Carbonari or that any of them, except Passano, had been mixed up in political matters before; and, finally, that there was no prospect of getting further evidence. After casting many aspersions upon the character of Doria, and making some excuses for the precautions taken by Governor Venanson, they accordingly recommended that all the prisoners should be set at liberty!

Lescarène, after considering the report, recommended on January 14th that all except Passano and Mazzini should be liberated unconditionally, and that those two should also be liberated, but should not be allowed to live at Genoa. Finally, on January 28th, King Charles Felix, at Turin, decided that Mazzini could not be allowed to live anywhere on the coast, but would have to move inland.

Mazzini decided he would prefer exile, as affording greater freedom for his revolutionary activity.

How can we account for the extraordinary blindness of the

commissioners and the leniency of the government? Only by assuming that Carbonaro influence was at work. The police, for instance, knew perfectly well about Doria, Passano, Mazzini, and their friends meeting in the evenings on ships in Genoa harbour because all three had been quite open about it. How, then, should they pretend to be only aware of meetings in the bookshop which Doria's cousin ran in Genoa? And how could the revolutionaries' evidence be expected to be other than mutually consistent – were they not bound to have concerted their stories together beforehand? Unfortunately for Doria, his grand plot to betray his fellow revolutionaries had misfired because the government he sought to serve was itself permeated by the influence of members of the powerful secret sect.

After the *débâcle* of the Mazzini arrest and release Doria tried hiding in Marseilles, and when that city became too hot for him he returned to Genoa, and to the friendly protection of Governor Venanson, who made him chief of his secret police! It was the removal of Venanson by the new king, Charles Albert (who had succeeded his uncle in April 1831, and who knew the Carbonaro leaders personally) that spelt Doria's doom. With the Carbonari and the government now in league to ruin him it was only a question of the means to be used. That was found in the desirable shape of his seductive mistress, Davino. Making a surprise and breathless entry into his bedroom at night, Davino persuaded him to keep her with him, saying she could not return to her brutal husband. He duly agreed, whereupon she spent the next few days in the country with him, endeavouring to murder him with various poisons, but only succeeding in upsetting his stomach. By testing the poisons on a cat (which duly succumbed) Doria proved her treachery; but he was infatuated enough to accept her confession and contrition. After this she did have the decency to desist from her attempts to poison him; but this put her into a difficulty with her masters, the Carbonari, whom she, too, now had to avoid. The frustrated Carbonari were obliged, in the end, to effect the arrest of the two of them, for adultery (and Doria, also, for having pistols under his pillow). Davino extricated herself by claiming that she had been enticed and then raped by Doria, on the night when she had fled to him; she thus escaped free. But Doria was duly sentenced to two years' imprisonment, and it was a much harsher imprisonment than that suffered by Mazzini.

The attitude of the Carbonari seems to have been what mattered in those days. To their sympathy Mazzini owed his light sentence, and his friends and Davino their release. To their anger Venanson owed his removal, and Doria his harsh imprisonment. But the Grand Master of the Spanish Lodge was not done with yet, for Metternich was beginning to be interested in him. In January 1832 the Austrian Chancellor started asking for his extradition to Milan, so that he might give evidence before the tribunal enquiring there into the activities of the secret societies. And the attitude of the Turin government was at last beginning to change. Charles Albert was coming to understand something of the danger in his midst. Mazzini, by then in exile at Marseilles, was planning movements more dangerous to the monarchy than Doria or Passano had dreamed of. Fear of Mazzini put a new aspect upon the Doria case, and in the summer of 1832 the Grand Master had his prison sentence commuted to banishment so as to enable him to go to Milan and tell the Austrians what he knew. He never returned to Piedmont but he never ceased to issue his warnings and pleadings to the government at Turin; and amongst the menaces which he described to the Austrians there figured most prominently the person of Mazzini.

When Mazzini was detained in the fortress of Savona during the investigation of Doria's case against him he had already finished his apprenticeship as a revolutionary. In future, he might collaborate with the Carbonari, but he would no longer take his orders from any Grand Masters or Supreme Lodges. Doria, he now knew, had betrayed, but this was not yet known to his friends, and it was necessary to warn them in his letters to his mother. As these were read by the prison authorities at Savona he used a prearranged code by which the first letters of every second word, when put together, made a message in Latin. It was thus that he set the Good Cousins to work to catch Doria.

Passano was with him in prison. He, like Mazzini, was Doria's dupe; so the natural thing was for Mazzini to try to concert a plan of action with him. "I have safe means of correspondence", he urged the Grand Master of the *Speranza* during the few moments when they met in the prison corridor, "give me the names!" Passano's reply, besotted as the old man now was with symbols, was "to tap me on the head and confer upon me I know not what indispensable grade of Masonry!" The veteran revolutionary had had enough; the only intrigues he was interested in now were those which could secure him an easier lot, in his imprisonment. As an experienced prisoner he knew quite a bit about how to gain concessions, and he was ready to help his less experienced companion to learn the tricks. But Mazzini was preoccupied with plans for action, and it now seemed to him as certain that Passano was a broken reed as it was evident that Doria was a traitor. Who, then, was left but himself? The revolutionary leadership which Mazzini determined at Savona to assume was his by right of succession. The defection of Doria and Passano had left him as the only possible leader.

For some ten weeks, from the middle of November 1830, Mazzini thus remained imprisoned at Savona while awaiting the result of the investigation at Turin. He had a healthy horror of imprisonment and wept tears of baffled rage at first. But there proved to be compensations in the life of a prisoner. The fortress which was his prison is situated high on a cliff and he had a fine view from his window over the sea and the sky, "two symbols", as he called them, "of the infinite". Soon he was dreaming dreams, conceiving a new kind of revolutionary society loftier, freer, and more dedicated. He had with him a Bible, a Tacitus and a Byron and there was the conversation of the Governor, Fontana, and of his cultured wife, a relative of Manzoni, who would invite him to coffee in the evening and would reason with him on the errors of the Carbonari. He could write, and receive letters; and, thanks to their prearranged code, the Ruffinis and Elia Benza could keep him in touch with the news. A maid, Caterina, brought him his meals; a kindly gaoler, Antonietti, asked him, every evening, if he had any orders. In his seclusion the ideas gleaned from his reading of the historians of Ancient Rome and of Italy, the visions of the romantic poets, and the utopias of the French reformers mingled with his experiences as a revolutionary and sorted themselves out into the characteristic concepts of his own future teaching. Italy, freed from the foreigner, united and republican, with her capital at Rome. Rome, for the third time in the history of the world, giving forth the Civilizing Word. An United Italy, initiator of a new epoch, the epoch of the Peoples. Italy wresting the initiative, in civilization, from France. And all this to be accomplished by sacrifice, by martyrdom, by relentless obedience to duty – as the Greek Hetairia had accomplished it. This was the Law of Progress, the Law of Humanity, ordained by God, inescapable Destiny. And his own mission was to elevate the Italian revolutionaries to this plane of thought and action.

Then suddenly, at the end of January 1831, he was released as a result of the self-imposed blindness of the senatorial investigating committee. He was back, now, in the real world, a world so different from his dreams. And he found that the Carbonari, far from being moribund, had achieved an uprising upon a considerable scale. Not this time in Piedmont, or in Naples, but in the Papal State they had raised the revolution, as a greeting for the new Pope, Gregory XVI. They had seized power in the Romagna, in the Marches, and even as near to Rome as at Terni. But there the movement had stopped. The populace of Rome, much more papal in sympathy than that of Bologna, had refused to rise; the poor of the Trastevere quarter had, indeed, come out in defence of the new Pope.

Mazzini was still a Carbonaro; now the hour of the Carbonari seemed to have struck. Clearly the opportunity must not be lost, the uprising in the Romagna must be supported by similar movements wherever else they could be organized. For the revolutionaries at Bologna had shown their intention of starting an Italian movement which should extend throughout the Peninsula, and the delegates who mustered there from the Romagna, the Marches, and Umbria called themselves the "Assembly of Deputies of the Free Provinces of Italy". It was a challenge to Good Cousins everywhere to throw in their lot.

These things were happening as the young Mazzini, accompanied by his uncle, Alberti, was driving over the Mont Cenis to that voluntary exile which he had chosen so that he might the

more easily organize the revolution. At Geneva he met the most
distinguished of the Italian exiles, the historian Sismondi, who
was now preaching a federal Italy to his assembled countrymen.
He also met Pellegrino Rossi, the future liberal minister of Pio
Nono, who would suffer assassination at Rome in 1848. But as he
held forth on his utopian visions he saw in their faces only a
reflection of the quizzical smile he had seen on the lips of
Guerrazzi, in Tuscany. So these men, he reflected bitterly, who
talked and wrote so much, were no real revolutionaries after all.
But then:

"a Lombard exile, who had always listened attentively to my talk
without saying anything, drew me aside and whispered in my ear that,
if I really wanted action, I should go to Lyons and present myself to
the Italians whom I would find collected together in the *café della
Fenice*".

Lyons was on the way to Paris, whither he and his uncle were
destined, so all he had to do was to hasten their journey. At
Lyons he found real signs of vitality, including some of the men
he had seen with his mother ten years earlier at Genoa, after the
abortive 1821 uprising. Amongst them was Carlo Bianco,
destined to be his close companion in exile and revolution.
Lyons was exhilarating. An incursion into Savoy was being
busily planned.

"The expedition comprised perhaps two thousand Italians and a
certain number of French workmen . . . the preparations were made
publicly; the tricolour flag of Italy was interwoven, in the *café della
Fenice*, the committee's meeting-room, with the flag of France; the
deposits of arms were well known to all; there was close contact
between the committee and the Prefect of Lyons".

The Prefect could not have allowed these irregular preparations
if they had been disapproved of in Paris, but Louis Philippe had
only been seven months on the French throne, and, as the product
of a revolution himself, he still appeared in the rôle of patron of
revolutions everywhere. The Carbonaro uprising in the Romagna
could never have been undertaken had not the new French king
made it clear that France would not tolerate Austrian intervention to suppress it, and the revolutionaries at Lyons felt
confident that they would not be interfered with.

But unfortunately for them the time had come when Louis was

turning respectable. He was now regarded by the Powers as securely enough established to warrant their according him official recognition – on the understanding, naturally, that he ceased to patronize foreign revolutionary movements aimed at the unseating of legitimate monarchs. So Mazzini and his new friends found, one morning, that all was changed.

"As I was repairing to the *Fenice* full of hope that action was imminent, I saw a crowd gathering to read a government announcement posted on to a wall. It was a harsh proclamation against the Italian project, an instruction to the exiles to dissolve their band and a brutal warning that the full rigour of the law would be brought into play against anybody who attempted to violate the frontiers of friendly states and to compromise France in her relations with other governments".

Some supposed that Louis only meant to wash his own hands of responsibility while leaving the Italians free to act. So Mazzini proposed

"that the problem be solved by sending a nucleus of armed men, to serve as an advanced guard of the expedition, and by mixing in with it as many French workmen as possible, on the road to Savoy; and this was done. But a troop of cavalry caught up with them and scattered them by force . . . then began the scattering of the exiles. Some were conducted, handcuffed, as far as Calais, and were put on board for England".

Again, as at Geneva, a relentless revolutionary appeared at Mazzini's elbow and determined his next action. This time it was Gaetano Borso, who had fought in Piedmont in 1821 and since in Spain.

"He told me that he and a few other republicans were leaving, that same night, for Corsica, whence, in arms, to join the insurrection which was still alive in Central Italy; and he asked me if I would like to go with them. I accepted at once. I hid this sudden decision from my uncle, leaving him a few lines begging him not to worry about me and to say nothing for a few days to my family; and I left. In the *Diligence* which carried us to Marseilles I found Bianco . . . we travelled almost without stopping to Marseilles; from Marseilles to Toulon; and from Toulon, on a Neapolitan merchant ship, across the most tempestuous sea I have ever seen, to Bastia. . . .
"Carbonarism, brought there by the Neapolitan exiles, was then uppermost in the island and the people made of it what every man should make of an association he has freely accepted – a sort of religion. As was fitting at the outset of a great undertaking, many

who had sworn vengeance against each other were reconciled within it".

To reach the mainland, from Corsica, with the band of upwards of two thousand armed men amongst whom he now found himself, ships were needed.

"There was wanting money with which to charter ships, and to enable us to leave something to help the poor families of those islanders who were going to follow us . . . Two of our men, Zuppi and a certain Vantini of Elba, who later on founded some hotels in London and elsewhere, were sent to the Provisional Government of Bologna to offer it help and to ask of it the necessary money".

But the Provisional Government, naturally enough, declined to assist revolutionaries on an island subject to France. So

"from that inept government, which trusted only in diplomacy and shrank from arms, they had the reply of barbarous foreigners: *whoever really wants liberty risks himself for it*".

Disaster overtook the revolutionaries of Central Italy. Francis IV of Modena, who had flirted with the revolution, dropped this dangerous game as soon as he saw that Metternich meant, after all, to intervene. And this Austrian intervention, made possible by Louis Philippe's new respectability, soon settled matters in Modena, Parma, and the Papal States. But it is worth noting that the uprising lasted altogether close on two months – from the beginning of February to the end of March 1831 – that it extended the whole way from Parma, in the north, to Terni, near Rome; and that the revolutionaries at Bologna clearly proclaimed, for a time at least, national rather than merely local purposes. But Mazzini poured particular scorn, during the next few months, upon the behaviour of the revolutionary leaders of the Carbonari, in this their latest uprising, and he made of their 'ineptitude' the occasion for his founding his own society of Young Italy. It is not, therefore, to be wondered at that he antagonized them; and this antagonism would have a serious effect upon the outcome of his own conspiracies.

Chapter 3

MARSEILLES: YOUNG ITALY

The end of March 1831 saw Mazzini stranded in Corsica and the Carbonaro revolt at Bologna collapsing.

"All hope of action having disappeared, and having spent what little money I had, I left Corsica and made my way to Marseilles where my uncle claimed me again, in the name of my family.

"And in Marseilles I turned once again to the old idea of Savona, the founding of Young Italy. Thither poured the exiles from Parma, from Modena, from the Romagna, more than a thousand of them. Mingling amongst them, I came to know the best, in that year – Nicola Fabrizi, Celeste Menotti, brother of poor Ciro (executed by Francis IV at Modena) Angelo Usiglio, Giuseppe Lamberti, Gustavo Modena, L. A. Melegari, Giuditta Sidoli, a woman rare in her purity and the constancy of her principles . . .".

These are names we meet often in the saga of Mazzini – especially that of Giuditta Sidoli. They were the little band who were going to form the nucleus of his own new association. There were perhaps forty of them at first, mostly at Marseilles, or on the Ligurian coast near Genoa. They had all been mixed up in Carbonaro movements and it would be wrong to suppose that they were now waging war upon that old vast revolutionary body in which they had been nurtured. The parent association was in the habit of spawning smaller offspring – "economies" was the technical term for them. Such, already formed, were the *Apofasimeni* and the *Indipendenti*. It was generally supposed that Mazzini's Young Italy was just another such body; and so, in a sense, it was, at least for a time. And just as the members of Young Italy often remained Carbonari, so they might also be members of the other "economies" as well. They might likewise be Freemasons. Mazzini only insisted that they must not be members of societies with purposes specifically opposed to his own.

The differences between Young Italy and the Carbonari were

at first far less conspicuous than were the similarities. Having himself received his revolutionary training as a Carbonaro, Mazzini, when he came to make out the articles of his own association at Marseilles, some time in the early summer of 1831, made them out on the pattern of those of the parent body. So we find that each member of Young Italy is to choose a pseudonym drawn from one of the warrior families of the Middle Ages – the name he chose for himself was Strozzi, which had been his name in the Carbonari. Every member, as in the earlier body, is to furnish himself with a dagger, a rifle, and fifty cartridges. There is the same secret greeting between members, the one Cousin's hands crossed and spread out with the palms flat on the heart, the other's crossed with the palms extended outwards to indicate an open heart, and the greeting *what is the time*? with the response *time for the struggle*, followed by the inter-locking of the index fingers to symbolize the link of a chain. The numerous grades of the Carbonari are reduced to two, those who are simply enrolled, and those who are also enrollers, as Mazzini had been himself. The enrollers are to have their greeting code-word changed every month or two. There is to be a central congregation (for the time being at Marseilles) and provincial congregations are to be formed throughout Italy. There is to be an entrance fee and a monthly subscription, which can be varied locally. No longer will they call themselves Good Cousins; they will be Brothers, or, as Mazzini himself more simply called them, "the Good". They are to try to insinuate themselves into positions of public responsibility; traitors are to be "eliminated" – and so are tyrants. Members are to swear not to reveal, whether for fear of torture or for favour of reward, the existence or the laws or the purpose of the Association and, if they can, they are themselves to destroy the betrayer.

Most of this belongs to the Carbonaro tradition. On the other hand, after some months Mazzini felt that Young Italy had made sufficient progress to enable him to imprint it with a hallmark more specifically his own. Members are now forbidden to join other associations (but there was little attempt to enforce this) and the oath requiring the elimination of tyrants and of traitors is omitted. It is reasonable as well as charitable to suppose that the invitations to assassination and murder included in the earlier regulations were uncongenial to Mazzini personally, having been embodied only as a concession to the very strong Carbonaro traditions of most of the members. In future years he was to show himself opposed to acts of vengeance against traitors[1] though his attitude towards assassination remained equivocal.

The real originality of Young Italy, as Mazzini came to shape it during the summer and autumn of 1831, at Marseilles, consisted not so much in its preaching an United Italy, with her capital at Rome (Unity had already been the avowed objective of Foscolo, of Santarosa, of the movements of 1821 and 1831, and of the Carbonaro Chief, Buonarroti), nor in its preaching a Republic (the favourite ideal of Buonarroti) but rather in its insistence that the bounden duty and mission of Italians was to strive for these things and to be willing to suffer martrydom for them. The Italian people were no longer to think about claiming their democratic "rights", as the French had claimed theirs in 1789; they were to think about the mission of Italy in the world, the mission of an Italy of free Italians, regenerated by their struggle. Their sense of mission would enable them to win their rights, as it were incidentally. And it would lead them to look no longer to France for their salvation, as the revolution of 1831 had looked to France – all members of Young Italy must be Italians. Nor would they want any longer to look to princes to lead them, as they had looked to the Duke of Modena in 1831 or to Charles Albert in 1821. And their sense of a new mission would likewise free them from looking to the older men, those who had won laurels in past revolts, because the older men would believe in the older approach. They would look to the young. Those over forty years of age were at first supposed to be excluded from Young Italy; but it is not surprising that Mazzini was soon prepared to make exceptions in favour of older men provided that they were "young in spirit".

It is more surprising that he was still ready to appeal to

---

[1] He insisted upon having his name cleared, in the French courts, when it had been falsely said that the murders at Rodez in Southern France, of two Italians, suspected spies of the Duke of Modena, had been carried out in obedience to the orders of a secret tribunal over which he had presided.

princes – even to Charles Albert himself, the prince whom he regarded as having betrayed the revolution of 1821.

In April 1831 Charles Albert, as we saw, had succeeded his uncle as King of Sardinia. Despite an ostentatious display of traditionalist sentiment he had never lived down his revolutionary past; he was still mistrusted by the legitimists on account of his association with the Carbonari in 1821, and his uncle had sought to keep him from the throne. Small wonder, then, that the Carbonari believed that he might yet be ready to embrace their notions; and we can safely assume that it was pressure upon Mazzini from his Carbonaro associates, at Marseilles and back in Genoa, which induced him, for all his now ardent republicanism, to appeal to the young king to head the movement for Italian unity. The Carbonari had looked upon Mazzini as their literary luminary, the man who knew how to compose, in several languages, a stirring and effective address. Clearly, at this exciting moment in the spring of 1831, with Charles Albert ascending the throne, the brilliant young secretary of the *Speranza* Lodge must be induced to use his talents once more. And Mazzini, from Marseilles, responded to their desires, using, in fact, the very phrases which he had used on their behalf in addressing himself to Charles X of France, two years earlier ("Sire! if I believed you to be a commonplace king, of foolish or tyrannical mind, I would not send you these words . . . Italy knows that what you possess of royalty is more than the purple . . .").

Mazzini secured the printing of this Open Letter privately, at Marseilles, and posted copies of it to the addresses of such friends and accomplices as he could think of, not only in Genoa, and Piedmont, but in the other Italian states as well. It was an eloquent appeal, but also a highly menacing one. It starts by finding excuses for the king's defection in the revolution of 1821, explaining that he was not, at that time, his own master. But now he is free. Now, as king, he can act in accordance with his own nature; indeed it is made very clear to him that he will be well advised to do so: "there is not a heart in Italy whose pulse did not quicken at the news of your accession; there is not an eye in Europe that is not turned to watch your first steps in the career now opened to you". An alarming prospect, this, for Charles

Albert, but not one which he needed to take too seriously, for the eyes of Europe were, in fact, turned, as always, upon Paris, and Louis Philippe was making it only too clear that he was now determined to support the forces of order rather than those of revolution. It was therefore inconceivable that Charles Albert, scarcely more than a petty princeling, living precariously between the great powers of France and Austria, should head a revolutionary crusade. Even Mazzini is prepared to recognize that the rôle for which he is casting the king will not be an easy one. Europe, he explains, is divided into two camps, "power and right", "movement and inertia", kings striving to "maintain their usurpations" and peoples striving to assert "the rights assigned to them by nature". If Charles Albert tries to maintain the "usurpations" (i.e. the traditional rights of the House of Savoy), then he signs his own death warrant, for "blood calls for blood, and the dagger of the conspirator is never so terrible as when sharpened upon the tombstone of a martyr". What he has to do is to set up a democratic constitution and to recognize "the right, power and sovereignty of the nation". And this nation is not merely Piedmont, it is the whole of Italy. Mazzini assures him that his mission is none other than to unite all the states of Italy in the struggle for Italian independence. And he need not worry about France, or Austria, or the Italian princes, because the people will prove his sure ally – this last assurance, if he recalled it in 1848, must have brought a bitter smile to the king's lips for, after seventeen more years of Mazzinian propaganda, and with a now friendly France and an embarrassed Austria, the people proved quite unwilling either to rise behind him in effective numbers or to unite.

"Sire", Mazzini concludes his letter, "I have spoken to you the truth. The men of freedom await your answer in your deeds. Whatsoever that answer be, rest assured that posterity will either hail your name as that of the greatest of men, or as that of the last of Italian tyrants. Choose".

Charles Albert chose, and Mazzini, till then a voluntary exile, was banished under penalty of imprisonment if he should try to return. For there was little of the Carbonaro left in Charles Albert.

Mazzini's Open Letter created something of a furore in Italy, even though it was only signed "an Italian" and it was some weeks before its authorship was certain. By mid-June a copy had been put into the hands of the Genoese police by one of the more timid of Mazzini's lawyer friends, who had received it through the post. It was soon openly on sale in Tuscany; copies had turned up in Naples by September. Mazzini claimed later that he had written the letter at the request of others, and we may assume that those others were his Carbonaro friends. He also claimed later that he had never had any hopes or even intentions for the success of the appeal. The idea of Charles Albert leading the progressive movement was only fit for "the weak-minded who abounded then and abound now". At the time (June 1831) he wrote to an advanced veteran revolutionary, Michele Palmieri, in exile in Paris:

"I send you a writing which I have addressed to Charles Albert; not that I have any hope in him; he is a coward, if not worse; there is no hope of salvation by a man who, to justify himself with Italy, would need all the energy which Genius could give to an idea conceived and planned at the highest level. But I was anxious that the traitor-prince should not be able to say 'the word liberty was not uttered; opinion was uncertain, and I made no move for fear of making matters worse'; and I also wished that the people should not be able to deceive themselves on account of a few frightened and treacherous concessions".

But no reader of the Open Letter will easily believe that it was quite insincere. Certainly, an United and Republican Italy was already Mazzini's goal, as it had already been the goal of many Carbonaro leaders, including Buonarroti, the Great Chief, in Paris. But before that goal was achieved he knew well enough that there would have to be struggles and fighting, especially against the Austrians, and in these struggles princes might play their part. In 1833, eighteen months after his Open Letter, when his plan was an army revolt in Piedmont, he was still thinking in terms of using Charles Albert as general of a purged army. There were obvious dangers in using princes, but there was no necessary reason, in Mazzinian principle, why Charles Albert should not be employed as an instrument, during the period of transition; behind Charles Albert, or any other prince, he always saw a Committee of Public Safety, with himself in control. When he

published his Letter, as when he published a similar letter to Pio
Nono in 1846, his hopes may have been slender, but they were
real. Always Mazzini was an opportunist of means, though not of
ends, and Charles Albert was a possible means, as Victor Emmanuel II, Napoleon III and even Bismarck were later on. Some
of his Carbonaro friends, the men of the 1831 revolt in the
Romagna, and even their leader, Ciro Menotti, a man as lofty in
his political idealism as Mazzini himself, had used that palpably
unreliable prince, Francis IV of Modena, in their designs for
Italy. The idea of using self-seeking princes for the regeneration
of Italy was as old as Machiavelli and it was certainly part of
Mazzini's thinking. When, in later years, he sought to explain
away his appeal he did so because a new party, a "Moderate
Party", had grown up which thought the *goal* for Italy was that
she should become a federation of states under constitutional
princes. With that ideal, which appealed to so many wise and
moderate men in 1847, Mazzini would have nothing whatever to
do; and he would not have his Open Letter of 1831 used against
him for the Moderates' purposes.

"Sir", he wrote to his Paris publishers in April 1847, "you asked my
permission to reprint a certain letter addressed by me to King Charles
Albert. . . . I am unwilling that my consent should be interpreted
either as counsel or as advice. Be kind enough to look to this, and I
am satisfied".

"The men of freedom await your answer", he had written to
the king.

Who were they?

They were not a large band, in 1831, but many of them were
resolute and some were idealists. They were the exiles of the
revolutions of 1821 and 1831, some of whom had spent the
intervening years fighting in Spain, or in Greece, or in South
America, or wherever else they could find some revolution to
support. Already they could count many martyrs for their cause
such as Santorre di Santarosa, slain on the Greek island of
Sphacteria, or Ciro Menotti, hanged by Francis IV of Modena,
or Ugo Foscolo who had died in exile in London. But it would
also not be unfair to call many of them professional revolutionaries and for some a harsher name would be more appropriate.

Mazzini's father tells him, in prison at Savona, the court's decison: either he must live in a small island town of Piedmont or he must go into exile.

Drawing by G. Mantegazza.

Mazzini's own visions and his own devotion to a cause lying outside himself certainly raise him to a plane as lofty as that of any leader of the Italian Risorgimento, even though his fanaticism led him into policies which some have always found it impossible to condone. He had, by now, sublimated his adolescent resentment against aristocracies, monarchies, Austrian soldiers, and Catholic hierarchy into a passionate faith in the People, especially when banded together as Peoples, and especially when constituting an United and Republican Italy. As for the individual, let him embrace duty, sacrifice, martyrdom. Would he pursue Art? Art should be "nothing but a hymn of war" until Italy be freed. Would he dally with Love? "the caress, the kiss, which today is profaned by those who do not understand all its mystery, would become sacred . . . were it the reward for the virtue of a citizen".

These were lofty, if rather puritan sentiments, loftier, certainly, than most of the Italian exiles gathered at Marseilles could aspire to. It is easy to call them mere sublimations of primitive passions but they were lofty sublimations and Mazzini himself believed in them. Certainly his practical work, which took most of his time, was conspiracy and intrigue which would stop at little to upset the existing order, to throw out the Austrians, and to unify Italy. But the New Italy which he preached was to be a sublime Italy, a regenerated, virtuous, and generous Italy; an Italy of Italians rather like Mazzini himself. A dream perhaps, and a romantic one at that; but a dream which Doria and Passano could not have dreamt and one for which Mazzini was prepared to work and to suffer, himself, throughout his life, not merely to lead others (as often proved necessary) to their imprisonment and death. It was a dream distilled from notions much too optimistic about human nature, and in some ways it led to harm. But it was generous, as well as dangerous.

Those whom he gathered immediately round himself, during that summer of 1831 at Marseilles, were a very small band of devoted disciples. Closest to him were three, Luigi Amadeo Melegari, Angelo Usiglio and Giuseppe Lamberti. Melegari was the toughest and most energetic of the three; after the collapse of the 1831 revolt he had escaped in a fishing-boat from the coast

c

north of Pisa, and a vessel bound for Marseilles had eventually picked him up. He was the man who looked after the party organization at Marseilles, who saw the contraband copies of their journal, *La Giovine Italia*, safely smuggled on the boats, who upbraided the Chief if he thought his leadership was slackening, and who, in the end, was prepared to shoulder the whole revolutionary organization at Marseilles after Mazzini had moved to Geneva in 1833. He disliked Mazzini's love affair with Giuditta Sidoli and he disliked still more his new Religion of Humanity. He considered it was merely vanity to desert the Ancient Faith, and it is an interesting commentary upon the practical significance of Mazzini's theology that his right hand man scorned it. But Melegari was a fearless and a loyal servant and as such Mazzini used him and abused him unsparingly, not expecting him to follow his own romantic religious flights, but expecting him to produce, somehow, money, rifles, and even ships. Usiglio and Lamberti were both more personally congenial to the Chief. Both were from the Duchy of Modena, Usiglio from the capital city, and Lamberti from Reggio. For their participation in the revolution they had been compelled to flee, had found themselves at Marseilles, and had joined Mazzini. Lamberti shared the Chief's secret lodgings, and spent much of his time checking the proofs of *La Giovine Italia*. Both were devoted, but neither was physically strong. They served chiefly as secretaries. Very useful, too, was G. Ciani, from Milan, who helped to pay the costs, and who planned the despatch of the journal, via Switzerland, into Lombardy. But most useful of all, very probably, was that eccentric and beautiful woman, the Principessa di Belgioioso, at that time in Marseilles, who lavished money, from her large fortune, upon Mazzini's projects.

Most of the foundation members of Young Italy at Marseilles came from Modena and were the product of the 1831 uprising there. In their attempts to organize revolution in Italy they had to rely, at first, upon that small personal following which Mazzini had been building up within the Carbonari.

"Without an office, without assistance, immersed the whole day and part of the night in work, writing articles and letters, interviewing travellers, enrolling sailors, folding up pieces of paper, doing up parcels, alternating between intellectual and manual work . . . we lived as true equals and brothers, with only one thought, only one hope, devoted only to one spiritual ideal; loved and admired by the foreign republicans for our tenacity of purpose and capacity for uninterrupted work; often, since we spent our money on all this, we were in extreme poverty, yet we were cheerful as could be, and smiling with the smile of faith in the future. Those years between 1831 and 1833 were two years of young life, pure and joyful in their devotion . . .".

Their difficulties of writing, printing, and packing, in secret, were surpassed by their difficulties in distributing their contraband propaganda. But here Mazzini's Carbonaro experience and contacts stood him in good stead. He had his acquaintances at Leghorn, notably Carlo Bini. And there were many upon whom he could rely at Genoa, and at other places along the Ligurian coast, such as Porto Maurizio, Elia Benza's home, or Taggia, where the Ruffinis were often to be found at the villa of their uncle, the Canon, who had educated them as little boys. Moreover, the Carbonari had cultivated the sailors whose ships plied along the Mediterranean littoral of Italy, Corsica, France, and Spain. The sometime secretary of the *Speranza* was well enough known to these seamen, on whose ships, when they lay in Genoa harbour, he had convened secret meetings. How many of these sailors were already, before Mazzini's Savona imprisonment, something more than Carbonari, something more like personal disciples, we do not know; but it is probable that, in the harbour of Marseilles, he found ready-made the nucleus of Young Italy's postal service.

"Approach the men of the sea, who land on your shores", he advises a friend in Rome; "those men are our best friends"; and later he tells how "there was a young man called Montanari, who sailed in the Neapolitan boats and represented the society on them; he died later on of cholera in the south of France; others, employed on the French boats, helped us wonderfully. And until the anger of the governments developed into a frenzy, we entrusted the packages to these men, merely writing upon a package intended for Genoa the address of a firm not under suspicion in Leghorn, on one intended for Leghorn an address at Civita Vecchia, and so on. The package was thus exempted from scrutiny by the customs and police at the first port of call and was safeguarded by our man on the ship until his comrades of the society were warned, came on board, divided up the papers and carried them off, concealing them about their persons".

As the police became more active, so the penalties became more severe and the rewards to informers more tempting. So

"there began a duel between ourselves and the petty governments of Italy which cost us effort and expense but which we fought with good success. We sent the papers packed inside barrels of pumice stone, then in the middle of boxes of fish amongst which we worked, at night, in an old warehouse which we rented. Ten or twelve of these boxes would be numbered and despatched by commercial firms, unaware of the secret, to other firms, equally unaware, in different towns, where one of our men, warned of the arrival, would come and buy the box whose number gave the clue to what it contained".

They used many other devices, for instance, on one occasion, the false bottom of a trunk. The discovery of this trunk was something of a disaster. At the end of June 1832, Mazzini sent in it some old clothes, intended for his mother's attention, and addressed on her behalf to the firm of Ricci Brothers at Genoa. A customs officer saw that the trunk had a false bottom, and when he had opened the hidden part he found it contained, in print, five copies of the first number of *La Giovine Italia*, seven other revolutionary writings, and, in manuscript, thirteen letters together with some instructions to Elia Benza for a mission he was to undertake, on behalf of the society, to Naples. It was a rich haul. Two of the letters were particularly secret. One, to Elia Benza himself, contained a list of men upon whom he could rely at Naples, and the formula of the chemical he should use for revealing letters written in invisible ink (an acid solution of iron) and one for the ink itself (precipitate of iron potash) together with a list of the current Carbonaro signs of recognition and passwords at Naples. The other important letter was to Jacopo Ruffini. It is dated June 16, whereas the one to Benza is dated April 16th – some indication of how long Mazzini had to wait for a ship to take the trunk. In it he explains his difficulties: "As I write I am still uncertain whether I can despatch the letter or the trunk; but that devil of a captain Andrac knows and cares nothing about it". The letter contains much miscellaneous information about the comings and goings of members of the society and their agents, but the really significant thing in it is a first reference to Ramorino in which it is disclosed that he is to be the general in charge of the invasion of Savoy, which Mazzini was already planning, but which did not take place until January 1834. The general, it appears, has already been promised 40,000 francs from Lombardy, for his preparations, is now pursued by the French police, and Mazzini does not know where he is.

Lescarène, Charles Albert's Minister of the Interior, took the discovery of this interesting trunk rather lightly. But he sent an account of the episode, and copies of the letters, to Naples, thus prejudicing the chances of Elia Benza on his mission there and embarrassing the Neapolitan Congregation of Young Italy. He also censured the police for not immediately arresting the agent of Ricci Brothers, and also Maria Mazzini, as distributors of seditious literature, so that their houses, which would be likely to contain revealing documents, might be searched before they had the opportunity to destroy them (Maria Mazzini did, in fact, destroy her collection of letters from her son after this episode). To the king he reported that the captured documents only confirmed what was already known; they showed that Young Italy was in no position yet to take effective action, if only for lack of funds; it would be best to let matters take their course while redoubling vigilance and allowing the fear to grow that more had been discovered than actually had been. It might, he thought, be advisable to remove from the Genoa area the brigade of Aosta, with which it was clear that Mazzini had contact; but this recommendation the king ignored as unnecessary. It was unthinkable to him that there could be disaffection in his devoted army and he still seriously underrated Mazzini.

Meanwhile the Governor of Genoa wrote to the Minister that the police had, in due course, visited Mazzini's mother, who had fainted, and was now ill, and that none of the local fraternity of Young Italy dared visit her house. "Since the recent event they are all filled with alarm and they complain of the imprudence of the *avvocat Masini* (*sic*) who has so badly compromised them."

There is a casual air about police procedure both during and after this episode which is reminiscent of the time of Mazzini's arrest in November 1830. If Sardinia-Piedmont was a police state, it was a wonderfully inefficient one. But, if the government was casual, Mazzini's organization, too, was amateurish. He could not afford such discoveries as this.

Under pressure from Austria and Sardinia the French government sought, that summer, to expel the leading exiles from Marseilles. Louis Philippe was becoming still more respectable, so that the host of émigrés of all nations swarming around the docks at Marseilles would have to scatter. Nor could the irregularities of the *rue Pavillon*, where Mazzini had his lodgings at number 27, be overlooked any longer. An expulsion order was served upon him there, and the little printing press of Dufort, further down the street, where the revolutionaries used to congregate, and where *La Giovine Italia*, together with much other revolutionary literature, was printed, had to close.

Mazzini, however, though ordered to leave France, only left the *rue Pavillon;* he did not leave Marseilles save to go for a few days to Lyons, which he visited to throw the police off the scent. And in October the beautiful Giuditta Sidoli (also an exile from Reggio in the Duchy of Modena) received him into her house at number 57 *rue St Ferréol*. This remarkable woman was a real mother to the exiles. She was ardent as they were for the Cause, having been married into it at the early age of sixteen and lived in revolutionary circles ever since. Her own family were the aristocratic Bellerios of Milan but her husband, Giovanni Sidoli, had been one of the revolutionaries of Reggio, and the two had lived the lives of exiles till the husband had died of consumption, at Montpellier, in 1828. Giuditta had returned to Reggio, with their four children, but the revolutionary life was in her blood and the uprising of 1831 in the Duchy had found her inspiring her late husband's friends to deeds of valour and herself sewing tricolour flags. When it was over and she had become, in her own right, a proscribed revolutionary, she had entrusted her children to her traditionally minded father-in-law (who duly had them educated by the Jesuits) and had taken, again, the path of exile, finding herself, by February of 1832, in Marseilles, with her old friends around her once more – and with Mazzini.

More than one of the fraternity became bewitched by her; but for Mazzini she became the grand passion of his life. He was not, however, to live in her house for long, for he was by now the one in whom the police were really interested and Giuditta's house, which attracted all the Italian refugees, was altogether too conspicuous a place for him. He evaded one attempt to secure his arrest and expulsion by having a friend, of similar appearance, despatched to Geneva in his place whilst he himself passed amongst the police in a uniform of the National Guard! He found his last home at Marseilles in the house of Démosthène Ollivier, an ardent republican and the father of Napoleon III's future premier, Émile Ollivier. There he remained off and on (he was at Lyons for some weeks in the spring of '33) until he left Marseilles for good in June 1833 and settled at Geneva.

Life had become much more difficult. The editorial and printing staff of *La Giovine Italia* were now scattered and Mazzini had to entrust the printing of the periodical to a Frenchman, Victor Vian, and to French operatives, with the result that directing the paper became "a horrible torment" for him.

"The French compositors did not understand a syllable of Italian, and an elderly Sardinian who boasted of knowing our language was obstinate and stupid; fully three times I corrected the proofs; it was time wasted, and we published the first number full of printing mistakes".

He also published an apology to his readers. Soon he hired a press, and he and his friends printed the next number themselves.

He was obliged to write most of the journal himself for want of support from other writers. By November 1832 he was writing to Charles Didier, in Paris, who had congratulated him on the first number:

"I will tell you frankly . . . that *La Giovine Italia* lacks collaborators. When I started I was promised help by all our best intellectuals, Libri, Benci, Giannone, Berchet, Pecchio, etc. Not one of them has fulfilled his promise and I am pretty well alone at the moment. None the less the journal will appear; we count upon overcoming by our obstinacy the inertia of our countrymen".

The only writer of distinction who contributed was the historian Sismondi, and to secure his contribution Mazzini had to allow him to take a federalist line which ill suited his United Italy programme. Gioberti – not yet famous – contributed, but under a pseudonym, 'Demofilo'. Mazzini begged at least his own intimate circle to contribute under their own names but they refused.

Even Melegari, Jacopo Ruffini, Elia Benza, and Guerrazzi insisted upon publishing their articles anonymously – it is hardly surprising that those who were still in Italy preferred to remain anonymous.

Such were the conditions under which, in three years, altogether six foolscap numbers of *La Giovine Italia* were issued – three in 1832, two in 1833, and one in 1834. They were rather more than two hundred pages each. On August 25th 1832 Mazzini wrote: "This second number . . . of which I have printed some thousands of copies, cost me 1,396 francs – meanwhile the number of subscribers does not increase nor of collaborators; most do not pay me. . . ." Yet precariously and irregularly the journal did somehow circulate amongst a few of the educated classes – lawyers, doctors, occasionally priests – from Genoa right down the coast to Sicily, conveying incitement to Italians to revolt against all existing authorities, and an appeal for sacrifice, for a Third Rome, for Italian Unity, and for an Italian initiative in a new Europe. The number of copies which actually reached those who were capable of understanding them and who were brave enough to pass them on to a friend rather than pass them to the police or destroy them cannot have been large. But the governments were not to know, from the few copies handed in, how many might be in secret circulation up and down the country, and Metternich found it worth while to send for a couple of numbers for his personal perusal.

In May 1833 Charles Albert's government fixed a penalty of up to five years' imprisonment for the crime of acting as a distributing agent for seditious journals and books. This Piedmontese law was proclaimed because evidence had been found that efforts were being made to seduce the army from its allegiance. But until May 1833, when this disturbing evidence came to light, the striking feature of the government at Turin had remained its indifference and its clemency. Nothing illustrates this more remarkably than does its treatment of the ablest and most dangerous of Mazzini's agents in Genoa, his old university friend Elia Benza. Benza had been a Carbonaro of the *Speranza* Lodge and had been duly denounced by Doria. Moreover, when he had been arrested, the case against him had been much strengthened

by the seizure of compromising letters to him from Bini of
Leghorn, letters which contained references to a certain Tausch,
son of the Austrian consul at Leghorn, and at that time much
preoccupied with a plot to murder Metternich. The case against
Benza was serious. It was for this reason that the Commissioner
of Police, Pratolongo, invited him to dine privately with him at
his house so that, when he had heard the accusation, the two of
them might, at leisure and in comfort, work out the most suitable
replies for Benza to make in court. A gentlemanly officer was
Pratolongo; he had been just as well disposed over the prosecution of Mazzini, and it is a pleasure to learn that later on
Mazzini's father cured him of a disease. "Bravo my father for
curing the Commissioner Pratolongo", wrote Mazzini to his
mother in 1840, "he was kindly to me". The only sentence imposed upon Benza was that he should return to his house at
Porto Maurizio and behave himself – he would be under supervision. However, in the summer of 1832 Mazzini had sent
him that letter, hidden in the false bottom of a trunk,
entrusting him with a mission to Naples, to establish contact
with the local congregation there. Although the police seized the
letter they made no attempt to arrest Benza, who received a
further letter from Mazzini and duly set out on his mission.
Having accomplished it, and being by then aware that the police
knew what he was doing, he could hardly return to his home on
the Ligurian coast, so he sailed instead to Marseilles, joined
Mazzini, and made a few contributions to the journal. Yet in
October 1832 he coolly returned to Porto Maurizio. The police
abstained from arresting him, contenting themselves with
another vague surveillance, and letting it be understood that, if
he behaved himself, and quietly practised his profession as a
lawyer (which he proceeded to do) all would be well. And so it
was.

Such was the "ruthless tyranny" of Charles Albert's government in the hey-day of Young Italy's campaign. Small wonder
that Doria, exasperated by the obtuseness of the authorities,
was insisting, at Metternich's Milan enquiry, that Carbonaro
influence was still uppermost amongst the police of Piedmont.

Jacopo Ruffini, at Genoa, was another who was supposed to be under police supervision, and not without good reason. But after the arrests following the Doria disclosures he had prevailed upon the police to allow him to go to his uncle, the venerable canon, at Taggia (next door to Porto Maurizio) where he could see Benza and where, probably, he also saw Mazzini en route from his prison at Savona to his self-imposed exile. By May 1831 the police were growing suspicious of Jacopo's continued stay so close to Benza and they peremptorily demanded his return to Genoa. But he knew how to handle the Piedmontese police. He took along the canon, as his witness, and explained that he had been suffering from an inflamed throat, showing the marks on his neck where the leeches had been applied. This ingenious idea worked. He was duly allowed to stay at Taggia "for the sake of his health". Encouraged by the success of his ruse he thought of something even better. The repercussions of an earthquake, he explained, had been felt at Taggia. It was no longer safe for him to remain in his uncle's house there. Let him, therefore, remove to Porto Maurizio! But this was too much, even for the authorities. The Military Commissioner at San Remo was informed by the Governor of Nice (then part of the Kingdom of Piedmont-Sardinia) that Jacopo Ruffini could move, if he liked, to San Remo, but in no circumstances could he reside at Porto Maurizio. Nevertheless he did go to Porto Maurizio and then proceeded to plead that he had not enough money to move again to San Remo. Whereupon the Military Commissioner required his immediate return to Genoa, and he went.

Chapter 4

MARSEILLES: EXECUTIONS, AND GIUDITTA

Neither the Letter to Charles Albert nor the discovery of the trunk with the false bottom nor even the circulation of *La Giovine Italia* had sufficed to awaken the authorities at Turin to the reality of the danger from Mazzini. What they had failed to appreciate was that, unlike the Carbonari, or the general run of the romantic revolutionaries, he really meant business, he meant to clear out the existing authorities and to found a New Order. And that Order would be his Order because he was determined that, during the critical early stages of war and revolution, he would himself be leader. Now that Young Italy was making headway he would tolerate no dictation from the other revolutionary groups, the other off-shoots of the Carbonari. Nor would there be any summoning of a Constituent Assembly "until a late stage, when the war is over, or far advanced". Till then there would be

"a Central Junta, a provisional government vigorously constituted by a few strong men, a kind of Committee of Public Safety which will occupy itself with the affairs of the revolution, publishing its purposes, and only those guarantees which it is suitable to give to the people . . .". "I love liberty", he wrote about the same time, "I love it perhaps even more than I love my country; but, my country, I love her before I love liberty".

Making Italy, making her a unity, a powerful unity capable of fulfilling a mission in Europe – that was the job. It was a question of *making Italians* even more immediately than it was a question of giving them liberty.

It was in May 1833 that Charles Albert's government at last began to take Young Italy seriously. Mazzini's wider horizons, beneath their firmament of God, Progress, and the like, remained,

of course, quite beyond the vision of the prosaic functionaries of
Turin, as they were generally beyond his own followers. But his
plans were realistic enough, and it came as a shock to the
government when it discovered what they were: invasion of
Savoy from France or Switzerland, invasion of the Ligurian
coast from the French coast, revolution in Savoy and Liguria,
and, most serious of all, corruption from within of Charles
Albert's army, with plans to acquire arms from disaffected
garrisons. It was when they discovered all this that the king's
government struck.

Mazzini knew well enough that so widespread a conspiracy
could not be kept secret for long and he had been pushing ahead
feverishly with it all. To further its success he was now ready to
throw overboard some of his most cherished principles. Had he
been preaching Italian initiative, Italian self-reliance, urging his
countrymen not to look for salvation to the French? But – what
a help it would be if Frenchmen, from Lyons, would help in the
Savoy invasion, or Frenchmen from the riviera would invade the
Ligurian coast! It was no use being too doctrinaire. He told
Melegari (who had written an anti-French article for the journal)
that he must swallow his prejudices:

"I, too, if I had anything to hope for from the mud which covers us,
from the inertia, greed, cowardice, which (amongst us Italians I can
say it) characterizes most of our fellow-citizens, if, I say, I could drag
out of them the spirit they had in the Middle Ages, that strong,
indomitable spirit which knew how to respond to ideal concepts . . .
but don't let us fashion Utopias, when those in Piedmont say they
won't move if the French won't move . . .".

He would not even insist upon his principle that there must be a
new kind of leadership, a break with the professional revolutionary class, the condottiere revolutionaries of fortune, who had
mixed themselves up in all the European movements since the
era of revolution had started in 1789. The congregations of
Young Italy in Piedmont were insisting that they would only
follow General Ramorino, who was precisely this type of
professional, ready to "draw his sword" in Italy or in Spain, in
Poland or in Portugal, "in the cause of Liberty". It was not what

Mazzini wanted; he wanted to direct military operations himself as well as to control the political side of the movement. But, if the congregations insisted upon a professional soldier, he would yield. It was a serious concession. But at least he would see to it that his own political authority was not undermined. "The Commander-in-Chief must be excluded, for ever, from power. That, and the bands of volunteers, must be our guarantee against him – whoever he may be".

Realism is the key-note of Mazzini's urgent preparations. Money and guns. Incessantly he appeals for money to buy rifles and to pay the volunteers. At the end of 1832 he writes to a friend at Geneva, who has appealed to him for help towards the cost of a new journal in French:

"I will speak frankly to you. I am, as you say, not rich; but the 500 or 1,000 francs which I would contribute towards the cost of printing . . . I shall devote to the purchase of 50 rifles. What are 50 rifles? – they are much more than are some volumes of French writings; they arm 50 men, and so form a little band auxiliary to the parent bands. Suppose, then, that we all, you, Pepoli, Bossi, and myself and whoever else possible, did the same thing, we should have the equipment for five or six little bands, in other words for two or three hundred armed mountain troops. Let me tell you that, from the valley of Fontana-Buona alone, on the eastern riviera of Liguria, I have had requests for 500 rifles. And I have always said, and I shall say again, that if all of us do not make a beginning by giving even the 20 francs which is the price of a rifle, and steadfastly collecting equipment, thus making a start towards collective action, we shall achieve nothing. The example could be decisive".

Soon after, he was fishing in deep financial waters.

"A certain person", he writes to Melegari, "has offered me a loan of 100,000 francs, and more if I need it, for the coming uprising. He offers it as broker for persons unspecified . . . 25 per cent interest . . . as guarantee . . . a traveller to be allowed to go into Italy, make contact with the Congregations, discover whether the prospects are really good. This traveller to be the broker himself . . .".

It sounds as though the broker were one of Metternich's spies. At all events we hear no more of his scheme.

By the spring of 1833 Mazzini was quite certain that the whole of Italy was ready to rise in overwhelming numbers. It was only a question of which region should take the initiative.

"Yesterday", he wrote in April, "I had the latest communication
from Naples, which told me that all is ready for the complete revolution of the Kingdom *twenty days after receiving the word from me here.*
So it is with the whole of Italy. There remain a few doubts in Piedmont, and for this reason they are pressing the need of equipment
there; *money* and *guns* . . .".

He was on a brief visit to Lyons when he wrote this, trying to
interest the French republicans in giving some help. And the
letter was written to Paris, to Belgioioso (husband of the more
celebrated Principessa), and was intended to rally the Carbonaro
committees there to the support of Young Italy. He was preoccupied with trying, above all, to gain the active support of the
great Buonarroti, sometime founder of the *Filadelfi* (anti-
Napoleonic republicans in the French army) and, after 1821, of
the *Apofasimeni* (Italians sworn to strive for an united Italian
republic). Buonarroti was still widely recognized as *de facto* head
of the entire network of associations loosely called Carbonari,
he was still Europe's premier revolutionary, and his support or
opposition could be decisive. Mazzini had already secured an
article from him for *La Giovine Italia;* now he told a friend to see
Buonarroti in Paris:

"If he asks you about Italy, or about ourselves, tell him tremendous
things about us: that the Kingdom of Naples, Rome, the Romagna,
Tuscany, Lombardy, are ready, and impatient; that the region of
Genoa is also ready; that in Piedmont there are many active elements
but there is also much division, and the cousins ought all to strive to
heal this".

Here was a strong hint that the old Carbonaro element was still
giving Mazzini trouble, and an appeal to their leader to rally his
supporters behind the programme of Young Italy.

"Point out to him the danger of prolonging the present dangerous
state of things on account of the police – that there is need of arms –
and of a gesture. If you say all this, I swear that you will not be saying
what is untrue". And lastly: "preach the republic and equality
(Buonarroti's personal predilections) to him like mad (*a furia*)".

Mazzini's aspirations appeared, however, to his fellow revolutionaries, and especially to those at Paris, to be chimerical.
Certainly his plans were far reaching. He saw the two extremities
of the peninsula, Piedmont and Naples, rising first, and the

central provinces, Rome and Tuscany, inevitably caught up in the general conflagration. As each province emancipated itself it would send two deputies to his Central Junta. This was the body which he called a "sort of Committeee of Public Safety". It seems odd that he should have been surprised that some of the other revolutionary leaders saw in him a potential Robespierre and the heads not only of Charles Albert and of Francis IV of Modena rolling in the dust but the heads, too, of the Mirabeaus and the Dantons – the leaders, that is, of rival revolutionary groups. Already Buonarroti was more than suspicious of him and entirely opposed to his plan to stimulate the revolution in Piedmont by invading Savoy. But he did not try to prevent his own followers from enrolling in Young Italy, and his own right-hand man at Marseilles, Carlo Bianco, was also Mazzini's chief adviser on military matters.

So long as Mazzini's relations with Buonarroti remained at least outwardly friendly he might continue to hope that, in the event, most of the affiliated groups of the Carbonari would receive their instructions to collaborate with him once he had won an initial success. What mattered most to him was to secure the friendly co-operation of a new "economy" of "Reformed Carbonari" which had appeared upon the scene in Piedmont and in Tuscany and was called the *Veri Italiani*, the True Italians. This society had very much the same aims as Mazzini, looking to an united, republican and independent Italy, and its emergence represented Buonarroti's reply to the challenge offered by the revolutionary achievements of the Greeks and the Poles – and of Mazzini. Endeavouring to swallow his indignation at the fact that Marseilles friends of his, Enrico Mayer, a well known Swiss revolutionary, and Michele Accursi were on the Supreme Lodge of this new society in Paris, Mazzini did his best to gain control over its local lodges in northern Italy. And he seems to have been succeeding until the Grand Master, Gaetano Ciccarelli, in Paris, sent a certain "Capitano Belluzzi" to Tuscany to sever the connection and to undermine Mazzini's influence. By the spring of 1833 Mazzini was complaining that Carbonaro principles were being resurrected in Florence, Pisa, and Leghorn, and Belluzzi was writing, with exultation, that Young Italy would be ruined.

"To all this", writes Mazzini, "I can see but a single remedy: war, open war: war not against the *Veri Italiani* as such, but against the Central Junta".

By the month of May 1833, with the great revolution scheduled to start in a matter of weeks, and Mazzini assuring everybody that all was ready, and under his control, the real position was entirely different. No doubt the initiative rested with his own disciples of Young Italy, but the other societies were awake, too, and there is every reason to suppose that the majority of those, especially in Piedmont, who might be prepared to back the revolution once it had started, belonged to one of the other groups of "Reformed Carbonari" whose leaders, from Paris, were disinclined for any action which did not stem from a French initiative, were loyal to Buonarroti, and were denouncing Mazzini. Increasingly he was coming to understand this, but he despised his adversaries and trusted in the number of his own adherents, which he estimated at between fifty and sixty thousand, and in the appeal which his ambitious goal would make. He expected to see all the other groups tumbling over each other to fall in behind him once he had taken the initiative.

But the differences between himself and the other leaders were real and deep. Their first principle was the friendship of France; what Mazzini called "preaching the French initiative". That was why they stayed in Paris and maintained their contacts with the French government. And their second principle was secrecy; they detested Mazzini's open propaganda in the columns of his journal. They did not believe in making broad appeals on matters of principle and trying to exhort Italians into a different outlook towards life. Buonarroti believed both in unity and in the republic for Italy, but he regarded it as madness to go into battle proclaiming the purpose of creating them. He knew that neither principle made any wide appeal, and that the republic was regarded as so radical a notion that it frightened moderate elements, reminding them of the reign of terror in Paris. It was better, in his view, to keep these objectives in the background, and so try to win the confidence of men who were only looking for a measure of constitutional reform.

The strain upon Mazzini by the spring of 1833 had become

terrific. On the one hand he was stoking up revolutionary fervour
and forming new congregations of Young Italy up and down the
peninsula. On the other he was trying to prevent a premature
outbreak, especially in the Romagna, which "would ruin everything and set back the national movement for twenty years". His
friends on the Ligurian coast were clamouring for action; but
inland, in Piedmont, the congregations were not ready and were
quarrelling amongst themselves and with the other societies. Yet
he was confident that he would be able to give the signal for
action before the end of August, and he was even more confident
that the movement would succeed once it had started.

But as spring turned to summer, a rather sordid combination
of carelessness, cowardice, and indulgence amongst members of
the lower ranks of Charles Albert's army, who had been seduced
from their military allegiance and enrolled in Young Italy, led to
investigations which the Turin government, at last thoroughly
roused, pursued with vigour, thus dealing a very serious blow to
his plans. It had naturally been important to Mazzini to secure
converts in the army; but he was shrewd enough to realize that
this was the most dangerous work of all, because "it is impossible
to conspire in the army without discoveries. There is espionage,
drunkenness, and foolhardiness". He therefore wanted to leave
this work till the last moment and then only enrol a few soldiers
in key positions. But he was faced by the difficulty that he could
not get money out of the congregations of Young Italy until he
could prove that he had penetrated the army and won access to
the arsenals at Genoa, Alessandria, and Chambéry.

The man particularly entrusted with the dangerous job of
seducing the soldiery at Genoa was Jacopo Ruffini. A fanatic as
avancé as his friend and Chief, he had already contributed a
peculiarly audacious article to *La Giovine Italia*, explaining that
a soldier's oath of loyalty was not binding if it was sworn to a
government like Charles Albert's. But, as events were shortly to
show, the quality of those whom he and his friends seduced
from their military allegiance was sometimes not of the highest.
As soon as suspicion fell upon them they were liable to betray
their new masters as readily as they had betrayed their old. Such

a one was Quartermaster Sacco. He and his friend Sergeant Allemandi were both enamoured of the same girl, and, in her presence, Allemandi struck at Sacco and accused him of having disclosed to her more about the conspiracy than he should have. Enquiring into the cause of the quarrel the authorities began to perceive the deeper implications, and a search by the military police disclosed letters which indicated that the house of one Lorenzo Boggiano, ostensibly a brothel, was actually a meeting place of the conspirators. Boggiano excited suspicion still further by committing suicide and Sacco, seeing that the fat was now fairly in the fire, joined with another Quartermaster, Turffs, and a gunner, Piacenza, and the three turned King's Evidence. By denouncing their comrades in the conspiracy before they had themselves been accused they were guaranteed, by the Piedmontese penal code, their own immunity from prosecution. So the police went with them through the streets of Genoa, and at house after house the renegades gave the conventional signs of Young Italy, the doors were confidently opened to them, and the arrests were duly made.

It was thus that the Ruffini house received a visitation and that Jacopo himself was arrested. His brother Giovanni was also sought but the family, with some ingenuity, contrived to substitute the elder brother, Ottavio, for Giovanni. Since Ottavio was innocent of all connection with Young Italy he was soon released. Giovanni escaped to Marseilles, followed by his younger brother, Agostino, and their mother. Jacopo, confronted in court by Turffs, and by the other traitors, denied everything, including his membership of Young Italy. But the evidence against him was overwhelming, and, disgusted with his comrades, he committed suicide in prison by cutting his jugular vein with a splinter of metal torn from the surround of his prison door.

The suicide of his closest friend came as a violent shock to Mazzini and remained with him all his life. It was not merely that the intimate relationship between his own and the Ruffini family made it particularly poignant; it was also that he believed that the suicide had been caused by the police deceiving Jacopo into thinking that he, Mazzini, had betrayed him. Years later he would cry out, at night: "Jacopo, Jacopo, I did not betray!" The story of the supposed police trick was recounted by Mazzini's disciple and biographer, Jessie White Mario, and has been repeated since. But, as Alessandro Luzio demonstrated as long ago as 1923[1], there was no occasion for the police to trick Jacopo or any of the others into making false confessions, for the evidence against them produced by the renegades was overwhelming. Jacopo's suicide is much more likely to have been due to his disillusionment at being betrayed by the very men he had himself enlisted. He was a highly strung young man, as were most of his family. His eldest brother, Vincenzo, had already committed suicide, for reasons unknown, while a student at the University of Genoa. The second brother, Ottavio, would commit suicide in 1839. There was a streak of instability in the family history, on their mother's side.

Jacopo's suicide was on June 19th. Meanwhile, at Alessandria and at Chambéry arrests and trials, similar to those at Genoa, were already taking place, mostly as a result of the disclosures made by those seeking to save their own skins. There was a sub-lieutenant, Paolo Pianavia, at Taggia, who had probably been enrolled by Jacopo Ruffini. He was already in prison at Alessandria when he decided to betray his military associates in the conspiracy. The inducements held out to him by the minister Lescarène, on behalf of Charles Albert, were not very generous, but they were graded according to the value of the revelations which he might make. "If they are sufficiently important", wrote the minister to the Governor of Alessandria, Galatieri, "he will not have to suffer an ignominious death". This meant that he would be shot in the chest instead of in the shoulders. "If they should be extremely important his life will be spared. It they put the courts into the position of being able to convict some of those supremely guilty, the remission will be such as greatly to reduce the penalty". According to Mazzini, writing to Celeste Menotti on July 23rd,

"The revelations of the officer Pianavia are the principal cause of all the subsequent arrests. He was far removed from being an *agent provocateur* – fear of death made him a traitor. Seven sergeants were shot beneath his window in Alessandria, while he was in prison; and

[1] *Carlo Alberto e Giuseppe Mazzini*, Turin, 1923, p. 139.

the eighth was to be himself if he did not make a revelation. His brother, a lawyer, was sent to him from Genoa, to induce him by frightening him. Every kind of moral torment was applied. And he revealed. Having taken the first step on the road of infamy he saw that he was lost in the eyes of the Cousins, and ruined with the patriots, and he allowed it all to be dragged out of him. Then it seems he was seized by a veritable fever of revelation; the Governor, by continual threats, by incessantly saying: *not enough; you cannot escape death if you do not reveal more*, brought him to the point of making false accusations against innocent people. Now, which of the two is the more infamous, he or the government?''

Mazzini did not want to turn indignation against the traitors, he wanted to turn it against the government, and we are bound to treat with caution his accounts of police brutality. A remarkable instance of his clemency towards the traitors was the case of Giovanni Re, whose disclosures were responsible for undermining the movement in Lombardy. His own opinion of Re he showed in a letter to Melegari:

"at one time excellent, a tireless traveller, enthusiastic, he has revealed all he knew both of Lombardy and of Piedmont. Set at liberty, he is in the Ticino, where he has deposited with a lawyer a long and detailed statement of his infamies and revelations, declaring them false and calumnious, etc. A traitor then and now. See what men are like! All the arrests in Lombardy, which amount to thirty, are his work . . .''.

Nevertheless he would not allow Young Italy to be revenged upon Re. He felt the behaviour of such traitors to be a disgrace to the movement, but he refused to allow his comrades to pursue the vendetta against them. This was creditable to him, especially when it is remembered what a large part the barbarism of vendetta had played in the life of the Italian secret societies. But any obloquy which he could help to heap upon the government came as grist to his mill, and he was so successful in heaping it that even to this day a legend, which owes much, in the first place, to his propaganda (and later to the Piedmontese historian Brofferio) was handed down about the brutalities of the military governors (and especially about Galatieri of Alessandria – since shown to be false), about the iniquity of civilian prisoners being tried by military courts (though this was required, in cases of treason, by the Penal Code), about forged documents, inadequate provision for the defence, and terrorist tactics to extort confessions, although the reliable evidence all points to a scrupulous fairness in the conduct of the trials.[1]

From the point of view of Charles Albert and his government the discoveries were extremely serious. Whole regiments had been infected with Mazzinianism. The conspiracy was, in fact, so widespread that it was imperative, for the reputation of the army, which he had very much at heart, that the king should prevent the extent of it from being disclosed. So, although he set up a special commission to keep him in touch with the trials, he gave instructions that prosecutions should only be undertaken where they were absolutely necessary for security reasons, and very often, especially amongst the aristocracy of Genoa, a written promise of good behaviour was the only inconvenience to which suspects were put. Considering that, besides the evidence of treachery within the army, there was placed before the courts detailed information of plans to seize barracks, government offices and arsenals, to arrest and, if necessary, to kill officials and governors, to assassinate the king, and to effect an invasion of Savoy by foreign troops, it is at least understandable that the government took firm measures to meet the situation, and it is rather surprising, in the face of the publication in Italy of the judicial proceedings, that some English historians have continued to repeat the ancient accusations concerning arbitrary and "panic" ferocity on the part of Charles Albert's government. The total number of executions arising from the arrests amounted to fourteen. The condemned were brave men; some of them, notably Andrea Vochieri, a lawyer of Alessandria, very brave. And they deserved the halo of Mazzinian martyrdom which was soon accorded to them. But they were also guilty.

From the disclosures made in these Piedmontese trials of June and July 1833 it became too clear to admit of any doubt that the

---

[1] Such is the impression left by the court records, and also the opinion of the leading Italian authorities, Alessandro Luzio, *Carlo Alberto e Giuseppe Mazzini*, pp. 125–231, and Arturo Codignola *La Giovinezza di Giuseppe Mazzini*, Vallechi, 1926, p. 177, etc. More recently, however, Arturo Codignola (*Mazzini*, U.T.E.T., 1946, pp. 55–68) follows Cesare Spellanzon (*Storia del Risorgimento*, Rizzoli, 1934, Book 3, p. 648, etc.) in drawing attention to the fact that, though the trials were properly conducted, and the evidence was overwhelming, the sentences were severe and reflected the fear of the king and the harshness of some of the governors, notably Galatieri.

nerve centre of the whole conspiracy was Mazzini at Marseilles. He had already been exiled for his Letter to Charles Albert. It now remained for the military court at Alessandria to sentence him to death – a sentence to be "read and published, loud and clear", in front of his father's house at Genoa, and to be preceded by a flourish of trumpets.

The disclosures were devastating to Mazzini's plans because they revealed and destroyed the vital part of Young Italy's effort, its penetration of the army. That he continued as though nothing had happened, intensifying his efforts throughout the peninsula, until he brought matters to a head soon after the new year, is thus the more remarkable.

Moreover his embarrassments were personal as well as political, for at this moment of acute crisis in the affairs of Young Italy there was also some crisis – perhaps illness – in the life of a baby newly born to him by Giuditta Sidoli. This event had serious repercussions upon the fraternity at Marseilles, which centred itself upon Giuditta's house in the *rue Ferréol*. For not only did she leave abruptly, but Mazzini himself disappeared with her. At the very moment when the trials were being conducted in Piedmont, and the revolution was being betrayed, he could not be got at. Nobody knew where he was, and nobody knows for certain today.

Mazzini's difficulties were made even more embarrassing by the arrival at Marseilles of Jacopo Ruffini's two younger brothers and of their mother, Eleonora. Giovanni had arrived first, after nearly suffering shipwreck in a voyage vividly described in *Lorenzo Benoni*. Agostino had followed with their mother, and these two had been met at the port by Mazzini and Giuditta Sidoli. From Mazzini's point of view it was not a very fortunate moment for them to have cast themselves upon his protection; no doubt he greeted them affectionately but all we know of his reaction to their arrival is that he took away young Agostino's passport, which was made out in the name of François Duchesne, adopted it as his own, and disappeared with it, accompanied by Giuditta, thus mortally affronting the two Ruffini brothers and their mother, none of whom in after years ever quite forgave him.

For this they have been much blamed by historians, and there was no doubt something ungenerous about the behaviour, in later years, of all of them. But with Eleonora Ruffini's predicament at Marseilles it is impossible not to sympathize. She became separated from her two sons. After a few days the news of Jacopo's suicide in prison reached her. And the man to whom they had all looked for a lead, who had been directly responsible for bringing them into disaster, had simply disappeared – with Agostino's passport.

Perhaps the predicament of Giovanni and Agostino was even worse than that of their mother, for she was a more dominating personality than either of them. Eleonora Ruffini was a remarkable woman and even, after her manner, as they all called her, "holy". At all events, she shared with Mazzini's mother the honourable title, amongst the exiles, of *Madre Santa,* just as Giuditta Sidoli was the *Mater Dolorosa.* But, whatever her sanctity, she was also an eccentric, and when she and her sons and Mazzini were all eventually reunited at the *Hôtel de la Navigation,* on the *paquis* at Geneva, in the following month, life was not altogether easy; it was clearly something of a relief to her sons, and no doubt also to Mazzini, when, in November, she finally decided to return to Genoa.

We know of Mazzini's disappearance with Agostino's passport from Agostino's diary.[1] But he gives no dates, other than the month, and it is difficult to deduce from Mazzini's and Giuditta's letters the exact sequence of events. The most tenable hypothesis is that Mazzini and Giuditta left Marseilles together, about the middle of June,[2] to go to Montpellier, a city already known to Giuditta since it was there that her husband had died. Mazzini then went through a nervous crisis, which was probably why

[1] Cod. 1. 443. Mazzini's friend Angelo Usiglio excused his Chief's behaviour on the grounds that he only knew of the arrival of Eleonora and her sons, and of Jacopo's imprisonment, two hours before his own planned time of departure. His letter is published by Eugenio Artom in his book *Un Compagno di Menotti e di Mazzini, Angelo Usiglio,* Modena, 1949, Appendix 11, p. 188.

[2] In the National Edition of Mazzini's letters there is yet another letter from Marseilles, dated June 29, i.e. one day after he had started writing from Geneva! This letter must have been written much earlier, probably on May 29. Mazzini, as often, only put the numeral, without the month. The month was added, later, by Melegari, and in making these later additions Melegari was not always accurate. The letter concerns his plans to break with the *Veri Italiani,* and is clearly earlier in date than one he wrote on the same subject on June 1.

Giuditta decided to go on with him to his destination, Geneva. But on July 4th she left him there and went back to Montpellier, where she remained till the end of September, when she went back again to Marseilles. Thence, on October 10th, she set sail for Leghorn, in an attempt to rejoin her previous four children at Reggio. But she left Mazzini's baby at Marseilles, in the care of Démosthène Ollivier, in whose house Mazzini had been living before his departure. This we know from the testimony of Émile Ollivier (the later French premier) who insisted, on several occasions, that his father looked after Mazzini's baby by Giuditta. In his *L'Empire Libéral*[1] he says:

"(Mazzini) hid himself for a year in my father's house. . . . The police ended by finding him, and obliging him to leave Marseilles. He took refuge in Switzerland, leaving in my father's charge the child which a beautiful Italian woman from Reggio, his companion in exile, gave to him, and which died soon after".

And in a letter to the Italian historian, Alessandro Luzio, he wrote:

"My father was an intimate friend of Mazzini. It was in his house that Young Italy was conceived and that the child died which he had by a Modenese lady. Unfortunately Mazzini's extensive correspondence was seized and lost after the coup d'état".[2]

Mazzini's letters to Démosthène Ollivier, were they available, would no doubt throw more light on the matter, about which Mazzini and Giuditta both preserved an absolute secrecy, even from the Ruffinis. From the letters between the lovers during the year 1835 we know that Démosthène was a wretched correspondent and that Mazzini was trying to get information out of him about a mysterious "A", who keeps appearing in his own and in Giuditta's letters, whose health is constantly poor, and about whom there is no further mention in his correspondence after that year. There can be no doubt that "A" was their child or that it died either in 1835 or in 1836,[3] and it is unlikely that the various people who claimed, a generation and more later, to be natural sons of Mazzini had any right so to style themselves. Their separation from each other and from their child was an anguish

---

[1] Vol. I, p. 257.
[2] A. Luzio, *Giuseppe Mazzini* (Treves, 1905), p. 118.
[3] The problems relating to this child are discussed in the Appendix.

to both parents. Giuditta wanted to send money to Démosthène Ollivier; Mazzini made it clear that that was his business, complained that Ollivier's attitude humiliated him, and held out hopes that he would soon be taking charge himself. One is left with an unhappy feeling that, though Ollivier had clearly been the soul of generosity to Mazzini at Marseilles, his household may not have been the best one in which to leave a baby. But the historian is as much in the dark, today, about the poor child's life as the unhappy parents were in its life-time.

If Mazzini had left Marseilles, in June 1833, so as to stand by Giuditta in some personal crisis, it seems that what actually happened was that she had to look after him. The first we hear from either of them, after the departure, is a letter from Mazzini to his mother, begun on June 28th but posted at Geneva on July 3rd, to which Giuditta added the following postscript:

"*Mia Signora,*

"In a moment of such bitterness as this, when I am separating myself from Pippo, I feel the need for you to remember me, and the promise of affection which you made me. It is true I never replied; that must have seemed discourteous but I had tenderness – a warm tenderness in my heart. Please remember me and love me – I love you and will never forget you. I did not write to you because I could not tell you all the truth about Pippo's health, because he would not let me, and I had not the heart to abuse the faith you had in me by deceiving you. But now Pippo, although very weak, is a little better – he is in need of much care – but he will improve – the love of those friends whom he calls brothers, and of their mother [the Ruffinis, who by this time had reached Geneva] will take the place of that other kind of love, and will help him to endure his many trials. It is a relief to me, now that I must leave him, to see him surrounded by them. The fits of sobbing are growing less. But I would not suppose that the climate of England could suit him [Mazzini's mother had been urging her son to go to England] – indeed I would think it most harmful – both for his health and for his spirits.

> I embrace you with all affection,
> Giuditta."

Clearly Mazzini had had a nervous breakdown. And now Giuditta was leaving him, to go to Montpellier, where she would rejoin old friends. Already Mazzini felt sure it was the end of their life together. Already he had heard her sobbing in the night, crying out for her children at Reggio. His mother wanted him to marry her. It was impossible, because she was determined to return to her family and because he could not deny his vocation. But he always regarded himself as married to her "in the eyes of God" and his passion for her remained stronger, far, than hers for him. More than a year later he showed her he was still hoping to have their child with him, in Switzerland – hoping, perhaps, to have Giuditta, too:

"[Démosthène Ollivier] enrages me; it takes five letters to get a word out of him; he is unpardonably inconsiderate and very indelicate. I am always dreaming of how to become independent of him – but I should have to improve my position; and I shall try to – So . . . once more I speak to you about this; or rather no; it should be my concern; the reunion once affected, it will not matter what is thought. – But, write to me, write to me. . . . I am in doubt, and as a result I am afraid . . . and I keep looking at your picture – if you only knew how serious and silent it appears to me, in the absence of news of you, and how it is transfigured when I put it in front of me after having received one of your letters; they are the same features – but animated, lit by an indefinable smile, by a smile of love, which brings me perilously near to breaking it, so as to overwhelm you, to give me the illusion – it is you – it is my Giuditta, my love, my life, my present, my future, my whole existence – for, now I know it, my very existence was in you – I had not come to feel it till I came to love you".

But Giuditta, generous and impulsive, was not cast in Mazzini's mould. She had other close friends at Marseilles, including Melegari, whose fury at her sudden disappearance with Mazzini may have been prompted by something more than the embarrassment in which the Chief had left the affairs of Young Italy. When she finally reached Florence en route for Reggio she grew very friendly, very soon, with that lofty Tuscan patriot, Gino Capponi, and we find her dropping notes for him in the right-hand aisle of the *Duomo*. There was also, in Florence, a Francesco Fontanelli, an emissary of Young Italy, who made an even deeper impression upon her. And throughout the year 1835 her letters to Mazzini cooled, while his to her remained at fever heat.

Mazzini's sudden flight from Marseilles to Geneva has generally been attributed to the activity of the French police, consequent upon the discoveries in Piedmont, while his convulsions and moral crisis have been attributed to the executions, and especially to Jacopo's suicide. All these factors no doubt contributed to what happened, but that some crisis connected with Giuditta was what actually determined his immediate course of action is made clear by his subsequent letters to the infuriated Melegari and Bianco, who felt that they had been left in the lurch. On July 8th he wrote to Bianco:

"You have blasphemed against me. – You had reason to, but I could not do otherwise. I could not write to you. I did not know what to say to you . . .".

And the next day, to Melegari:

"I have received your letter, of five lines. You are angry: Why? I do not know – I know that you are wrong. If my silence has perhaps made you imagine that I had forgotten my country, you are wrong. . .. But I should not and cannot justify myself. Believe that I belong wholly to our country; and let us leave the matter".

And again to Melegari on the 18th:

"If I have concealed anything from my friends it was not for my own sake but for others; not for love of mystery quite alien to me; but in duty bound, and arising from a delicacy which anybody with sensitive feelings ought to understand . . .".

Dora Melegari, daughter of Mazzini's friend, and editor of the Chief's letters to her father, says of Mazzini's departure with Giuditta:

"Where did they go? It is impossible to say definitely; certainly the great exile left his friends for a little time without information about his movements; they were shaken, agitated, distressed; they did not know where to find their Chief, and they believed themselves abandoned".

On July 13th Giuditta wrote from Montpellier to Melegari:

"I cannot justify myself; appearances are too much against me in the eyes of my friends, and I am ready to take all the consequences in as much as my assurances that I am deserving of pardon do not suffice to obtain it for me".

And on the 28th Mazzini wrote to him:

"It grieves me to have caused you sorrow. – Yet it is my story; an intimate story which I shall not relate in full even to myself – a story more compounded of irreparable wounds than can be apparent to anyone who does not know all my affairs. I have wanted, I swear it, to do good to all with whom I have been brought into contact – and always I have done harm to them and to myself. I shall leave my story, in a few pages; but to whom? – the terrible thing is I don't know . . . to you I can say that if you understand me, and think where I was, and perceive what tied me, then you ought to have the key to it all; you should be able to see those duties which were all-powerful for me".

If Mazzini did leave the story in a few pages they have not been discovered.

Chapter 5

GENEVA: WAITING ON NAPLES,
WAITING ON PROCIDA

Neither the arrests in Piedmont nor his quarrel with his friends
nor his own illness and sorrow caused any limitation of the scope
of Mazzini's plans for Young Italy. In the middle of July 1833,
only about a fortnight after Giuditta's departure from Geneva,
he was writing to a collaborator:

"It is in no spirit of mere youthful enthusiasm or exaggerated desire,
but in cold blood, and after the most precise calculation of which I am
capable that, with my hand on my heart, I say to you: if we allow the
year, the season, to pass without acting, we are lost. If we act
resolutely, if we strike a spark of live fire, Italy will be a volcano. We
are so situated that if the voice of insurrection is raised in any part of
the peninsula it can give us victory. You say that this voice cannot
come from Turin, or from Alessandria, or from Genoa? – let it come
from the provinces, from the riviera. – It cannot come from Piedmont? – it will come from elsewhere; that we take for granted; it
being understood that we do not intend to cause it to be raised in
Modena or in Bologna, or in a weak or sleepy place; we intend to
cause it to be raised in a place of the first importance. – But, when
it is raised, it is necessary, it is vital, that Piedmont should respond;
respond in whatever way is best but quickly, and without hesitation.
Given the initiative, the Ligurian rivieras, Savoy, and a few bands of
Piedmontese, Piedmont and Lombardy will be ours at a stroke. . . .
Within a month, Charles Albert and Austria will think they have
beaten us; they will think that the season is over and that the rest of
the year will be quiet; all their thoughts will be turned towards the
spring. It is the moment to catch them. All that quantity of supporters
which we have, scattered everywhere and disorganized, will act with
us. Everybody, thinking us strong because we go ahead after a
reverse, will be with us . . .".

And finally (his correspondent was a trader, Pietro Olivero, in
Switzerland)

"work out to the very best of your ability how many men and what
supplies you can muster to bring into being some bands of troops, one

of which will move down from the Simplon pass, the other from the St. Bernard, at the same time as the Savoy venture and the one which we shall launch elsewhere".

The one to be launched elsewhere, which was to provide the initiative, was to be in the Bourbon Kingdom of Naples.

"On Naples", he wrote to Melegari on July 23rd, "everything depends. . . . Two months ago they made a spontaneous offer; and unless a strange feeling of diffidence has come over them between then and now it is impossible for them to refuse now. The message in my letters, despatched to three different centres, admitted of no objection. But I count now upon nothing. The Italians seem to be in love with the executioner who mows them down, one by one, wherever they still deceive themselves that they are safe. Meanwhile my hands are tied, and with plentiful resources at a number of places, with the ferment in Piedmont, with all in readiness for following up an initiative elsewhere, I am obliged to speak words of uncertainty to everyone on account of this wretched delay at Naples. Failure to grasp the opportunity has ruined Piedmont. A delay of a few more days will ruin Naples".

But the delay went on, and, as week followed week, Mazzini went on writing, interminably, day and night, in his hot little room at the *Hôtel de la Navigation* at Geneva. Many of the Marseilles fraternity were now with him there, including his "Chief of Staff", Bianco. So were the Ruffini family. But Melegari was still at Marseilles, where his presence was useful because he could organize the project for an invasion of the Ligurian riviera from the French coast.

The initiative was no longer, however, since the disasters of June, to come from the north but from the south of Italy. Earlier in the year Mazzini had been holding back the centre and the south of the peninsula, warning them that the failure of a premature movement could throw the whole programme of Young Italy back for twenty-five years, and insisting that the initiative must come from Piedmont. Now, having lost his grip upon the situation in Piedmont, he was urging the Neapolitans to give the lead. He reminded them they had been ready to give it in May. Their reluctance in July seemed to him inexplicable. Yet the explanation was simple enough; during the intervening two months the arrests had shown that the authorities knew far more about the movement than had been supposed, and that

Mazzini's direction of it, while not lacking in faith and courage, had been deficient in prudence. The disclosures at the trials had indicated that too much was known by too many lower-grade members. The Neapolitans, like everybody else, were disillusioned by the news from the north.

Yet Mazzini, in whom the events of June had bred a new fever for immediate action, on the widest scale possible, could see nothing but hopeful symptoms everywhere in Italy, and even in Europe. It was only necessary somewhere to strike the spark:

"By a general movement I don't mean the utopia of an instantaneous and simultaneous movement from one end of the peninsula to the other. The idea of such a movement, even before this crisis, was chimerical. Revolutions are not planned at a minute's notice. I mean by a general movement a situation in which there is absolute *certainty* that an uprising in one region will be followed in a *very short [brevissimo]* time by all the others. We have this certainty and it is founded upon positive evidence".

On August 13th, to Melegari, he is more explicit: he announces that the Central Congregation has decided that:

"the Italian movement shall take place by 'irradiation' from the countryside into the capitals, a method which has the advantage of immediately popularizing the revolution by compromising all the country districts which, even were the movement to have a favourable outcome in the capitals, might well remain inert and passive as they did in 1821. . . . As soon as Naples has taken the offensive, and the movement has reached the frontier, and is ready to cross it, the general explosion should take place. Simultaneously Piedmont will be attacked through Savoy by General Ramorino, and from her own countryside, with the insurrection of the valleys of Aosta, Ivrea, Canavese, etc., above Turin. The country districts of Lombardy will rise, up to the Valtelline, threatening the Tyrol. Those of Liguria should then revolt; but quickly, with the energy and speed of a thunderbolt. They can, so they should. . . . We speak of a popular uprising, of a movement towards the capitals, of a general and popular demonstration which, by proving at home and abroad that the Italian nation has risen, gives the signal for the insurrection of Europe. All this has been made ready – France is determined to act; Spain and Germany are ready to follow. We know their troops and their dispositions and we are sure of it . . .".

This was no calculated exaggeration, intended to stir up timid and fearful supporters. It was written to Melegari, who needed no stirring up, being disposed, at this time, towards

action at least as bold as that envisaged by his Chief. It was
Mazzini's considered opinion that a spark struck in Naples would
set the whole of Europe ablaze. As for Italy, "In the few days
after the uprising in Naples all the land of Italy, from Faro to the
Po, ought to be freed".

The Neapolitan Congregation thought otherwise, and it continued to hang back.

We catch glimpses of Mazzini's feverish life:

To Melegari:

"I have had to correspond with Naples; with Genoa (and this has cost
me immense mental strain because it was necessary to be exact and
also felicitous in my replies); with Leghorn, with Ancona, and very
lengthy instructions for Ghino [Bianco] so that the few days of his
stay where he is [Lyons] may prove profitable in the matter of the
talks he is to have with the French republicans – then there are all the
instructions for the travellers. My hand trembles while it moves from
the writing to the coffee-cup . . . .".

To his mother he sends a letter with a very oddly disguised
reference to his hopes from Naples:

"As usual I have no time to write to you; it is the second night's sleep
I have lost. I am in touch with a saint. Soon you will hear the *oremus*
which I am offering up to the honour and glory of Saint Januarius; he
has become the saint of my choice. Why? – a whim".

His mother would understand the meaning of this allusion to the
patron saint of the Neapolitans.

It was part of the plan that from Naples the insurgents should
invade the neighbouring Papal State, and Mazzini's preparations
there give us a reminder of the grim reality which lay, un-
publicized, behind his romantic aspirations.

"You can rest assured that I leave no stone unturned anywhere, and
especially in the Papal State. . . . On the twentieth day [after the
Neapolitan outbreak] the first guerilla band from Ancona, of more
than a hundred men, will start marching – commanded by the famous
Constantini, called Sciabolone. They have rifles, daggers, etc. . . . .".

And the instructions under which they were to operate included
the following:

"At the first sortie each band should attack and kill the known Centurions [auxiliary Papal police] in the locality and all the known enemies of the Federation [Young Italy]; it will not be a bad plan for every congregation to make a list of them. . . . They will respect religion; but they will kill without pity priests whom they find at the head of the brigands [the Centurions]; the houses of the brigands and of such seditious priests will be set on fire . . . in every region where they can make an incursion their first care will be to disarm the enemy's military posts . . . to take into custody the representatives of the government, the police chiefs, and the persons in public positions, whether secular or ecclesiastical, using towards them such courtesy as is suitable and killing them if they attempt to escape . . .".

But still there was nothing from Naples. The rising there was due to take place on August 11th, but by August 17th Mazzini's only news from Italy was of further arrests in Lombardy and in Tuscany.

"With all these arrests in Tuscany I foresee that the 4,000 lire [promised] from Florence will also vanish. It is maddening – but, for the rest, I am content. I am content that the persecutions are now revived everywhere".

And again on the 17th to Melegari:

"The Neapolitan revolution will kindle that of the Papal State. The revolution of the Papal State will kindle that of Tuscany. The Tuscan revolution is destined, by the insurrection of Siena, Montepulciano, etc., to confirm and strengthen the insurrection at Perugia – by that of Leghorn to open up a port – by that of Prato, Pistoia, and Pisa to give moral aid to the insurrection of the Duchy of Modena, to effect . . . a rapid demonstration on the Ligurian riviera, bursting forth with a picked band of young men towards Sarzana, by ways of Massa and Carrara . . .".

and so on. Apparently there was no limit to what would happen in Italy and Europe if only Naples would rise.

". . . in spite of Leghorn [where Guerrazzi, stigmatized as 'proud' and 'ambitious', was sceptical about Mazzini's plans] I am certain of Tuscany if Naples does her duty. All depends upon that. When you hear that the two bands of Neapolitans have marched twenty paces over their frontier, from that moment the cause of Italy is safe".

Mazzini's confidence is the more remarkable because it was based upon no knowledge of the Italian peninsula. Apart from a boyhood holiday at Florence he had never been further into it, from Piedmont, than to Leghorn. He had not seen Bologna or

D

Perugia, Ancona or Rome, nor had he any first-hand idea of that Kingdom of Naples which was so different from all the rest. Yet he had planned the whole movement, down to the details of the valleys through which the guerillas would march. He depended upon his travellers, who carried letters which were written in invisible ink. Sometimes the vital message was written across the lines of what purported to be an ordinary commercial letter. Sometimes it was written at the top or at the bottom of the ostensible letter. Sometimes it must have been quite indecipherable, as we know from his own not infrequent despair at receiving letters which he could not read. And sometimes his letters would fail to arrive at all because it was his habit to send them in a bunch, with the pages deliberately arranged in the wrong order, to his friends at Marseilles or at Genoa, for them to rearrange and distribute amongst suitable travellers. And for further concealment he would give enigmatic or cypher addresses.

At all events his confidence was misplaced. The Neapolitan Congregation failed to move. There were arrests at Naples, and these may have been the cause; but since the initiative was to come from the provinces, with the first movement in the Abruzzi, these arrests at Naples should not have paralysed the uprising if the revolutionaries were, in fact, working along the lines adumbrated by Mazzini.

To Mazzini the diffidence of the Neapolitans remained incredible.

"I am in a kind of moral agony. – We are at the 20th [August] – the revolution should have taken place on the 11th; there is no news at all . . .".

On the 21st he writes:

"I have letters from Naples written on the 8th; they were ready, then, and safe. Between the 8th and the 11th there are only two days. *Perdio!* that in a mere forty-eight hours there can be destroyed an insurrection planned in ten provinces!"

And to Melegari:

"The 23rd and nothing new! . . . I am writing today, fulminating, by a thousand different routes which will converge upon Naples. Those men will ruin the whole of Italy, and especially Lombardy, if they do not act, and quickly. . . . Are there no steamships? – is there no means of rapid transport? – Have you anybody you can send to Naples? I think it is the only thing to do, if it is possible. The traveller should present himself at one of the addresses which you have, especially to that of Geremia Mazza, *Strada Nuova Santa Maria d'Ogni Bene*, No. 52, on the third floor . . . the ticket which I enclose for you would suffice; the writing on it is covered with starch . . . the traveller would need no other instructions than to urge, to demand the performance of the thousand promises – made not only to me, directly, but to the congregations, to Florence especially, telling them the precise date, and to Ancona; he must tell them that Italy is being lost on account of them, that all are ready to respond to their initiative, that the travellers are en route, that the word has been spread, that they will be taken and shot one by one, and that they will cause the flower of Italy to be shot, that the position in Piedmont is improving hourly, that Ramorino is coming post-haste from Oporto – let him tell them whatever is likely to demonstrate the urgency of the matter. Let them act; I know that they can; they can in ten provinces even if they cannot in the capital. – Think of it! They were still determined upon action on the 8th! Upon Naples depends everything, everything – more than I can say".

But by the 26th he had abandoned hope. He declares that he is dead, dead not only in a personal sense but in a political sense. He had lost his political honour throughout the peninsula. Who would believe that for a year he had laid his plans with the Neapolitans, concerted everything with them? Who would not consider him an impostor who had tried to raise the revolution on false pretences? Best, now, that he should take all the blame on his own shoulders and so leave the others free to carry on the struggle. They would always be able to say that he was a despot, that he acted on his own, concentrated all in his own hands – and then was mistaken. If he were to publish all the correspondence it would vilify the Italians; better that he should be vilified than that all the nation should be. Better that he should die – but he would try to do so with a gun in his hands, and in his own country.

On the 29th there was a moment of anticipation. A letter arrived from Ancona, written on the 18th. Eagerly he seized upon it, sure that, at last, he was going to hear what had happened in the Abruzzi. But he was destined never to know what was contained in that letter. Try as he would, with all the known reagents, he could not discern a word of its invisible writing.

Mazzini's youthful confidence in an uprising of the whole of

Italy never quite recovered from the fiasco of this non-starting enterprise. Something died within him. His next adventure, Ramorino's Savoy expedition, had, by comparison, a desperate, half-suicidal quality about it. He did not embark upon it with the serene optimism which he had still felt in August 1833, an optimism which had somehow survived even the arrests in Piedmont in June, even the parting with Giuditta. No doubt it is dangerous with advanced romantics to be categorical as to which are the genuine crises in their lives and which the transient; their language is so exaggerated that, if one takes it at its face value, one has to assume that they pass through a death and a rebirth every month or two. It was habitual with Mazzini to say that he had "died", that all personal life was over for him, that he was incapable any longer of feeling happiness. Indeed we meet him saying that in one of his earliest letters that have survived, one written in the spring of 1825, when he was only nineteen, to Elia Benza: "I do not remember for some four years having lived for a day – one single day – happy. You may very likely have some-times seen a smile upon my lips, but it does not come from the heart". The refrain reappears intermittently until, with the departure of Giuditta Sidoli from Geneva in July 1833, he insists that his individual life is over, that he lives now only for his political life. But in August 1833, when the Neapolitans failed to rise, he said he had died politically, too. And it is true that there came then the first real challenge to his political faith. For Mazzini was then confronted with Italian revolutionary groups, governed by congregations of Young Italy, which had promised to act, had received the order to do so, and had entirely failed to respond, although everything depended upon them. This was more serious, far, than what had happened in Piedmont in June, where drunken or amorous sergeants had let slip secret informa-tion and terrified subordinates had turned King's Evidence. It was but in human nature that things of that sort should happen; no revolutionary could hope altogether to avoid them. But at Naples, in August, the Association had failed to respond to his leadership or to honour its undertakings, and if that were the sort of response which the Chief could expect how would he ever be able to make his plans for the Italian revolution effective?

The defection of Naples meant that the initiative would have, after all, to be taken by the north. The plan for invasion of Savoy from Switzerland and France, led by General Ramorino, and for an invasion of the Ligurian coast from the French coast, would have to be put into operation without waiting for movements elsewhere and would itself become the signal to the rest of the peninsula. This was not the order of events which Mazzini preferred, but it had now become inevitable. The Piedmontese congregations had foisted Ramorino upon him, they were suspicious of him, reluctant to part with any money, and still much influenced by their contacts with Paris, especially through the *Veri Italiani*. His own hand would have been greatly strengthened in dealing with them, and also in dealing with his friends from Milan (who were the best off, financially) if he could have pointed to a general uprising, spreading from the south, the course of which he alone could control. As matters had turned out, however, his position had been much weakened, instead of strengthened, by his efforts in Naples. He was regarded as having misled the Piedmontese congregations, and it had become hopeless for him to attempt to wean them away from their devotion to the idea of Ramorino's leadership of the northern movement.

If a professional military man had to be accepted as leader then the choice of Ramorino seemed to have much to commend it. He was a native of Genoa and he had taken part in the Piedmontese uprising of 1821. In his youth he had received the best military education that Europe could provide, for Napoleon himself had sent him to school at Versailles and later to the military academy of Saint Cyr. He had fought at Wagram, and on the Moscow campaign he had been awarded the Cross of the Legion of Honour. By 1813 he had become a *capitaine* of the *Grande Armée*. Scorning to serve the Bourbons he had settled, after 1815, in Savoy. It was in 1821 that he turned professional revolutionary condottiere. The brochure put out about him in 1833, for the benefit of prospective employers,[1] stated that, when the call of duty came, in 1821, he had cast all personal interest upon one side, made his way down the valley of Aosta into Piedmont, and

---

[1] *Biografia del Generale Girolamo Ramorino*, by "*Un Italiano*", Paris.

demanded a battalion with which to attack Chambéry. But since
the same brochure, anxious to depict him as a soldier born and
bred, also explained that his commercial ventures since 1815 in
Savoy had not been successful, it may be that the weight of his
personal sacrifice in coming to the aid of the revolutionaries had
not, in fact, been too crushing. Certainly, if the emoluments
which he secured from the Piedmontese revolutionary leaders on
that occasion were on the same scale as those which he later
secured from the Poles, in their uprising of 1831–32, when he
acquired his reputation as the "Hero of Ignawe", he was liberally
rewarded; for his Polish contract enabled him to live in the best
hotels and to draw substantial pay in gold.

In so far as he could tolerate the idea of any professional
military leader Mazzini was predisposed in favour of Ramorino.
Already, in June 1832, he had been in touch with him, in the hope
of securing an invasion from France.[1] For that project Lombard
members of Young Italy had already promised 40,000 francs.
Thus far there had been no return on this speculation, for the
general had since been in Portugal, drawing his sword in the
cause of liberty on behalf of Don Pedro. Since the Piedmontese
congregations were adamant that they must have him, Mazzini
now had to offer him further inducements. By the autumn of
1833 his one chance of getting the Piedmontese to act had become his ability to produce the general, and he recognized this so
clearly that he was ready to misinform them about his success in
the matter, just as he had been ready to tell the Neapolitans that
Ramorino was on his way from Portugal at a time when he
certainly was not. On September 4th he wrote to Melegari: "Tell
[the Piedmontese] we have Ramorino with us, we shall, in fact,
have him within four days – Tell them whatever you think
best. . . ." Actually, Ramorino did not arrive until October 8th,
when Mazzini at last met him. It was probably a disappointing
meeting for both of them for Mazzini could not produce the
money he had promised to pay for recruitment.

"Ramorino is here as I write – full of enthusiasm and faith. I had
already solemnly promised him – on the authorization of others –
50,000 francs – he had been free to spend up to that amount to secure

[1] V. 87.

men, arms, information about Savoy; with those funds he would be
answerable for everything. Now he comes, and there is not a penny.
All have withdrawn their offers, on account of the Naples business. – I
have written to everybody again, and in so pressing a fashion that I
hope they will yield".

Amongst those who had failed to send the money they had
promised was that distinguished liberal Carlo Cattaneo who had
undertaken to send 2,000 francs. But he was unimpressed by the
plans for the invasion of Savoy, and his money had not been
forthcoming. Mazzini's reply was that his name would be
"published on a List of Infamy on the day when twenty or thirty
of us depart for the frontier". He tells Melegari to

"speak to him coldly and firmly . . . Cattaneo has forty or fifty
thousand francs of rent – a thousand times I have written to him at
Genoa; a thousand times he has promised; never has he given. If he
shows himself yielding make him understand that it is assuredly now
no matter of redeeming his promise with two or three hundred francs.
If he shows himself uncertain about the amount make him understand
that for less than three or four thousand francs, at least, he would not
avoid what we are now threatening".

So serious was the disadvantage at which Mazzini was put by
the failure of the Neapolitans to rise that he was driven to pretend
that, after all, they were about to do so, although he knew very
well that they were not.

"You have perhaps inveighed a bit too much, if I am not deceived,
against the Neapolitans", he tells Melegari. "We, too, will inveigh
against them, without restraint. But for the present something else is
needed. It is necessary to simulate letters, in invisible ink, purporting
to bring to us from the Neapolitan provinces the message that they
are ready; that a delay has been occasioned by some mistake on the
part of the leaders . . . but that it is being repaired, that they will
soon act, that, in any case, the least sign of an initiative on the part
of those in Liguria or Piedmont would cause them to rise *en masse* –
etc.".

Pardonable devices, these, in a revolutionary leader, or even in a
politician, yet inconsistent with Mazzini's reputation. The
Neapolitan disillusionment had undermined his faith in his own
followers and had altered his methods. He was ready, now, to
adopt some very strange expedients. We find him conniving at
the expulsion of Italian refugees from the Swiss Canton of the
Ticino because it would tend to drive them westwards towards

his own insurgent formations around the lake of Geneva.[1] He
rejoiced at the arrests and imprisonments which occurred in
Tuscany in the autumn because he thought they would stir the
Tuscans to resentment and so to action.[2] He was willing to have
suspicion of complicity with Young Italy deliberately cast upon
innocent people, such as Braida, a popular criminal lawyer in
Genoa, because, if they were arrested and imprisoned, it would
tend to incite the populace. He recommended ingenious devices
for planting false clues and getting the wrong people arrested:

"It would be a good thing to pretend to pay attention to the gossip of
somebody who drinks a lot, and who is vain – one of our own men –
and, to name somebody, the choice should be amongst the many who
in reality do nothing for the cause, such as Porro and the others . . . all
these contrivances are repugnant to me, but, if they really help, the
means are always sacred in whatever colour they may present themselves".[3]

Giovanni Re, as we saw, who had betrayed secrets to save his own
life, is not subjected by the Chief to the vendetta; but he is
criticized for missing the admirable opportunity which his arrest
gave him for betraying some of the more inconvenient of the
Carbonari. "There are men, in our army, whom a word from
those arrested would have sufficed to imprison because of their
conduct in 1821; and their arrest would have done us a lot of
good". Mazzini explains that he would not stoop to this sort of
thing himself, but since Re is in any case dishonest why should he
not use his dishonesty to some advantage to the cause? "If I
were arrested I would not accuse [innocent men] because I am
honest; but he [Re] is not. . . .".[4]

No attentive student can miss the coarsening in the quality of
Mazzini's words and behaviour in the autumn of 1833. His life
with men whose inspiration was so much less lofty than his own,
and who were continually letting him down, was inevitably
affecting him. He felt the change in himself: "I feel more and
more that I ought to withdraw myself for I do not feel any more
the energy and *inspiration* – allow me the word – which I had".

To this period of desperate expedients belongs a strange

---

[1] IX. 124.
[2] "Apart from the loss of money, which grieves me greatly, I am very pleased
about the arrests in Tuscany" (IX. 40).
[3] IX. 88, 89.   [4] IX. 92.

episode, ignored or misrepresented hitherto in England, namely
Mazzini's attempt to procure the assassination of Charles Albert.
To ensure the success of the invasion of Savoy the most helpful
first step, in Mazzini's view, would be to procure the assassination of that traitor-king who had once been a friend of the
revolutionaries but who had nipped the revolution in the bud in
the previous summer and, in Mazzini's eyes, was now beyond the
pale of sympathy.

A tool for the purpose was ready to hand in the shape of an
exile from Parma, Antonio Gallenga, who was a member of Young
Italy and had been rebaptized into the society with the name of
Procida. He presented himself to Mazzini at the *Hôtel de la
Navigation*, at Geneva, and offered to go to Turin to kill the king.
Mazzini accepted the offer, giving him a thousand francs from the
funds of Young Italy, and despatching him to Pietro Olivero
who, at Locarno, was by way of procuring passports for those
who wanted to enter into Piedmont. Mazzini's backing for
Procida, in his letter to Olivero, is unqualified. The young
would-be regicide is ". . . . one of us, a man to be respected above
others, he is so holy and so good. It is essential, at any cost, to
find a passport for him, as he will tell you. – Everything depends
upon it". He encloses a note for Procida and recommends him, if
he runs into difficulty at Turin, to go to the *Café d'Italia*, outside
the *Porta Palazzo*, just past the butcher's shop on the right hand
side, to ask for one Domenico Bazzi, an architect, and to present
the note.

Procida duly made Bazzi's abode at Turin his base for operations, his plan being to conceal himself in the corridor of the
royal palace and stab the king on his way to hear Mass. But, if
his soul was as lofty as Mazzini believed, his daring was less
remarkable, and his feet grew colder each day that he remained
at Turin. He could not bring himself to run the risk of obtaining
a dagger for his purpose in the city, so he adopted the odd expedient of sending a confederate, Antonio Sciandra, all the way to
Geneva to borrow one from Mazzini. Probably he also wanted to
lay further facts before the Chief. At all events Mazzini gave
Sciandra the stiletto (*pugnaletto*) which he was in the habit of
keeping accessible on his desk, and waited anxiously for news.

Undoubtedly Procida had arrived at Turin at a very dangerous time, when the police were peculiarly active. The arrests were continuing, Gioberti had now been arrested, so had an important ally of Mazzini, Francesco Allegra. "If", wrote Mazzini, "for lack of the Neapolitan initiative, and of money, we cannot act, Young Italy, as a secret society of conspirators in Piedmont, is dead, or as good as dead". On September 12th he wrote to Melegari: "Procida is silent – He has gone away from Turin – He has gone on a holiday – I fear the worst. On the 10th he was not . . .". Here, in the manuscript of Mazzini's letter, there follows a blank caused, in the opinion of the experts consulted by the editors of the National Edition, by chlorine *recently* applied, i.e. applied shortly before the year 1910 when the volume was published.[1] The letter continues: " . . . but hope is not lost – He must return soon". On September 18th:

" . . . I await impatiently the letter which will tell me of the deed . . . *Perdio*, Procida? . . . I tremble at these delays. His secret is in the mouth of a traveller. It is certain that he reached Domenico [Bazzi] at Turin; he is of the best but every man has a friend, and so it goes. I am fearful of seeing this decisive stroke go up in smoke – but decisive absolutely".

Once again the hand that would erase the dangerous words has been at work; it has attempted – this time not quite successfully – to erase the words from '*Perdio*' to 'absolutely'.

On September 20th there comes the hopeful hint from Mazzini that a double murder is now possible: "If this stroke of Procida's does not come off it will be a great disappointment – and it will do us great harm. The Duke of Modena is at Turin – Procida and Bazzi could do well! But today I despair of all but ourselves to do deeds . . .". And again appears the attempt at erasure – there has been a similar attempt to erase every subsequent reference in the correspondence to the Procida plot, but it has been clumsily done, and patient study of the originals, at Genoa, is rewarding.

---

[1] If the erasure was, indeed, recent, it was probably made when Dora Melegari, daughter of the conspirator, published his correspondence with Mazzini in *La Giovine Italia e la giovine Europa*, in 1906. But a more likely time would have been when Mazzini caused grave embarrassment to Melegari, in the year 1856, by publishing the story of Procida's attempt in the *Italia e Popolo* and including in it a reference to the fact that Procida had been sent to him by Melegari. By that date Melegari was a rising politician. See below, p. 158.

Neither a double nor a single murder was forthcoming. Procida had started boasting about his plans to a certain notorious conspirator, Antonio Angelini – Mazzini had sent Angelini to Turin, but, apparently, for some different purpose. The police swooped upon Angelini's house but missed him. Procida was staying in the same street, so he and his accomplices thought that the police were after them, and they fled the city. Mazzini thought Procida was going to Lyons, and wrote to him there; but at the end of September he reported that he was at Chiavari, on the Ligurian coast. "He will return to Turin if he doesn't, as I fear, slip home to Parma". And on October 3rd to Melegari:

"I greatly fear that Procida has weakened and that the lost time will have cost him dear. His secret is already in the hands of five people, and not through me, but through him, by his own choice, by formal statement; it is a petty vanity which it seems to me ought not to find place in a spirit like his. Do not speak with him, or with others, do not write a legible line . . .". But ". . . I have provided already, and somebody from here, where I am, is leaving for Turin – I believe it will decide matters; but that cannot be before the 14th. – God help us! – That all should be lost – all!".

Meanwhile Melegari was beginning to feel rather sorry for Procida, who would certainly be going to his own death whether or no he compassed that of Charles Albert. So Mazzini reminds him that Procida's name will live as a legend, and he will become one of the martyrs of Young Italy. "You grieve to think of Procida, and I will not gainsay you, but, in dying, Procida begins a second life even amongst men, and he knows it, and this thought will comfort him in his death".

The young man, however, was not of the stuff of which martyrs are made and, despite a last appeal on October 8th from Mazzini, who wrote that he had faith in him as the "man of the epoch", the would-be assassin left Turin without having attempted to do the deed.

Later on Procida joined himself again to Mazzini in Switzerland. But he separated himself once more and this time he proceeded to enter the service of the king he had planned to assassinate, receiving as his reward a minor diplomatic post in Germany. Stung by the attacks which Procida then made against his former friends, Mazzini, in the year 1856, published his own version of what had occurred in the autumn of 1833, as counter-blast to Procida's account. The turncoat, in consequence, was obliged to resign his position as a deputy in the Turin parliament, and to renounce politics. But he became Italian correspondent of the London *Times* and, in Mazzini's words, "poured out in its columns, twice a week, outrages and calumnies upon Garibaldi's volunteers, upon the army of the south, upon the working men's associations, upon the party of action, and upon me". He was not, in short, a pleasant character, and it seems strange that Mazzini thought him "so holy and so good" and that, after twenty-eight years of bitter disillusionment with his behaviour, he could still remember how

"his eyes glistened while he talked. . . . He finished by convincing me that he was one of those beings whose determinations stand between the conscience and God and whom Providence, from the time of Harmodius, has occasionally sent to earth to teach despots that it lies in the hands of a single man to put an end to their power".

Chapter 6

GENEVA: THE SAVOY INVASION

When Mazzini met Ramorino on October 8th it was agreed between them that the "positively final" day for the invasion of Savoy should be November 12th. That day, however, came and passed and there was no sign of the general. As week succeeded week Mazzini alternately threatened and cajoled him, but always without effect. It was an odd situation. The congregations in Savoy and Piedmont were still insisting upon Ramorino, but Mazzini's friends on the lake of Geneva – Polish, German, Danish, French, and Italian – were imploring him to go ahead and act, without waiting for the general, while he himself wanted not, indeed, Ramorino, but the men Ramorino would bring with him. Forty thousand francs had, in the end, been paid over, and a thousand volunteers had been promised.

But as the delay went on Mazzini began to lose the confidence of the other revolutionary leaders in Switzerland. Several of them were quite ready, themselves, to assume the rôle of Ramorino; they had never before heard of a revolutionary committee which, when the hour to strike had come and passed, was still unable to move because it could not find its leader. Even Harro-Harring, the Dane, whose dearest dream was to die, on the field of victory, with Mazzini gazing approval into his eyes, was moved to remonstrate with his much beloved master. But the advice was wasted upon the Chief. His face would cloud over when aspersions were cast upon the personal character of the chosen leader. He would pace up and down, throwing away cigar after cigar, demanding faith. Or he would raise his shoulders and say "I cannot renounce my confidence in the heart of man". Whom could he trust if he could not trust the general? In any case it was too late. "The future will decide. Ramorino is destined to be our chief; he holds all our destinies in his hands!". He held, too, their secrets; if they dropped him there was much information of which he could dispose on advantageous terms. Harro-Harring contented himself, in his memoirs, with the rather surprising reflection that the purity of Mazzini's soul was such that he could not conceive of treason; and he returned to his employment, which was to maintain contact with the Polish contingent. He had served in the Polish revolution, and many of their men were his personal friends. So Mazzini was by way of sending him off to make contact with their leaders, who had their headquarters at the "Red Lion" at Lausanne. Harro-Harring claimed that he spent no less than 157 francs on *diligences* between the two cities.

Of the Polish leaders Charles Stolzman was the most responsible; he was clear enough that Mazzini was mistaken in pinning his faith upon Ramorino, and he said so. Stolzman was a man of integrity who commanded Mazzini's respect. His mistrust of Ramorino was grounded in his disbelief in the legend about that worthy's being the "hero of Ignawe", and also in his dislike of the general's personal immorality. The German leader, Hermann de Rauschenplatt, was another who pressed Mazzini to fix a date and stick to it, and to throw over Ramorino. But Mazzini, although he was prepared to address Rauschenplatt as "General", and to speak of him as leading an "army" (he commanded the allegiance of twenty Germans, only, at Lausanne), did not get on with him personally. This was a great grief to Harro-Harring, who adored them both and insisted that the German was the soldier, with the shining sword, while Mazzini was the philosopher, the Socrates, the Christ, the Divine Man.

The advice given to Mazzini to drop Ramorino was not altogether disinterested, for amongst those who gave it were some who might expect themselves to be given his position. One such was Rauschenplatt. A candidate more congenial to Mazzini was the more modest Bianco, who was the recognized military leader amongst the Italian exiles and had the great advantage of being *persona grata* with Buonarroti. He spent much of his time at Lyons, trying to enrol the Italian exiles in France. But he was averse to leadership. "Me, I am only Bianco", he said, when urged to assume the rôle of commander. But it was agreed that

he should be Ramorino's deputy, when the great day came. A
less reticent man was the French "General" Damas. He had few
doubts about his capacity to lead the invasion, and for some
time Mazzini seriously toyed with the idea of letting him do so.
He always claimed to have three hundred followers, but when
Harro-Harring went to see him at the "Red Lion", at Lausanne,
in November, he admitted that he scarcely had one hundred
left because the rest had found it more profitable to take up
smuggling. A veteran of the Napoleonic days, he alternately
bored his listeners with his anecdotes and shocked them with his
indiscretions. In the end Mazzini dropped him because Damas
insisted – not without some justice – that the Savoyards were
more French than Italian, and that it would be best to lead the
invasion waving the tricolour of the old French Republic, which
was the only flag to which they were likely to respond.

The question of the flag seemed crucial to all concerned.
Melegari, for instance, wanted it simply to bear the words *Unity*,
Independence, *Liberty*. Mazzini was horrified. There *must* be
Equality, too.

"Liberty is little, is nothing, if it is not the necessary means for
founding Equality, for reconstituting a People. – Liberty is the
critical part only. Liberty, by itself, is Protestantism in religion.
Liberty, by itself, is Romanticism in literature. Liberty is a negation
– of itself it constructs nothing".

And there was another concept as important: Humanity, the
Chief insisted, must also appear on the flag.

"We shall be invading with the Poles, the French, etc. To all these
patriots from other countries who have come to die with us and for us
have we no word to offer? Should we not show that on our banner
there is something upon which they can seize for themselves? If we
put *Liberty, Equality, Humanity*, on one side, and *Unity* on the other,
we say everything – everything".

But the quarrel went on. Melegari wanted to inscribe a war-cry
against the foreigner – *guerra al barbaro* – but there was the
difficulty that a lot of *barbari* were about to fight alongside the
Italians. Bianco wanted Young Italy's device, *God and the People*.
But that seemed too vague. In the end the flag bore the inscrip-
tion *Liberty, Equality, Humanity*, on one side, and *Independence*

and *Unity* on the other. So they compromised, and did what Mazzini wanted.

December came, then January, but still there was no Ramorino. Rumour had it that he was engaged in losing at the gaming tables of Paris the 40,000 francs he had received from the revolutionary committee. But it would also seem that he had run into genuine difficulties in his recruiting campaign in France. In fairness to him it should be recognized that the economic situation was against him. He was not lacking in courage, and enjoyed an enormous reputation; there is no reason to suppose that he would not have succeeded in raising a fair body of troops and in leading them into Savoy if conditions had been more propitious. But, after the collapse of the European revolution of 1830-31, there was a slump on the revolutionary market generally. It was a very bad period for recruiting revolutionaries; there were, as Damas had found to his cost, more profitable and less dangerous forms of lawlessness open to such men. Moreover, as a result of the purges of foreign exiles undertaken by Louis Philippe, the Rhone valley was no longer the reservoir of cosmopolitan insurgents that it had been as recently as 1830. Nor was service on behalf of Young Italy likely to be very popular in the autumn of 1833. Too much had happened, and had failed to happen, that had lowered the credit, in revolutionary circles, of her ruling committee at Geneva. And finally, 40,000 francs, though a difficult sum for Mazzini to raise, was not a large one with which to enrol and equip a thousand troops in France for the invasion of Italy.

It remains seemingly strange that Mazzini continued to insist upon waiting for Ramorino. If the Piedmontese congregations of Young Italy had any confidence left in their Chief they could hardly have held him to his undertaking to produce the general after the latter had failed to appear in November. Nor is it very easy to believe that the revolutionary committee was so deeply committed to him that it could not throw him overboard. Harro-Harring tells us that the German contingent simply could not believe that any revolutionary committee could be so incompetent as to tie itself, and all its plans, to one particular general.

Mazzini urges Ramorino to take the route into Savoy.

Drawing by G. Mantegazza.

Signing the pact of Young Europe.

Drawing by G. Mantegazza.

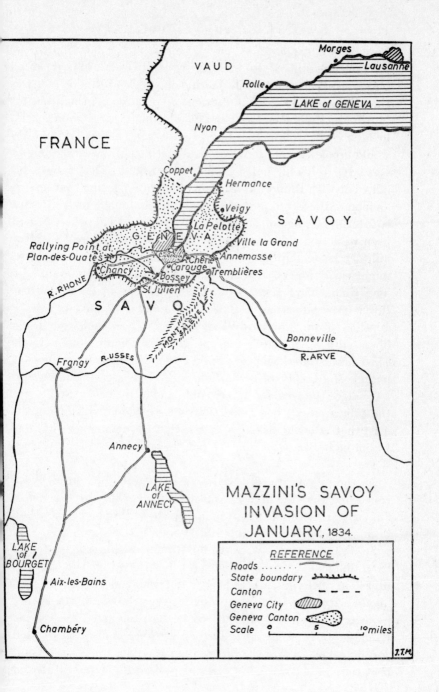

VAUD

Morges
Lausanne
Rolle
LAKE of GENEVA
Nyon

FRANCE

Coppet
Hermance
Veigy
SAVOY
La Pelotte
G E N E V A
Ville la Grand
Rallying Point at
Plan-des-Ouates
Chêne
Annemasse
Chancy
Carouge
Bossey
Tremblières
R. RHONE
St Julien
S A V O Y
MONT SALÈVE
Bonneville
Frangy
R. USSES
R. ARVE

Annecy

LAKE
of
ANNECY

MAZZINI'S SAVOY
INVASION OF
JANUARY, 1834.

LAKE
of
BOURGET

Aix-les-Bains

REFERENCE
Roads ....
State boundary
Canton
Geneva City
Geneva Canton
Scale 0   5   10 miles

Chambéry

J.T.M.

115

Perhaps the explanation may be found in the fact that, if he were not permitted to lead the expedition himself, it suited Mazzini rather well that Ramorino should lead it. The fact was that the general's very limitations were a recommendation for him in Mazzini's eyes. He knew he could "manage" Ramorino, and he later made it clear that he had always intended to do so.[1] He would brook no victorious general dictating political programmes – as later in his life he had to suffer Garibaldi. That danger did not exist with Ramorino, who was fond of repeating that he was "a man of the sword, not of words", and had made little attempt to interfere in the politics of Poland or of Portugal, where he had been in action. If, on the other hand, Mazzini were to let the military leadership pass to one of his fellow revolutionaries, he might easily lose control of the whole movement. It would be a long time before a constituent assembly could determine the future government of Italy; the Austrians would have to be expelled from Lombardy-Venetia and the whole peninsula liberated first. Mazzini's conception of his rôle as Young Italy's Chief necessitated that he should remain in control during that period. His theory of revolution, indeed, was one which would have made it logical for him to command in the field as well – but the congregations had ruled that out. In the circumstances the least that he could do was to ensure that the commander was one whom he need not fear on the political plane.

As the new year, 1834, dawned, it came to be agreed by all concerned that the invasion must be undertaken by the end of January or the whole plan would have to be dropped – there had been altogether too much publicity about it.

So January 2nd saw Giovanni Ruffini setting out at 6 a.m. from Marseilles, where he had been helping to plan the coastal invasion, for Lyons, where he was to try to concert the arrangements with Ramorino's representatives. Giovanni, the future popular author, and destined to be Senator and *Conte* of the Kingdom of Sardinia, already took a rather more sophisticated and detached view of the proceedings than did the other revolutionaries, and he was more particular about his comforts. He did

¹ Letter of May 1834. IX. 371.

not care for leaving Marseilles so early on a January morning and he was appalled by the "boredom, cold, snatches of sleep, and fatigue" inseparable from a 54-hour journey in winter. However, by January 10th he had finished at Lyons and reached Geneva, where he found that most of the revolutionaries had been suffering from influenza. But Mazzini he found filled with elation at the now assured prospect of action by the end of the month, and it was quickly agreed that, whether Ramorino arrived or no, the mobilization should, in any case, take place not later than January 30th.

But what was planned between the revolutionaries was quickly learnt at Vienna and Turin. There were spies everywhere; a whole nest of them at the "Red Lion" at Lausanne, others at Lyons, Marseilles and Geneva. From Paris one of them was writing at the beginning of January giving an accurate picture of the plans for the invasion and asking Metternich for instructions as to whether he should himself enlist with the insurgents.[1]

Metternich saw to it that the Swiss cantons were kept informed of the revolutionaries' plans, so expulsion orders soon reached the refugees from the governments of Fribourg and Berne. The first effect of these orders was, as already mentioned, to favour Mazzini's plans by causing the exiles to move westwards into the more tolerant canton of Vaud, on the western shore of the Lake of Geneva, where they were in a better position to join in the invasion. On January 27th, however, the canton of Vaud, too, ordered a general expulsion. But its effectiveness depended upon the sympathies of the local prefects, police, and people, and at the little town of Nyon, on the western shore of the lake, which had become the chief centre of the revolutionaries, the prefect had long been a friend of Harro-Harring, with whom he enjoyed discussing political and religious problems. This prefect did his best to shelter them all, but soon even he was obliged to follow the example of his more compliant colleagues at the towns of Rolle and Morges, farther east along the shore, and to issue expulsion orders.

[1] Some of what he wrote is printed in R. Barbiera *Figure e figurine del secolo che muore*. Milan, 1899, pp. 233, 234.

By the end of January action had thus become a necessity.

For the Poles and the Germans January 29th (Wednesday) was the day of mobilization, and the rendezvous was Nyon. The little town became a camp and the prefect became powerless. After escaping from arrest, and careering along the western shore as far as Lausanne, to round up supporters and encourage stragglers, Harro-Harring met his friend Rauschenplatt, and the two commandeered a char-à-banc and drove back in triumph to Nyon.

Thursday January 30th was spent in waiting at Nyon for instructions.

At last on Friday January 31st the news leaked out that Ramorino had arrived the day before at Rolle. He was now at Geneva. The main party, at Nyon, had not seen him, but he had appointed a Colonel Grabski to command their column, and, since the troops of the canton of Vaud were now menacing, Grabski agreed that they should proceed that night, in open boats, across the lake to a point on the opposite shore near Hermance.

It was a moment of spiritual elation and a mood of self-sacrifice prevailed. Harro-Harring gave his sword to Grabski, to make him look more like a commander, and his pistols to Rauschenplatt, who was to lead the German column.[1] Then the company marched off into a wood nearby to arm themselves with rifles at one of Mazzini's secret *caches*. They should also have found coats there, but these had unfortunately been confiscated by the authorities of Vaud. Worse still, when a detachment of the party reached Rolle, where they should have found a boat in which to cross the lake, it was not there – it, too, had been confiscated by the gendarmes. It took them three hours of marching before they found another, and then they could not get into it until they had emptied out the planks with which it was filled – a noisy process which created much interest on the part of the local inhabitants.

Eventually some 160 Poles and Germans, coatless and in two

---

[1] Harro-Harring's account of the expedition is given in his *Mémoires sur La Jeune Italie et sur les derniers événements de Savoie* (Paris, 1834).

open boats, pushed off across the lake on the last night of January and arrived on the other side in broad morning daylight. The obvious plan would have been to stay on the lake until dark and then land and march by night to join the main body which was mustering just south of Geneva. But they had no bread. And without coats or bread they could hardly spend another ten hours in open boats on the lake. When they landed they were promptly arrested by the gendarmes of the Canton of Geneva, an operation which was facilitated by the fact that, on Grabski's orders, they had left their arms hidden in the bottom of the boat.

Such was the initial disaster which overtook the main group of Polish and German auxiliaries. They comprised the most promising fighting material amongst the revolutionaries and almost the only professional soldiers. Their detention, however, was not expected to last very long, and Harro-Harring, with a few followers, had managed to avoid detention altogether. For they had been marched, under arrest, to Geneva and had there been liberated by the direct intervention of the mob on their behalf. They were thus able to join Mazzini, Bianco and the others.

It is not clear why Ramorino had chosen to appear first at Rolle; there were few exiles there owing to the prolonged hostility of the local prefect. Still, it was something that he had arrived, at last, somewhere near the scene of action; he had sent his messengers on to Mazzini and Bianco, at the *Hôtel de la Navigation* at Geneva, and Mazzini had replied immediately. The mobilization, he wrote, had not only begun, it was almost complete. The hidden depots of arms, upon which they depended, were already in danger. Arrests were being made by the cantonal gendarmes. It had become imperative to act at once, and the night of Saturday, February 1st, had already been fixed for the attack. He reported 300 men ready on the frontier of Savoy, 60 Poles at Geneva, 140 Poles in the Canton of Vaud, 100 Italians between Geneva and Nyon, and at least 150 Germans and Swiss on the borders of the lake. Every day ten or a dozen of Charles Albert's troops were offering to desert to him. Bianco added a note, by the same messenger, saying it was imperative Ramorino should come at once to Geneva. Meanwhile he himself had taken charge of the mobilization.

Ramorino, by his own account,[1] duly arrived at the *Hôtel* in time for dinner on the Friday evening. There he met Mazzini and Bianco, and a conference took place. He was told that there would be about 780 men in the party, altogether. If this is true (and it is approximately the number promised in Mazzini's letter of the previous day) it was an exaggeration, certainly, on Mazzini's part, and Ramorino had some reason to be disillusioned by the numbers that actually turned up on the following day. He was, however, in no position to complain. He had arrived late. But worse, so far from arriving at the head of an army he had, in Mazzini's words, arrived "without men, without arms, without a horse, with two generals, one adjutant, and a doctor". What, then, had become of the 40,000 francs? Three-quarters of it was lost. But 10,000 francs, Mazzini admits, Ramorino had previously returned; and, in order to understand Mazzini's policy, it is necessary to notice that, for two months at least, he had known that Ramorino was not going to turn up with an army.

True to his policy of keeping a close eye on his general, Mazzini secured that his friend Celeste Menotti should be a Staff Officer at Ramorino's G.H.Q. Menotti thus became custodian of the book of mobilization orders, and later on he refused to hand it over to his general on the ground that he thought he should hand it over to the provisional government which was employing them all, i.e. to Mazzini.

The eve-of-invasion conference between the crusaders for liberty can hardly have been a very cordial affair; all the same important decisions were reached. Ramorino agreed to the committee's plan that the general muster should take place at Plan-des-Ouates (four miles SW. of Geneva, near the Savoy frontier, and on the road to St. Julien) at 11 p.m. on the following evening – Saturday. He could hardly do otherwise since it was far too late to change the plan. He did, however, produce original orders of his own for the Poles and Germans out on the lake. They were

---

[1] Dupont published Ramorino's story of the invasion, some two months afterwards, in Paris, under the title *Précis des derniers événements de Savoie.*

not to cross the lake from Nyon, or to march to Geneva. They were to move round, to the west, through the mountain valleys, cross the Rhone at Arvilly and Chancy, and take the fort of St. Julien from the rear. Perhaps this would have been a good plan. But since, as already described, that party was already crossing the lake, it was irrelevant what Ramorino decided they should do.

By 8 a.m. on Saturday morning Mazzini and Ramorino were together again. The Chief of Young Italy persuaded his general to sign a proclamation, for the benefit of the Savoyards, about liberty. Soon after came the bad news from the lake; but a little later came the more encouraging information that the Poles and Germans had been allowed to re-embark, with their weapons, provided they left the shores of the Canton of Geneva for good. So Ramorino sent orders that they should carry out their re-embarkation peaceably, and proceed up the lake, landing again on its eastern shore, just beyond Hermance, in the territory of Savoy, and march from there southwards, to Veigy, and thence to Annemasse, where he would reinforce them. This plan vitally affected Ramorino's movements with his main body, influencing him to move backwards, towards Annemasse, in the hope of a reunion with the Poles, instead of forwards, to St. Julien, and along the main road to Chambéry.

The scene that Saturday at Carouge, just south of Geneva, was one of cheerful confusion. From all directions the exiles were filtering in, so were the cartloads of arms and ammunition. The populace was friendly, and there was little attempt at concealment. On the other hand, the government of Geneva was becoming more menacing, and the police paid a visit to the *Hôtel de la Navigation.* When the time came to move towards the rendezvous at Plan-des-Ouates Ramorino found it prudent to slip out, unobserved, and make the journey on foot, with Celeste Menotti. There were also some ominous warnings from Bianco, who informed his superior that Genevan troops had been sent to exercise near Plan-des-Ouates, and also that the Sardinian government had reinforced its garrison at St. Julien to 500 men. After surveying the site at Plan-des-Ouates Ramorino decided to go through with the plan for the general muster there, but he issued orders to accelerate is because of the danger from the

Genevan troops. The revolutionaries were now to rally at 9 p.m. instead of 11 p.m. It was later to be an important part of Mazzini's case against Ramorino that this anticipation of the agreed time prevented many from ever joining the main body, and that there were inadequate arrangements for guiding late-comers as to where they might find it. Ramorino argued that almost all had reached Carouge by Saturday afternoon and that the three main groups, the Italians, the Savoyards and the Poles, all received the revised order in plenty of time from their respective commanders there.

At 9 p.m. Ramorino ordered a count of those assembled at Plan-des-Ouates and found there were 160 – 50 Italians, 50 Savoyards, and 60 Poles. Harro-Harring, his bitterest opponent, says there were 270, and that there were 40 cartridges and a rifle for each man. Bianco says there were 233. Mazzini says there were 223, but that there would have been 600 if the time of the muster had not been advanced. It is hard to believe that a two-hour anticipation made as much difference as that; the claim comes from a justificatory document put out by Mazzini's committee just after the event. Later, in a franker letter of May 1834, Mazzini claimed that "perhaps 200" volunteers had been lost through this cause. It still seems a high estimate. At all events, it is clear enough that the actual muster, even if we accept Harro-Harring's figures, was a far cry from the 700 and more men promised by Mazzini. It was also a small force with which to attack the garrison of St. Julien, now reinforced to 500 men. Bianco later argued that they could have made the attack because part of the garrison of St. Julien was demoralized and part was even ready to join the invaders. There was also a story about an envoy from St. Julien who urged them to come at once because the garrison had been temporarily withdrawn. It was said that Ramorino wasted precious time checking up on this story; but clearly he would have to do so – in the previous year Charles Albert had invited attack upon the fortress of Fenestrelle by a feigned withdrawal of the garrison. Neither Bianco nor the Polish leaders were holding out any such hopes as these at the time, and it is hard to see how Ramorino could reasonably have reckoned upon anything but stiff opposition at this key fortress.

Even so, it is possible that he should have risked the attack because, as Mazzini knew, the hopes of success in such an enterprise rested upon showing great daring.

The general argued that it was ludicrous to suppose that he could attack St. Julien with such a force as he possessed, amongst whom the Poles alone were seasoned soldiers. He maintained that the Italians did not know how to handle their rifles, and that the doctor he had brought with him soon justified his place in the party by treating an Italian who had shot off his own finger. He claimed that it was essential to effect a union with the party from the lake and that the Poles in his own party threatened to abandon him forthwith if he did not lead them back to a reunion with their comrades.

The leader of the Savoyard group, Rubin, recommended that the whole party should encamp for the night at Bossey, some four miles to the north-east of Plan-des-Ouates, and still just within the territory of the Canton of Geneva. He knew the curé there, who was likely to give them refreshments, and to respond suitably to the gift of liberty, and, in the words of the Vice-Intendant of Faucigny,[1] to "emancipation from the shackles in which he had been living till then". So to Bossey Ramorino led his little force. A third of the men were needed to push and pull the two carts in which arms and ammunition jostled each other dangerously. Some thirty volunteers, who had arrived too late for the muster, filtered in to Bossey, but there was still no sign of that influx of Savoyards from across the frontier which everyone had expected. There was a theory that there might be some at the frontier town of Annemasse; moreover at Annemasse they might hope to join the party from the lake. So, in the small hours of Sunday morning, they moved on towards that little town on the River Arve. As they approached the bridge at Tremblières Ramorino thought it was time for them to make a demonstration, to attract volunteers, so he ordered a roll on the drums. Unfortunately there was only one man in a position to carry out the

[1] Jean Philippe Sage, who lived at Bonneville, and who collected his information from various witnesses. His account is printed in *Une relation inédite de l'expédition Mazzinienne de Savoie en 1834, Rassegna Storica del Risorgimento Italiano*, 1948 (Anno 35), p. 229.

order. "They promised me eleven drums and eleven drummers",
he complained, "but only one drum and no drumsticks could be
found". Moreover, though they forced the *douane*, the inhabitants of Tremblières, says the Vice-Intendant, remained "deaf to
the cries of liberty". The guard at the bridge even opened fire
upon them, but it then fled while its commander hid in a tub
belonging to the local tanner.

At Annemasse they found little more to encourage them.
There were no recruits from Savoy and there was no news of the
party from the lake. Nevertheless they made a determined effort
to show spirit. Thus the customs officers declined to be recruited,
so the invaders duly disarmed them, and took off their coats,
which they burnt, along with the official registers. This was
Harro-Harring's idea, and was intended to demonstrate that the
authority of Charles Albert's government was now abolished.
They next read a revolutionary proclamation, previously compiled by Mazzini, and dated "St. Julien, February 1st", pocketed
80,000 francs from the tills of the *douane* (for which Rubin gave
a receipt) and finally planted a Tree of Liberty. The Vice-
Intendant gives a clear picture of what happened at the foot of
the tree: "they harangued the crowd of curious bystanders,
whom they had attracted around them, by reading a proclamation at the end of which they cried *aux armes! . . .*". This was
intended to be the signal for a general rush, by the crowd, to the
recruiting booths. "But a profound silence and the utmost immobility on the part of the spectators made it clear that they
were not born for that kind of glory".

Probably most of the crowd were Swiss. It was a fine Sunday,
and a number of people had been making their way out from
Geneva and Carouge to see what was happening. Clearly it would
be curiosity that compelled them. It was also a weakness, from
the point of view of recruitment, that everybody knew that the
claim, in the proclamation, that St. Julien had already been
captured, was false. And again, as Mazzini later argued, Annemasse was not a promising recruiting centre. It was a frontier
town, its livelihood depended upon the customs, and it was therefore intimately linked with the royal government.

Possibly the situation might still have been saved, at least temporarily, if the Poles and Germans from the lake, so ardently hoped for by their compatriots in the main party, had at last made their appearance. But the circumstances in which that contingent now found itself were precarious in the extreme. For the Genevan government, having allowed them to escape, was taking every precaution to ensure that they made no further trouble by landing either upon Genevan or upon neighbouring Savoyard shores. So the party was reduced to rowing up and down the lake, trying to find somewhere to land, and being prevented from doing so by the Genevan troops, who had no difficulty in covering their movements. The message which reached Ramorino on Sunday night stated that they were then stranded in their boats opposite Coppet, unable to navigate because they had been deprived of their sails and their oars, and encircled by hostile craft.

As to Savoyard recruits, there were, eventually, a few. But Ramorino states that more took the convenient opportunity which the occasion afforded to provide themselves with rifles without taking the further step of enrolling in the force.

At 5 p.m. that Sunday afternoon Ramorino moved his dis-illusioned men a farther three-quarter-hour's march up to Ville la Grand. The crisis was at hand. Some, at least, of the Poles were saying that they would make their way back to Geneva if reunion were not effected with the party from the lake. There were already desertions amongst the Italians and the Savoyards. But the more fiery leaders, amongst whom we may place Harro-Harring, some of his Polish friends, and also, probably, Bianco and Celeste Menotti, were telling Ramorino that, at all costs, he must march forward, into the territory of Savoy, and that the population would yet rise and join them. And this remained the burden of Mazzini's exhortations.

But Ramorino had had enough. Disgusted by his companions in arms, who kept stealing the straw which he had reserved for himself and his General Staff to sleep upon, and who insisted upon clustering around his fire, instead of lighting fires of their own elsewhere, he managed to secure a bed for himself, for Sunday night, in the house of the mayor of Chêne, close by. But he was determined, before retiring to it, to effect the dissolution of his insurgent band. At 2 a.m., on account (as he claimed) of the continual reports of desertions, he had an alert sounded. The response from the tired, cold and disappointed men was feeble. But one who did respond was Mazzini, who moved forward to his post, convinced that the moment of action had at last come. Already he had a high fever upon him, and when he found that the alert was a false alarm he swooned and collapsed and, in a coma, was carried on a stretcher somewhere in the direction of Carouge, which was where he found himself when he recovered consciousness some hours later. Meanwhile Ramorino was holding a council of war. Celeste Menotti, as well as Mazzini, was absent, nor was any member of the Central Congregation of Young Italy present. Rubin, leader of the Savoyards, was not there – Ramorino says he had already deserted. But Bianco was present, and so was Antonini, who commanded the sixty Poles; the others were personal friends of Ramorino.

The dissolution of the band was agreed by this council. Bianco claimed to be exonerated from personal responsibility for the decision on the grounds that he had pleaded hard for an immediate attack upon either Bonneville or St. Julien and had been called away to the Italian column ten minutes before the dissolution was agreed.

While his officers were carrying out the dissolution, and the frustrated men were filtering back to Geneva, their general escaped to his prepared bedroom in the house of the mayor of Chêne. But he was not to occupy it for long before two or three enraged Poles, with whom was Harro-Harring, forced their way in and demanded that he should either lead forward those of them who still wanted to fight or he should die. He managed, however, to escape through his bedroom window, and thence made his way up to La Pelotte, and across the lake, and so into France. The mayor had offered to provide him with a safe-conduct, but since he was more afraid of falling into the hands of his recent followers than he was of the authorities he wisely declined this assistance.

Was Ramorino bribed to betray the expedition?

It has been freely asserted that he was. Harro-Harring says the general had received 350 to 400 thousand francs "from the Holy Alliance", that he tried to delay the mobilization, and that he deliberately engineered the troubles of the party on the lake; and the Vice-Intendant of Faucigny relates the rumour that he was bribed by the banker Heintch, acting on behalf of the Genevan government, which was frightened of the likely reactions of Charles Albert's government. He may have been bribed; but if so it is more likely that this occurred beforehand, in France (as Mazzini supposed) and that it accounted for his very late arrival. There is nothing about his behaviour during the weekend of operations to suggest that he was other than a cautious professional soldier who found himself out of place in a nest of revolutionary enthusiasts.

The Savoy expedition was not planned as an isolated movement. It was intended that as soon as the invaders had established themselves at Chambéry and at Bonneville a revolution should break out at Genoa, supported by a general rising along the Ligurian coast, itself stimulated by an invasion from the French coast. The government of Charles Albert would thus be caught between two fires. The garrison at Alessandria would declare for the revolution – and so on. However, none of these things happened. That the invasion from the French coast did not take place is perhaps the least surprising part of the failure, for that plan was, indeed, hazardous. A Neapolitan vessel, sailing from Marseilles to Naples, was to be seized, en route, by its "passengers", who would prove to be the warriors of Young Italy, and who would divert it to the Ligurian coast. Melegari, at Marseilles, was supposed to be planning all this. And the revolt at Genoa was to be organized by Mazzini's friends still in or near the city, including Elia Benza, Federico Campanella, Napoleone Ferrari, and disaffected elements in the garrison. It was timed to break out on February 11th, and the fever-striken Mazzini, still lying half delirious somewhere between Carouge and Ville la Grand, had not abandoned hope that this revolt would yet save the situation. A week after that terrible night of the dispersal he wrote to Melegari:

"The day fixed for Genoa is Tuesday (11th) – But the mistrust arising from our news may have changed their minds – As to that, everybody must act according as his conscience dictates".

On February 12th, to his mother:

"Of the state of our morale I won't speak. If there is any hope of raising it it is by letters, of the 11th, reaching us from Genoa".

To Melegari:

"Letters posted [from Genoa] on the 10th say nothing about the 11th. There have been some arrests amongst the popular leaders. I have the darkest forebodings for Italy, for myself, for everything. This incessant being on the brink of gathering the fruit, without daring, or being able to pick it, is something to drive one mad. We shall see tomorrow".

By the 16th he had given up hope.

"I am in a fury with men always irresolute, even unto death. . . . Our friends, it seems to me, have forgotten me, they do not write to me . . . they do none of those things which they had promised".

The movement at Genoa had, indeed, never come to birth at all. Discoveries, arrests, some treachery and some cowardice had caused the appointed day to come and go with a muster of men – but no leaders. Twenty-seven years later, in his Autobigraphical Notes, Mazzini wrote:

". . . it failed only because of the inexperience of the leaders, good men, but very young, and unknown to the majority. Giuseppe Garibaldi had a part in that second attempt [at Genoa] and saved himself by flight".

Mazzini's reference to Garibaldi is technically correct, but its implication is ungenerous and it was calculated to come as a shock to Italian and English readers who, by the time it appeared, had become accustomed to regard Garibaldi as an invincible Sir Lancelot. By the time he wrote them many years of quarrel had estranged the Chief of Young Italy from his once ardent disciple. Actually there had been nothing discreditable, though there may have been some imprudence, in the behaviour of the young sailor from Nice, then newly enrolled in Young Italy. On February 3rd he went on board the royal frigate *Des Geneys* of Charles Albert's navy, in Genoa harbour, with the rank of a mariner of the third class, performing a part of his *leva* – his compulsory military service. He was sworn, with his friend and companion Edward Mutru, to gain possession of the ship for the revolutionaries when the insurrection should break out at Genoa. He had already been active there in enrolling new members for Young Italy, from the services, using those same methods of free drinks, entertainment, and promises of promotion which had proved so fatal in the previous summer. He did not know that two of his recruits had already betrayed him – after their dinner – to the police, who had sent a certain de Medici along to get himself enrolled and find out more.

But Garibaldi forestalled him for he did not wait for February 11th. He heard there was to be an insurrection to seize the *Sarzano* armoury at Genoa on the 4th, so he pretended sick and went ashore in a dingy with Mutru, leaving his companions to gain possession of the ship. Thence the two went to the *piazza Sarzano*, at what they understood was the appointed time for action, waited an hour, and saw nothing. Then they heard of the arrest and scattering of their associates, and no doubt they also read in the papers of Ramorino's failure, for it was reported in the *Gazzetta di Genova* of February 4th. They wandered about the city together, but the piazzas were deserted and in the dance-halls there were only the usual diversions. So at midnight they went to bed at some digs they frequented in a humble quarter. At 6 a.m. Garibaldi was roused "as though by an invisible hand" and, having failed to rouse Mutru, who was sleepy, he ran out into the street, to the *Darsena*. On his way back he met a friend who said that Mutru had just been arrested. So he dived for the house of a fruit-vendor, Natalina Pozzo, in the *piazza Sarzano*, who disguised him as a peasant, and the next night he escaped through the *Porta della Lanterna* to his home at Nice, and thence to Marseilles.[1]

There were two other groups which had a part to play in the general plan of the Savoy invasion, and which met with discomfiture. One was a small group at Lyons, which the Marchese Gaspare Rosales (a comparatively wealthy Lombard, who spent

[1] Such is his own account, in the definitive edition of his Memoirs. But there are others, in which various of his Genoese friends performed prodigies on his behalf.

61,000 francs in the cause of Young Italy at this time) and
Nicolò Ardoino (who had been a member of Charles Albert's
Chambéry garrison) were responsible for organizing; these men
marched from Grenoble, but were dispersed at Les Échelles,
where they killed a *carabiniere* and one other, but lost two of
their own leaders who were taken and shot. The other was a
German contingent which marched from Zürich and Berne.
Mazzini was sarcastic about them: they advanced "more or less
in battle array, bearing German republican cockades, and with
oak leaves in their hats, showing everybody the purpose for
which they marched".

The most interesting, as well as the most important, problem
about the Savoy expedition is Mazzini's own handling of it.

In *Young Italy's Letter to General Ramorino*, which was the
party's published accusation against the general, he makes three
principal charges: Ramorino had turned up too late to plan the
mobilization properly; he had failed to bring an army; he had
failed to attack St. Julien or to march into the interior.

These accusations were all justified; yet they fail to disclose
the reality. First, Mazzini knew *by the beginning of December* that
Ramorino's army was not going to materialize. "At the beginning
of December he at last told me that it had proved impossible for
him to muster even a hundred out of the thousand men promised". And it was then that Ramorino had returned the 10,000
francs, and the obvious moment had arrived to dispense with his
services – if Mazzini wanted to do so. And second, we learn from
Mazzini's Autobiographical Notes that, far from being anxious
to secure Ramorino in time for him to organize the mobilization
properly, Mazzini was counting upon his not turning up until the
movement was well under way, in fact until St. Julien had been
captured. So far from arriving too late Ramorino had, in fact,
arrived too early.

"I hoped that Ramorino would confine himself to the secondary part
outlined to him, and that he would not come until the movement had
begun; but I was disappointed . . .". And, after he had arrived, ". . . he
wanted to assume from then on that command which I had wished
should only begin at St. Julien . . .".[1]

[1] LXXVII, 177.

But not only did Mazzini intend that Ramorino's command should begin at St. Julien, he intended that it should only last for twelve hours! In May 1834 he wrote a long and intimate letter on the whole subject – his fullest analysis of the Savoy expedition.[1]

"For myself I thought that Ramorino did not want to undertake the enterprise; but I thought, knowing him ambitious, that he did not want it undertaken by others, I thought that, keenly aware as he was of his own interests, he would have seen interest, glory, power, dictatorship, everything that he would want in leading that expedition – at St. Julien – then we should be in a position to break that instrument and we should have known how to break it. So I turned all my energies towards having him, towards overcoming the delays, towards using with him every kind of persuasive language that I could, and I succeeded".

Here, then, was Mazzini's plot. Ramorino was to be merely a tool – a tool for use during twelve vital hours only. Since they were demanding the general in Savoy and Piedmont he would present him to them, for a brief twelve hours, at St. Julien. Then he would take over control himself. And why would this twelve hours be sufficient? Because "I arranged that delegates from each [of the provinces of Savoy] should be collected at St. Julien, so that when they had made sure of our arrival they should run to give their districts the signal for the uprising".[2]

But if he meant to assume control at St. Julien it was equally important that he should have control beforehand – otherwise they might never get there. And this was where he failed – failed because Ramorino turned up about thirty-six hours too soon. Mazzini wanted Ramorino at St. Julien, but he did not want him even one day too soon lest he should interfere with the plans. When he did turn up, Mazzini tried to present him with a *fait accompli*, but in this he failed and Ramorino started to make difficulties at once. He was annoyed to find that the mobilization had already begun, and he complained about it. He had to accept the plan for a muster at Plan-des-Ouates, but he put his own man, Grabski, in charge of the Poles at Nyon, he anticipated the hour of the muster, and finally he completely ruined Mazzini's plan by failing to march upon St. Julien. Mazzini seems to

[1] IX, 366.   [2] LXXVII, 177.

E

have underrated him. Lazy, indulgent, perhaps corrupt, Ramorino was yet no mere cypher. In his previous campaigns he had shown an independent will of his own, if not always a wise one.

Perhaps, all the same, Mazzini might have made his plan prevail if he had carried the other leaders with him. But it is clear that he did not let even his most intimate friends and associates into his secret; had he done so, would Bianco have been warning Ramorino about the reinforcements at St. Julien? Would Rubin, the Savoyard leader, have suggested Bossey as a suitable place for them to spend Saturday night? Would the Polish leaders have been pressing the need for a reunion with their brethren on the lake?

The fact that the other leaders had never known his real plans made it very difficult for Mazzini to concert with them, afterwards, an effective defence of Young Italy, and weakened the attempt to throw the whole blame upon Ramorino. There is a remarkable letter, written only some seven weeks afterwards, on March 22nd, by Mazzini to Melegari,[1] in which he explains his difficulty. The other leaders were pressing him to draw up a long and formal statement, in conjuction with themselves, in reply to the 65-page pamphlet of self-justification which Ramorino had just published in Paris. But such a document, Mazzini explained, simply could not be compiled. The most, in his view, that could be done was for him to write a personal account – an account, as he put it, with plenty of *pathos*. Why? Because the other members of the Revolutionary Committee were either out of sympathy with him, or out of touch with him; and because he was not, himself, satisfied about their behaviour at the time of the expedition. So far as Bianco, Antonini (leader of the Poles) and Rubin (leader of the Savoyards) were concerned he was evidently dissatisfied about their actions at the time, and he even considered that some of the accusations in Ramorino's pamphlet were justified. In fact, for the *débâcle* that had ensued, he was as much inclined to blame them as he was to blame Ramorino. The real villain, in Mazzini's eyes, was Rubin; but he felt he could not say so without compromising Young Italy.

[1] IX, 258.

"We promised [Ramorino] formations which did not come – that is definite – why? Young Italy would need to say: Rubin, and all the Savoyards had promised us 300 men; Walcker and Simond had promised us 60 and more *carabinieri* – the money was paid – and they did not come. . . . So Young Italy had conspired admirably – It could not have done more. We cannot say all this . . .".

The most eloquent testimony to the mistrust in which the other leaders held Mazzini is to be found in his own later confession that "not wanting to give any excuse for the suspicion that there was dual control, or that I was governed by ambition, I took a rifle and buried myself in the ranks". He must thereby have weakened his hold over the general; and, in the long letter of May 1834 already quoted, he recognized it as his great mistake

"not to have raised the cry of insurrection against him [Ramorino] amongst the small troop which was disposed to look upon me with more favour than upon him at the first deviation from the straight line which led to St. Julien".

The heart of that bitter self-reproach which afflicted him afterwards was not a personal indignation against Ramorino, it was indignation against those who had prevented him from taking the lead himself. By then some were openly accusing him of personal ambition and were demanding a change in the leadership of Young Italy. But the fault, he retaliated, had not been his, it had been theirs. With burning sarcasm he reproached them with their sycophancy, their silly worship of a general in his uniform. ". . . We were young – we had nothing but willpower, energy, constancy, capacity to work, and perhaps intelligence – he had the title of general, and fame, and military *aplomb* – in short, a name". He was certain, by then, that he should have stood out against all the others, against the congregations in Piedmont and against the other national leaders, all of whom wanted a 'general' even though they might not want Ramorino. At all costs he should have clung to Young Italy's principle "for new undertakings new men". "I should have struggled against everybody; the Italian and foreign youth was with me; and I am full of remorse that I listened to other voices rather than to theirs".

Clearly he was right. His plan had fallen between two stools. He had tried to satisfy everybody and, unknown to anybody, to keep the real control in his own hands; and the situation had got the better of him. To have realized his audacious plan he would have had to remain in absolute control of everybody, including Ramorino, throughout that vital weekend, and that was beyond his physical powers. When he failed there was nobody at all, not even Bianco, who could act in his place, because not even Bianco knew what the plan was.

We know rather little about what Mazzini actually did during the critical Saturday and Sunday. He tells us that on the Saturday, after helping to organize the mobilization at Geneva, he crossed the lake, with Giovanni Ruffini, in a precarious craft, to the western shore. Most of the Italians were in the region around Ferney and he went to organize their movement towards the evening muster. These were the men who, many of them, arrived too late, owing to the change in the time; some of them turned up later at Bossey. Mazzini himself turned up in time for the muster at 9 p.m. We have already noticed that he was in the ranks, and that he makes no claim to have insisted upon the advance to St. Julien.

Harro-Harring gives brief glimpses of Mazzini at Bossey and at Annemasse, neither of which suggests that he was very close to Ramorino or to G.H.Q. He was always "with the Italians". No doubt he was striving to put heart into their contingent; but, throughout Sunday, the fever which struck him down during the following night must already have been raging in his body.

"I had presumed too heavily upon my physical strength. The immense work which for months I had taken upon my shoulders had prostrated me. For the whole of the last week I had not touched my bed; I had slept supporting myself against the back of my chair in half- or quarter-hour snatches. Then the anxiety, the fears, the presentiment of treachery, the unforeseen disappointments, the need to hearten others with the smile of a confidence which I did not possess, the sense of crushing responsibility exhausted both my strength and my faculties. When I took my place in the ranks a burning fever devoured me. Many times I came near to falling, and had to be held up by somebody at my side. The night was very cold and I had thoughtlessly left my coat somewhere. I marched in a trance, my teeth chattering. When I felt somebody – it was poor Scipione Pistrucci . . . – putting a coat on my shoulders, I hadn't the strength to turn and thank him. From time to time, when I saw that we were not marching on St. Julien, I rallied my threatened faculties, by a supreme effort, to run in search of Ramorino and beseech him, threaten him, to induce him to return to the road upon which we had agreed. And he humoured me, re-assuring me, with a mephistophelean expression, making promises, and insisting that the Poles from the lake were expected every minute . . .".

Then he collapsed.

"Between one delirium and another, in that glimmering of con-sciousness which returns to one at intervals, only to disappear quickly again into darkness, I heard the voice of Giuseppe Lamberti calling out to me: *What have you taken?* He and a few other friends knew that, fearing that I might be taken prisoner and tortured to make revela-tions, I had brought with me some powerful poison. And, burdened as I still was by the thought of the mistrust which had arisen, or I thought had arisen, in some of their minds, I took those words to mean that he was asking me how much money I had taken from the enemy to betray our brethren. And I relapsed, raving, into convul-sions. . . .

"As soon as Ramorino knew about me he realized his obstacle had been removed; he jumped on his horse, read an order of the day which dissolved the Column, saying that the undertaking was impossible, and abandoned it. They besought Carlo Bianco to lead them; he refused in the face of the new responsibility and of the evident break-ing up of the different contingents. The Column was dissolved.

"When I came to I found myself in a barracks, surrounded by strange soldiers. Close to me was standing my friend Angelo Usiglio. I asked him where we were. With profound grief upon his face he told me: *in Switzerland*. And the Column? *In Switzerland*.

"The first period of Young Italy was over".[1]

[1] LXXVII, 181–183.

Chapter 7

BERNE: YOUNG EUROPE

Something more than the first period of Young Italy was over; its very life, as a society, was ended. Only one more number of the journal ever appeared. Two years later Mazzini wrote: "Young Italy has been blown away". And after another two years he spoke of the society he had created as "inactive at home and demoralized abroad ... dead irrevocably and for ever". During the remaining three years of his Swiss exile he found it impossible to organize any more movements in Italy, and when, in 1837, he withdrew to England, he ceased to make the attempt. The sporadic local *émeutes* in Italy of the middle forties were not of his or of Young Italy's planning, though he tried to assist them with the broken remnants of his party machinery. And the revolutions of 1848–49, though Mazzini's ideas had their part in them, were not made by Young Italy. By 1848 Young Italy had ceased to exist; it had been replaced by groups calling themselves 'Mazzinians', 'Democrats', 'Republicans', organized in local popular clubs, groups which paid Mazzini homage but which obeyed neither himself nor any central congregation. At Milan, at Florence, and at Rome these groups would respond to Mazzini when he appeared amongst them; his was the magic name. But the initiative (save for ten weeks at Rome) belonged by then with other leaders and with other parties.

What, then, did Mazzini mean when he said "The first period of Young Italy was over"? He meant that the first period of his own apostolate was over. He wrote those words in 1861, by which time several more periods of his life had succeeded each other and the Italian Risorgimento had passed through several new phases. But Young Italy had never been reborn. By Young Italy he no longer meant his revolutionary brethren, the *buoni*, the sworn band, he meant a *credo* of his own, which remained with

136

him throughout the various phases of his tormented life to his death in 1872. He meant a *credo* which had once been mostly the monopoly of Young Italy, but which had come to be shared by other groups who followed other leaders. It was a *credo* which would remain alive, and would help Italy to become, in 1946, a nation "one, free, independent, and republican" (which was precisely what the original members of Young Italy, at Marseilles, had sworn to dedicate themselves to "wholly and for ever") though the practical task would mostly be achieved by new parties and by other leaders. In short, Mazzini's ideas influenced all Italians and many of them have been signally vindicated in the twentieth century. But his chosen instrument, his revolutionary association, was shattered on that cold February night, while he lay distrusted and delirious.

Many had always regarded the Savoy expedition as a crazy plan, and many more, when it had failed, counselled Mazzini to moderate his methods. Even his mother joined with his father in imploring him, not only for the sake of his well-being in this world but for his spiritual salvation in the next, to desist from pursuing such paths.

Vincenzo Gioberti of Turin, priest, liberal, and courageous supporter of Young Italy, who had sacrificed his position at court and was in exile at Brussels, wrote to urge the Chief to cease from fruitless revolts which could only prejudice the position of liberals and patriots everywhere and make worse the prospects of improvement. But Mazzini was not prepared to yield one inch. To Gioberti he replied that insurrection was the only way to raise up the masses and to prepare the future, that the Italians must learn to act for themselves, that "action is taught by action". This was his justification of the Savoy expedition. And to the protests of another liberal exile, Pier Silvestro Leopardi, in Paris, who urged upon him the merits of constitutionalism and federalism, he replied that he was not trying merely to improve the condition of Italy but to regenerate her, to make of her "a great people". "Nothing", he wrote, "is changed in the laws or the scope of Young Italy or in the means which she proposes to choose and to adopt. . .'

Brave words. But, in reality, all was changed. The national movement was checked, and when it revived it revived with hosannas for Mazzini, the pioneer and prophet, but with more practical support for Gioberti and the Moderates, the men whom Mazzini despised.

It was precisely in this darkest hour of defeat, when Young Italy was most utterly rejected and its leading members were scattered to Spain, Portugal, England and the Americas, that Mazzini, on April 15th 1934, chose to found his new association, Young Europe, extending the principles of Young Italy to other European peoples.

It is true that the *Pact of Young Europe*, despite its impressive title, was signed by only seventeen revolutionaries, representing Young Italy, Young Germany and Young Poland, and that the only Italian signatories, besides Mazzini, were the dramatist Ghiglione, Rosales, Bianco, the two Ruffini brothers and Melegari. But there was nothing limited about the scope of its vision:

"Assembled together by common consent for the general good, this 15th April 1834, we . . . have determined as follows:

"(1) Young Germany, Young Poland and Young Italy, being Republican associations . . . led by the same faith in liberty, equality, and progress, do hereby fraternally associate and unite, now and for ever . . ." (Young Switzerland, Young France and Young Austria were added a few months later).

"(2) A declaration of those principles which constitute the universal moral law, in its bearing upon human society, shall be drawn up and signed by the three national committees. . . .

"(3) In all matters not comprehended in the Declaration of Principles . . . each of the associations shall be free and independent".

The Declaration of Principles was intended to clarify the purpose of Young Europe; but the nineteen dogmatic pronouncements which Mazzini drew up were only likely to achieve that purpose with people who were already versed in his theology, and the reader who is interested in pursuing him into that realm is therefore invited to consult Chapter 11, at the end of this book, where it is discussed further. The general purport of the Principles may, however, be gathered from the following: Number Three declared that Young Europe's objective was "to constitute humanity in such wise as to enable it through continuous progress to discover and apply the law of God, by which it should be governed, as speedily as possible . . .".

Number Four stated that

"As our true well-being consists in living in accordance with the law of our being, the knowledge and fulfilment of the law of humanity is the sole source of good. The fulfilment of the mission of Young Europe will result in the general good".

This reads like Rousseau, both in its utopianism and in its obscurity. And Number Six, the longest, is hardly more helpful:

"Humanity can only arrive at the knowledge of its Law of Life through the free and harmonious development of all its faculties.
"Humanity can only reduce that knowledge to action through the free and harmonious development of all its faculties.
"Association is the sole means of realizing this development".

The clearest and most practical message contained in these Principles was embodied in Number Two:

"One God alone.
"One ruler alone – His law.
"One Interpreter alone of that law – Humanity".

By the time he wrote this he had read Lamennais, as well as Rousseau, and had found in the Breton priest a religious justification for his own innate hatred of all prelates, princes, privileges and aristocracies whatsoever. Only let them all be destroyed, and the reign of harmony and love would be ushered in, for, as he had already explained in Number One, Young Europe was "an association of men believing in a future of liberty, equality, and fraternity for all mankind".

Young Europe, however, also had practical objectives. Looking back in later life Mazzini wrote: "The ideal of the association of Young Europe was the federal organization of European democracy under one sole direction, so that any nation rising in insurrection should at once find the others ready to assist it . . .". This had likewise been the purpose of Young Italy in respect of the different Italian states. It had been its function to plan supporting action in Piedmont or in Tuscany to assist a revolt which might be initiated in Naples. After the depressing ex-

periences of 1833–34 in Italy, the same principle was to be
applied to the whole of Europe. It was thus that Mazzini began to
see himself as the centre of a whole web of European revolution
everywhere, as the heir, at Geneva, to the mantle of the
Carbonaro Chief, Filippo Buonarroti, in Paris. That mantle,
whether it cloaked Buonarroti or Mazzini, was really an hallucina-
tion; but it was one much fostered by Mazzini's enemies, and
especially by Metternich's spies, so that the hand of the terrible
Genoese conspirator was seen behind every dagger that was
thrust and every bomb that was thrown. His record, in the matter
of assassination, was equivocal; his position, at the centre of
Young Europe, was sinister. Few paused to consider that Mazzini
was now a hunted exile, living, half-hidden, amidst the Swiss
Alps, or that Young Europe existed only in his imagination, on a
piece of paper, and, confusedly, in the cloudy imaginations of a
handful of fellow exiles. But it is a testimony to the power of his
personality that so much was attributed to him.

To those, like Gioberti, who had warned him that the time had
come to work for gradual reforms, rather than for apocalyptic
upheavals, he had replied by drawing up the Pact of Young
Europe. To those, like Lamennais, who urged him not to expect
the impossible of Italian human nature, he replied in the following year by writing a pamphlet, *Faith and the Future*, the first
full and considered statement of his faith, and the work which
marks his transition from conspirator to prophet. His immediate
purpose was to persuade the Italian revolutionaries, whom he
found a-whoring once more after false prophets – Buonarroti, or
the *Veri Italiani* – and who were also turning to the leaders of the
Catholic revival – Lamennais, Buchez, Tommaseo, Manzoni,
Silvio Pellico – that his own message was, despite the Savoy
débâcle, the true one, and that it was necessary to regenerate the
Italians by action at any cost. A few sentences from this, his
most important publication, will serve to show the lofty regions
into which his imagination had now soared:

". . . Today we have to found the polity of the nineteenth century, to
climb through *philosophy* to *faith*; to define and organize association,
proclaim HUMANITY, initiate the new Age. . . .

"We part from every school that tries to reconcile life and death, and to reform the world by an extinct philosophy. We hold God Himself surety for the sacred doctrine of the people, and its sovereignty. . . .

"Ours is therefore no idle contest of words. . . .

"We fell as a political party; we must rise again as a religious party.

"When, at Young Europe's dawn, all the altars of the old world have fallen, two altars shall be raised upon this soil that the divine Word has made fruitful; and the finger of the herald-people shall inscribe upon one *Fatherland*, and upon the other *Humanity*.

"Like sons of the same mother, like brothers who will not be parted, the people shall gather around these two altars and offer sacrifice in peace and love. And the incense of the sacrifice shall ascend to heaven in two columns that shall draw near each other as they mount, until they are confounded in one point, which is God. . . .

"Then shall we expel from our ranks those who dishonour us [the Carbonari] the tribe of unclean hearts and canting tongues whose inconsistency between language and performance implies infidelity to our creed, who prate of virtue, of self-sacrifice, of charity, while vice is in their hearts, shame on their foreheads, and selfishness in their souls; who nail their immorality to our banner and hide themselves in the day of battle, to reappear when the danger is passed . . . nameless, feeble men who blame our war-cry because themselves they lack courage . . . who ape in their conspiracies the rusty tricks of the police, who mock at enthusiasm, deny the power of inspiration and self-sacrifice, call martyrdom quixotic, and try to regenerate the peoples by statistics. . . .

"*Faith* . . . speaks to us in the prophetic tones of Humanity, European in substance, national in form. It will teach the Fatherland of the fatherlands to the nations still divided; it will translate religion and social philosophy into Art; it will surround with its own beautiful light *woman* who, though a fallen angel, is ever nearer to heaven than we are. It will hasten her redemption, restoring to her the mission of inspiration, of pity, and of prayer, which Christianity divinely symbolized in Mary. It will sing the joys of martyrdom, the immortality of the vanquished, the tears that expiate, the sufferings that purify. . . . It will murmur words of holy consolation to those children of sorrow born before their time, those fated and puissant souls who, like Byron, have no confidants on earth . . . it will teach the young the greatness of self-sacrifice, the virtue of constancy and silence, how to be alone and yet despair not. . . ."

Mazzini did not found a Church of believers in the Faith of Humanity. Martyrs the cause of Italy would have; but they were not martyrs for the Mazzinian Church. There were few martyrs for Mazzinianism save Mazzini himself and there were not many who had even an inkling what he was preaching about. Whether what he saw was a vision of the truth, or merely a mirage of mankind somehow separated from sin, is a matter to which we must return when we consider his theology, but it is important to notice here that the years 1834–35, when he founded Young Europe and wrote *Faith and the Future*, were the parting of the ways for Mazzini. He might have followed the advice of Gioberti, trimming his sails to the wind of disapproval, and bending all his energies towards reconstructing his party upon a more realistic basis. He chose the opposite course, the course of still wider and more sweeping claims, which turned him from a party leader into a prophet. His influence became vaguer and more symbolic. He talked about Italy, he talked about Humanity, and it was evident that he had become a martyr. These things were not without their effect, both in the Risorgimento and later, in the twentieth century, when the collapse of the Austrian Empire and the rise of European nationalism turned many men's minds back to Mazzini. But such influences, strong amongst the poets, strong in England, and still stronger in America, were nevertheless intangible things. They were a far cry from the confident, dominating, post-Christian faith, organized as a new Church, which he invoked in *Faith and Future*, but which neither he nor anybody since has established.

Intended to rouse the European conscience, as Lamennais had roused it the year before with his *Paroles d'un croyant*, Mazzini's pamphlet, written in conscious imitation of Lamennais' style, fell flat and was scarcely read. This was not altogether the author's fault. He had had a desperate struggle to bring it to birth at all. It had been necessary for him to send the pages by post, and the delays were such as to lead him to suspect that they were abstracted and read by the police en route. "All the same", he wrote on October 4th 1835, "I shall finish it, and I believe it will attract attention". By January 18th 1836, he was afraid that the copies despatched to France (where alone the pamphlet might have found a public) had been lost. He was right; they had been confiscated at the French frontier. Few concerned themselves with the writing, but amongst the few was the Austrian ambassador at Berne, the Count Bombelles, who procured two copies and promptly renewed his attempts to have Mazzini expelled from Switzerland.

Mazzini retorted by repeating the popular doggerel describing Count Bombelles and his wife:

> "Le mari n'est pas bon
> La femme n'est pas belle:
> Pourquoi, donc, ces gens là
> S'appellent-ils Bombelles?"

For about a fortnight after his delirium of the night of February 2–3 1834, at Carouge, Mazzini remained convalescent and in hiding. He wrote some quite lucid letters, one to Melegari at Geneva, trying to dispose of what remained of the money so as to relieve the most acute want amongst the exiles, another in an attempt to keep in being the various stores of arms and equipment. Harro-Harring says he spent part of February 5th with the stricken Chief and was relieved to find that, contrary to rumours that he had committeed suicide, "sa force d'âme ne l'avait pas abandonné un seul moment".

But he would see none of his friends, especially his closest friends.

"It makes me ill even to think of it", he wrote to Melegari, about the 11th. "If Albera and Rosales (Lombards, and close friends) and the others have anything to write to me, anything that may yet be of use to the fatherland, let them write – I will reply. I will never yield – but I fear I can do nothing – I never had anything but influence – now I have lost that".

He would, however, like some books. "If you are at the *Hôtel* [*de la Navigation*]", he tells Melegari, "you could do me a service; have sent to me the trunk of books which is in my room or yours – or visit the hotel if you are near". He wants his maps, especially those of Italy and of Savoy, and he wants Buchez' *Introduction to the Philosophy of History* and Botta's *History of Italy*. The effect of the shock was to make him brood more deeply about the roots of his faith, and Buchez, with his religious interpretation of history, was now to share with Lamennais an important influence over him, despite the "deplorably" Christian theology to which both Frenchmen adhered.

With Melegari, however, who was a devout Catholic and regarded Mazzini's theological preoccupations as a waste of time, he does not discuss the books. Melegari must be kept on the job.

So he concludes his letter: "Goodbye; take care of yourself; you can still be useful and should be. The failure of an undertaking from abroad is not the Italian revolution. In the interior everything still stands".

Alas! the day that he wrote this was the day when Genoa should have risen – when in fact his friends were in hiding and Garibaldi was escaping across country to Marseilles.

From Carouge Mazzini changed the password of Young Italy to *Martyrdom*, and the reply to *Resurrection*.

The only one of the leaders he would see was Rosales. Better off than most of the exiles, the Marchese Gaspare de Rosales had nevertheless ruined himself for the cause, and was a marked man with the authorities because he had been principally responsible for organizing the ancillary invasion at Les Échelles.

"Tell Rosales I will see him – I can refuse nothing. . . . If he wishes it, I will see him; but alone. Let him come to me – for that it is necessary he should make arrangements with Durand [the proprietor of the *Hôtel de la Navigation*]".

It is hard to determine how far Mazzini's continued seclusion at Carouge was due to shock, and his need for solitude, or to his danger from the Genevan police on the one hand and from the dagger of his comrades on the other. Undoubtedly he was in real danger from some of his recent brothers-in-arms and was aware of it. Harro-Harring, with his unique experience of the ways of European revolutionaries, explains that it would have been the natural thing to demand the life of the President of the Executive Committee after such a disaster. Santarini, the spy in Austrian pay, reports accusations pouring in upon Mazzini's head from all sides.

Mazzini explained to Melegari that it was for the sake of the future of the Cause that he protected himself. "If I were alone" (without responsibilities) "I would not think of my own safety even for one little second – so tired am I of this life of suspicion . . .". The danger came from some of the Poles, not from the Italians. Harro-Harring insisted that the greatness of Mazzini's soul was such that "the love and veneration of his compatriots increased rather than diminished", and it would be wrong to discount his opinion even though he was a *dévot*. In general, Young Italy did not blame its Chief. It took the line, with some success, that he had been betrayed by Ramorino and that, himself, he was a martyr.

After a fortnight's concealment Mazzini at last decided to try to return to the *Hôtel* at Geneva, but he would only do so on his own terms.

"You will attribute them", he tells Melegari, "to fear; you will be wrong; but, in any case, apart from yourself and Rosales I will not, I cannot, see anyone – I except nobody at all, for the time being. I need to be alone; I need to compose myself, if possible, I need to see nobody, lest I should kill myself, or go mad. It will therefore be necessary to arrange matters like this: we three [the Ruffini brothers and himself] on one side of the hotel, the kitchen side, all of you on the other side, so that the crowd of visitors may be directed towards you, without disturbing me".

Meanwhile one of the Polish leaders wishes to see him. He may do so, but he must not come unaccompanied.

"Zaleski wants to see me. I don't want this to be at the hotel. He must come to me during the daytime, any time today, before I leave in the evening. See if you can arrange this with Mons. Durand, so that he comes, for instance, with Rosales . . . or with a Mons. Bourget, intimate friend of Durand, or with anybody who can manage it".

He did return, by night, but he stayed at the hotel for less than a fortnight. The Genevan government, regarding its hospitality as abused, and under pressure from a justly indignant Charles Albert and also from Vienna, was determined to be rid of him. So, with one or two others, he moved north-eastwards into the interior of Switzerland. Melegari, alone, stayed on at the hotel; most of the fraternity scattered to France or crossed the channel or the Atlantic. Mazzini spent a week at Lausanne, then moved on to Berne, where he and the Ruffini brothers signed the Pact of Young Europe on April 15th. He was still hoping somehow, somewhere, to stimulate another invasion of Italy which should be the signal for that general uprising of which he had not yet abandoned all hope.

Until early in May he remained in hiding at Berne without sympathy or comfort.

"Things are bad for these poor exiles at Berne. There is not the slightest sympathy on the part of the people with them. And what sympathy could there possibly be between peoples who do not understand each other? Here everybody talks German".

Soon (May 4th) he returned to the Lake of Geneva, at Lausanne, where he remained, concealed from the police of the Canton of Vaud, until September. From Lausanne he could keep in closer touch with those revolutionaries remaining at Geneva, and especially with Melegari. It was a better action centre than was Berne, though not as good as Geneva. And for a breathless week there had seemed a real hope of renewed action, for on April 9th a revolt had broken out at Lyons, and the barricades had promptly been put up in Paris as well. In so far as this action had been taken under the auspices of the revolutionary committees it had been taken under those of the Carbonari, who always favoured action in France; certainly it had no contacts with Young Italy and Mazzini started by being suspicious of it.[1] But then he saw how he could use it, and, on April 16th (when, in fact, it had already collapsed), he sent word to one of his own men at Lyons to try to prevent a surrender and to divert the movement into Savoy:

"The armed insurrectionaries, banding together, rather than surrender should move into Savoy; there they will be received with enthusiasm [!] and they will excite an insurrection. Put yourself at their head, with our banner, and with a proclamation of a few lines, Italian and French, addressed to the people and to the troops, making us responsible for the plan and for the advice, speaking neither of Frenchmen nor of Italians, but of the republican legion which fights for all – of European liberty, for which Savoy could, if she wished, become the rallying ground, etc., – of Italy which, without fail, would respond . . .".

But there was to be no new Savoy expedition.

Geneva, the cross-roads of the routes between France, Switzerland and Italy, remained at the heart of such revolutionary flames as still flickered. If he could have escaped arrest, Mazzini would doubtless have stayed on there, as did Melegari, since the city was the best Swiss base for any action in non-Austrian Italy,

[1] "Curses upon the French movement if it succeeds! And curses if it doesn't!" (IX, 287).

and it also lay on the direct route from Italy to Lyons, and on to Paris.

It is not surprising that Geneva was the centre of Swiss revolutionary preaching and plotting; acknowledged leader of the Swiss radicals was Jacques Fazy, who edited the *Europe Centrale*. Fazy was a French Carbonaro and a personal friend of Buonarroti. But he had become fascinated by Mazzini, at Geneva, and had launched his paper, in December 1833, with the idea of helping him; in fact the *Europe Centrale*, supported as it was, financially, by Rosales, Ciani, Belgioioso, and other Young Italy leaders, was regarded as a semi-official Mazzinian organ. Before the Ramorino adventure it had discussed the desirability of the "emancipation of Savoy" and had helped to create amongst the people of the Cantons of Geneva and Vaud that friendly attitude towards the revolutionaries which was so conspicuous during the weekend of their enterprise. After the disaster the paper had defended Mazzini against Ramorino and against his Carbonaro critics.

But Mazzini remained in continual fear of arrest at Geneva; it was necessary he should move, but it was also wise, so long as he still hoped to see action, that he should remain on the Lake of Geneva, if only at the other end of it, at Lausanne; so at Lausanne he remained, throughout the summer of 1834, receiving in the columns of the *Nouvelliste Vaudois* the support of a journalist friend of Fazy, Enrico Druey.

At some time soon after he reached Lausanne, Mazzini allowed himself to be drawn into a plan as dubious, morally and politically, as his involvement in the Procida enterprise; the project this time was no less than the assassination of Louis Philippe in Paris.

At the end of a letter of May 23rd, from Mazzini to Rosales, occur the two following paragraphs:

"There is a certain matter under consideration – and I have left it until last because it is one of those things which, if it does not succeed, I would treat as out of the question. I want to tell you about it because, if ever . . . [blank in the MS.] I should not speak of it again, and you could avail yourself of it as circumstances might dictate – There is a certain man who is ready to accept the role which was entrusted to that Procida whom you have seen, and then to four or five others – except that this man's goal is in Paris – You understand?

"I have considered for a long time whether this task, if it were really accomplished, might not win the initiative for us, and ought to be undertaken – Finally, for many reasons, too long to relate, I have decided in favour – He is a Pole – and, if it takes place, he will have with him the symbol of Young Europe – For the moment that is as much as I can tell you – I will write again about it – Remember that this is only for you. Understand, too, that probably the only cost will be a payment of 300 francs".[1]

A few days later (June 2nd) he wrote a long letter to Pier Silvestro Leopardi, in Paris, explaining just why he so hated Louis Philippe. The king, he explains has no party behind him because he represents no principle; he merely represents the *status quo*, peace at any price, petty material interests. Any war would be fatal to his régime, so he can never be expected to go to the aid of revolutionaries anywhere. For this reason he

"sacrificed Spain in 1830, Italy in 1831, then Poland – despite solemn promises – For this reason he has obeyed the commands of the North [Prussia and Russia] which ordered him to destroy the Associations [the secret societies]. For this reason he has made himself the head, once more, of the crusade directed by the governments against the exiles, whom he fears because they are republicans, and all his cunning is directed towards chasing them to America . . .".

Every time, and most recently at the outset of the Savoy expedition, the king has betrayed the hopes of those revolutionaries who have approached him . . .

"every time it came to the issue there was a withdrawal and a betrayal – We have the material proofs of the policy which I here outline to you – And because he knows this, because he knows that we shall never have faith in him, that from us he has no hope of securing revelations or anything else, he intends to chase us to America . . .".

Then comes the threat again: " . . . Before that happens something may befall him which will cut short his career in midstream . . .".

Yet Louis Philippe was not so obvious an enemy to Mazzini's plans as was Charles Albert or Metternich. He had failed, certainly, to fulfil the hopes entertained of him; but he was not dedicated, as the Austrian government was, to the hunting out

[1] IX, 347.

of revolutionaries everywhere, and he still harboured, in France, a very large number of them. Why, then, was he the prime object of Mazzini's hatred in the year 1834?

The real reason is to be found in the presence in Paris of those Italian revolutionaries who were still looking to the French king. Those men, in Mazzini's view, were the real cause of his failure in Savoy. Buonarroti and the Supreme Lodge of the Reformed Carbonari, together with Angelini and the other leaders of the *Veri Italiani*, mistrusting Mazzini and his plans, and utterly opposed to the Savoy expedition, had prevented or discouraged the enrolment of their followers, especially in Switzerland.

". . . [Buonarroti] thundered forth his excommunication against us; an excommunication powerful enough because all the elements in Switzerland which were indispensable to me were enrolled in the Carbonari. . . . I found myself, at a single stroke, undermined in the most vital part of my work, and I felt all the wheels of the machine stopping without being able to discover why".

In Mazzini's view they had thus ostracized Young Italy because they were still thinking in terms of a French initiative and of utilizing the king's pretended democratic sympathies. Some were moderates, like Pier Silvestro Leopardi, who now believed only in slow and patient reform, not in revolution, and who looked to the French Constitution of 1830, by which Louis governed, as their model. Others were still revolutionaries, prepared to back the Lyons revolt of 1834, yet aiming only at frightening Louis Philippe into radical measures and into supporting the revolutionary movement in Europe. But, in either case, so long as Louis Philippe remained king in Paris, king by virtue of a revolution and the 'will of the people', he would remain the centre of revolutionary hopes and would attract men's eyes towards France and away from local, native initiatives – like Mazzini's.

So all Mazzini's passions and prejudices came to a head in his hatred of Louis Philippe – his mistrust of the traditional idea of the French initiative; his enmity against the Carbonari, now sharpened by their share in bringing about his own failure; his personal rivalry with Buonarroti for the controlling position amongst the European revolutionary movements; and his republican dislike of trusting in princes and contempt for the idea that any king – Louis Philippe, Charles Albert, or Francis of Modena (an earlier favourite) could redeem a country. As an undergraduate he had been obsessed with the obvious enemy – Metternich. After the executions in Piedmont he was obsessed with Charles Albert. Now, in 1834, he was obsessed with Louis Philippe. These were the three who, at succesisve stages, seemed the most obvious obstacles in the way of his will to rebel. For the sake, then, of Italy, of France, of Humanity, he was prepared to help to contrive their death. But he would not do the deed. Assassination was not his personal vocation, although he thought it was a high vocation, fit only for elect souls. He wrote of it with great respect: "sacred the sword of Judith; sacred the arrow of Tell". There is awe in his language about Brutus, awe in his language about Procida. If it did not happen to be his own vocation, he would yet speak of it with the distant respect of a secular priest discussing the deliberate self-annihilation of a Trappist monk.

However, we hear no more of his Polish friend's plot. In July of the following year a Corsican, Giuseppe Fieschi, with four companions, threw a bomb at Louis Philippe, producing slaughter amongst his entourage – no fewer than eighteen killed – and widespread suspicion that Mazzini lay behind his attempt. But there is no evidence to connect Mazzini with this escapade, nor with the similar episode, twenty-three years later, when Felice Orsini threw a bomb at Napoleon III. Mazzini's later disavowal of regicide is, however, inconsistent both with his own earlier theory and with his own earlier practice and, though later in his life his English friends might protest when interested French or Piedmontese politicians raised the alarm that he was trying to assassinate Napoleon or Victor Emmanuel, it yet remained true that he had tried to procure the assassination of their predecessors in Paris and Turin. Mazzini would claim that the liberal constitution of Piedmont, after 1848, ruled out any question of violence against Victor Emmanuel. But Louis Philippe, too, had been a constitutional monarch.

In September 1834 it became necessary for Mazzini to move

away altogether from the Lake. Fresh pressure upon Geneva and Vaud to get rid of him had followed upon the apologies formally tendered by the Swiss Federal Diet at Chambéry, to Charles Albert, in June 1834. So he moved north-east again, to Berne, then north to Grenchen, then west to Solothurn, where he remained from October 1834 to January 1835.

There was no longer any real chance left of action. Throughout the winter his reports get more and more dismal.

"I have bad news from Genoa – and it may get worse – . . . and, if Genoa – the one vital place – fails, all is over . . . Young Italy is silent – Young Europe is silent. Young Switzerland is beginning here and there, especially in the Canton of Vaud . . . Young Austria does little or nothing . . .".

And by January: "Young Italy no longer exists in Modena – disclosures about members – about deposits of arms – arrests, flights . . .". By the following summer: "From Italy nothing, or bad – very bad from Lombardy . . . bad from Piedmont, as bad as possible from Central Italy . . . it would be as well to go back to the beginning as though nothing had ever been done in Italy . . .". On June 6th 1835, he reports that his friend Antonio Ghiglione is back from Naples where the committee is "pedantic, doctrinaire, cowardly; they conclude that it is best to wait for an *opportunity*. The opportunity seems to be a movement from abroad, from France. [They say that] if the whole of Italy, or at least Genoa, Turin and Milan would *guarantee* that they would rise immediately after their own movement they would move – For the rest, they are philosophers, materialists, *positivists* – enthusiasm, poetry, and even martyrdom are folly – and so on.

"They are all quite right – and I propose to explain the position to everybody, withdrawing, myself, from everything. . . .".

The decline and disappearance of Young Italy went on until, on February 14th 1836, Mazzini reported that it had been utterly scattered away.

Amongst the other constituents of Young Europe there was little that was encouraging to report. As was to be expected, the least satisfactory was Young France. In a letter of February 11th 1835, Mazzini admitted that he had founded Young Europe with the deliberate idea of combating the French initiative:

"Young France is going and will go badly . . . Young Europe is inspired by the idea of emancipating the peoples from French exclusiveness – and the French feel it – the French will never work with enthusiasm for anything which comes from abroad. . . . For the rest, the home of Young Europe is not France – its true territory is amongst those peoples who have not yet developed their own mission – but we lack resources – yet we make a little headway; the Poles, working alongside the peoples of Slavic and Germanic race, are helping us . . .".

It is doubtful, nevertheless, whether the whole organization had a practical existence outside Mazzini's imagination. At all events Melegari felt impelled, in August 1835, to put the question to him direct: "Young Europe, is she a dream or a reality? . . . Do Young Germany, Young Poland, Young Italy really exist?" And Mazzini gave him a reply intended to confirm his failing faith:

"Young Germany exists: provisional committees Schutz, Soldau, and Schüler – statutes enacted, those which I sent you – organized by clubs – diffused in France, Switzerland, etc.; very little and disconnectedly in the homeland – Young Poland exists; you know the committee – I sent you the statutes . . . it has existed *definitely* in the homeland for perhaps three months or more; there is some correspondence; it improves from day to day. . . . You ask whether Young Italy is not dying, etc.? – my withdrawing myself in no way destroys Young Italy – I withdrew myself from immediate practical conspiracy; not from the faith, not from the association; conspiracy in the homeland will be the business of the homeland; abroad we will see what will emerge, if anything emerges . . .".

But the difficulty was that Melegari was supposed to be the representative of Young Italy on the central committee of Young Europe. It was therefore desirable that, besides reassuring him that both bodies did in fact exist, Mazzini should give him a little education in their purposes:

"My real intentions amount to this: we all have the duty of trying to propagate Young Europe by every means – practically speaking, we have to collect together all the means by which the first popular initiative can become a European initiative – morally speaking we have to proclaim in every way possible the dogma of the Holy Alliance of the Peoples – Hence derives your mission – As to our national mission, in its practical application, we are, both abroad and at home, in a critical epoch – we must leave it to develop and see what emerges – The other associations have no business to see anything of our domestic affairs – For them Young Italy, a faith, exists, for all of us are Young Italy and preach it; Young Italy as a *conspiracy* withdraws into hiding . . .".

Young Europe, in fact, was meant to be more than a dogma;
it was meant to be an effective organization. Especially, it was
meant to keep the European revolutionary initiative out of the
hands of France, and out of the hands of Buonarroti. Young
Europe was Mazzini's own invention, a revolutionary federation
which did *not* have its central committee in Paris, a revolutionary federation in which Italians could meet other nationals
on equal terms, indeed – such was still Mazzini's personal
magnetism – a federation in which Italians might hope to take
the lead.

But Melegari's questions haunt him. How can Melegari be so
wanting in faith? How can he fail to see that, even if as a conspiracy Young Italy is dead, she yet lives on as an ideal?

"Of Young Italy it seems to me useless to speak to you;
indeed I do not understand how you can ask me if it exists".

Chapter 8

FROM LAUSANNE TO THE JURA:
FRIENDSHIPS AND INFATUATIONS

Mazzini lived at Lausanne, during the summer of 1834, in the house of a family called Allier. Allier was a Frenchman whom he had come to know at Marseilles two years previously; he was a lawyer, and a convinced republican. He could appreciate Mazzini's fighting spirit, his republicanism, and his egalitarianism; and he was glad to help in the production and diffusion of the manifestoes of Young Europe and of the final number of the journal *La Giovine Italia* which appeared, defiantly, in July. And his wife, née Lisa Mandrot, was the first – if we except Giuditta Sidoli – of a long line of motherly and affectionate women who would bestow love and care upon the improvident exile who so obviously, they felt, needed a mother or a wife to look after him. The sympathy with which he was surrounded in her house, during months of bitter disillusionment, was something for which he always remained grateful; it may, indeed, very well have saved him from collapse.

Yet life was not altogether smooth in the Allier household. Mazzini found that his host was hot-tempered, and in the first month of his stay he was called upon to use all his powers of persuasion to prevent a major scandal arising from a friend of his making advances towards the good Madame Lisa. And at the beginning of August Allier fought a duel with a fellow Frenchman – and killed him. There were quarrels, too, between husband and wife. Gradually Mazzini came to dislike Allier more and more until, by the end of September, he could bear to live in his house no longer. Whether the affectionate disposition of Madame Allier and the immense personal fascination which Mazzini always exercised over women had anything to do with his quarrel with her husband we do not know. It seems possible, and

Melegari, Stolzman and others blamed Mazzini in the matter. But if that was, indeed, the root of the trouble, the wife nevertheless returned, outwardly at least, to a proper subjection to her husband, for she wrote some chilly letters afterwards to Mazzini which puzzled and pained him.

One effect of the quarrel and separation was to intensify Mazzini's rooted dislike of the French. He continued to correspond with Allier and to encourage him to contribute to *La Jeune Suisse* – the paper which succeeded *La Giovine Italia* – and he saw him when they were both in Berne, although Allier was too proud to make the first advances. But he grew cooler and cooler and, by the following spring, he was telling Melegari (who continued to be friendly with the Alliers and to blame Mazzini) that their conduct was "strange, not to say unworthy" and that God could strike him dead if he ever again believed in the friendship of man or woman.

Much of the trouble arose out of money, for Allier's hospitality was very far from being free. He charged Mazzini not only for his board but for extras, and especially for cigars, which were the Italian's one physical indulgence. When Mazzini left the house he had to post 950 francs, in notes, to Melegari, to settle his bill with Allier, together with that of Giovanni Ruffini, who had boarded with him at the Frenchman's house. Yet Allier proceeded, six months after Mazzini had left, to send him a further bill of 127 francs, largely for cigars!

Mazzini recounts the story in a letter to Giuditta Sidoli:

"Laugh with me, for once, at men and their meanness. There is a certain man, young, with advanced ideas, puritan, melancholy, anti-social, and so on, who revenges himself for the breaking-off of every relationship between us by making me pay a bill which I did contract with him, but at a time when we were still seeing each other, so that I did not think of keeping the receipt for my payments. This man gave me hospitality for some time, hospitality paid for, be it understood, paid for down to the last farthing. However, I suffered much from him precisely on account of the notion that I was a guest. Twice we were estranged from each other, in no way by my fault, twice I took the first step to bring about a reunion; finally I was obliged to break off all connection with him; and here he is today sending me accounts I have paid and which he has not cancelled, begging me to be good enough to pay them. A noble vengeance! He is a Frenchman, and I think that my expressing some opinions unfavourable to France enters to no small extent into all this. He has been closely bound up with all the Italians; he has become disgusted with them all, or they have all abandoned him. Only one friend remains to him, in whom he has full confidence   and that friend, who is M[elegari] is his wife's friend".[1]

Mazzini paid up. But he told Giuditta that he had finished with Allier for ever.

The significance of the Allier affair is that it helped, in the end, to bring about the final separation between Mazzini and Melegari. For Melegari, who by this time had moved to Lausanne, became much attached not only to Madame Allier but to her three younger sisters Dora, Maria (known as Maddalena) and Elisa, and he soon discovered that Maddalena had conceived a hopeless passion for Mazzini, for which he chose to blame his Chief. Actually the youngest, Elisa, who was only nine, was Mazzini's special friend for whom, long after, he would include playful and affectionate messages in his letters. Maddalena, who was fifteen when Mazzini was at Lausanne, developed her passion for him unobserved; but after he left it grew much stronger, expecially when she heard that he was living, uncared for, in remote parts of Switzerland. When she learnt, three years later, that he was poverty-stricken in cold and distant London she became so desperate that her mother feared for her very life and begged Mazzini to return to comfort her. To the mother's entreaties Melegari, never slow to criticize Mazzini, added his own reproaches – if he did not come the girl would die.

Mazzini did not return, and it was for long supposed by historians that Maddalena died – the girl became wrongly identified with a later friend of Mazzini's, at Grenchen, who did die young. Actually, Maddalena's mother wisely sent her to France, at the end of the year 1838, and the change of air and occupation at last eased her desperate obsession. For three years, however, after Mazzini's departure for England in 1837, Melegari pleaded with him to return to save the child's life while Mazzini equally persistently, but surely wisely, refused. No doubt it was as well that he did refuse for Melegari's solicitous attentions on

[1] E. N. Appendix I, 271, 272.

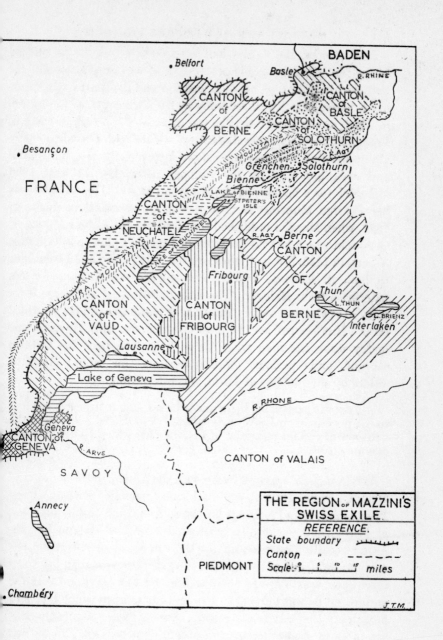

THE REGION OF MAZZINI'S SWISS EXILE

REFERENCE.

State boundary ⌁⌁⌁⌁⌁
Canton ⎯ ⎯ ⎯ ⎯
Scale: 0   5   10   15   miles

J.T.M.

behalf of poor Maddalena had a remarkable result; he offered himself in marriage to his protégée, and was duly accepted! He had greatly improved his own position and prospects by attending a course of political economy at the University of Lausanne, in which he did so well that he was appointed a professor there in 1843. After the marriage Maddalena, we are told, ceased to worry about Mazzini, who was never more mentioned between husband and wife, but only by the younger sister. By the year 1862 Melegari was a Senator of the Kingdom of Italy. By 1876 he was her Foreign Minister! But there was an awkward moment, in 1856, when Mazzini published that letter in the *Italia e Popolo*, at Genoa, in which he told the story of Procida's plan to kill Charles Albert, in 1833. For he there disclosed that Procida had been sent to him, at Geneva, bearing strong recommendations for his enterprise from Melegari. The rising statesman had some difficulty in explaining away what he now chose to call his "youthful error". But Mazzini said no more to embarrass him. He had some mercy upon the man who, for so long, had been his faithful servant, and – perhaps more important – for whom Giuditta Sidoli, by then settled at Turin, was interceding.

"I did not say everything there was to be said about Melegari, yielding to the prayers of an Italian lady whom I respect and love and to the influence of certain memories of the affection which bound Melegari and me together . . ."[1]

While Mazzini was still living with the Alliers, in the summer of 1834, Giovanni Ruffini, who had soon quarrelled with the testy Frenchman, found lodgings for himself, in comfortable quarters, at Berne, and eventually persuaded his Chief – whom he preferred to call Pippo – to join him there in September. But Pippo's mother, more out of touch than she generally was with her son's intentions, was alarmed to hear that he was leaving Lausanne and feared he was moving to some new base from which he could launch another Savoy expedition. Nor was she reassured by his attempts to secure her help in obtaining a passport. So he was obliged to explain to her, with less disguise than usual, the realities of his position.

[1] LXXII, 320.

"Whatever can you have deduced from my demand [for a passport] – that I am persisting in speculations, etc.? For what reason do you imagine I should want that document? – Do you understand my position? – here it is in two words: I cannot travel, nor stay still, nor let myself be known for even a quarter of an hour under my own name, whether in France, or in Switzerland, etc., without being immediately arrested – further, I am continually being hunted for . . . and understand that the reason for this is not what I am doing now, or planning, but the past. . . . If I stay here you understand under what conditions; never moving out of one room – never. – So what I was asking for was merely a further means of security, in the event of my having to go out, whether to change to another canton, or to another country . . .".

Maria Mazzini had suffered much during the past year; the sentence of death upon her son; Jacopo Ruffini's suicide; the disappearance of the other two Ruffini brothers with their mother; the return of Eleonora Ruffini, indignant with Mazzini and almost estranged from him; the disaster of the Savoy expedition and of its counterpart in Genoa. If only Pippo would desist from such enterprises and go to England! But she would continue to take his part against his father, and she would secretly send him the money that kept him alive, and would send it without old Dr. Giacomo's knowing. Employing the little disguises intended to mislead the censor Mazzini writes:

"Since this letter will not, I believe, be read by my uncle [pseudonym for his father], I will take the opportunity to repeat to you that I have received the order for 600 francs – and that I am always grateful to you for this . . . and for all that you do for me. I feel everything, understand everything – and – patience – One day, perhaps, we shall drown all our memories in an embrace. The cousins [the Ruffini brothers] are well . . . I have not yet changed my lodgings; but I shall change it soon, and shall rejoin my cousin".

So on September 21st 1834 he left the Alliers, and Lausanne, and joined Giovanni Ruffini at Berne; but the Austrian police were, for once, too efficient for him.

"Picture it", he wrote to Rosales, "after I had been three days at Berne, never going out, in one room, surrounded by other rooms, as is the best plan in the opinion of Usiglio, Ruffini and Lamberti – picture it I say that Bombelles [the Austrian ambassador] gave the number of my house to the *Vorort* [the Swiss government] – and the *Vorort* sent out an order of arrest – and I, you understand, received warning in time – and changed my plan and got away – But, my God, I begin to respect Bombelles!".

He and Giovanni got away to join young Agostino Ruffini at
Grenchen, at the foot of the Jura mountains, a region which the
younger brother had been exploring and enjoying very much.
Agostino was still only 22 years old, and his life was mostly a
series of *affaires de coeur*. At Bienne, close by, he had developed
a passion for Luisa Dorvillier, his inn-keeper's wife, who spoilt
him; at Grenchen he had met the captivating Elisa Yselin. Elisa
was the real obsession of his youth; but, alas! she had supposed he
was Mazzini! When she discovered he was not she broke off all
relations with him, remaining chilly even though he twice made
the journey to her home at Brugg to remonstrate with her.
Agostino's diary for this summer – written later – is frank and
cynical:

"Ridiculous love-making. 'Pippeggiato' (Obsessed like Pippo?). Always
in a state of excitement. . . . Nights at the duCommuns with Modena
and Giulia. Absurd conduct. Oh Muse! cover the horrid scene with the
veil of piety. For the rest, nobody at all to advise me and my own
head even madder than my surroundings. Mazzini and Giovanni
arrived at Grenchen . . .".

Even Mazzini, when he arrived, was infected with the holiday
atmosphere of the place, for he and the two brothers went out and
climbed the Weissenstein. At the top of the mountain there was a
tourists' book, and visitors were requested to state, amongst
other things, their religion. "Young Europe" the three entered,
boldly – "a little childish bravatura", Mazzini explains, "for the
benefit of Bombelles and Co.".

To drown his disappointment over Elisa, Agostino made up his
mind to go to Paris to study mathematics, a decision which both
Mazzini and Giovanni found commendable. "That young man",
wrote Giovanni to their mother, "is still too young, he needs
something to occupy him . . . all the better for him and for us if
he finds it in study".

Giovanni, for his part, took the line that he himself was now
too old to turn student again, and that it was up to him to
remain in Switzerland with Mazzini; so he returned with the Chief
to Berne. He was slowly turning into a man of the world, with a
pleasant easy-going cynicism, much preoccupied with what he
was eating and drinking, and unconsciously preparing himself

well for his future successful career as a novelist. Not that life was easy for him. One day he was arrested in Berne, in mistake for Mazzini. And the 500 francs which he and Agostino each received, quarterly, from their parents, was no more than the sum which Mazzini was by way of receiving from his mother. But he had fewer calls upon his money than had Mazzini, and he generally seems to have managed to do himself reasonably well. His picture of the fare he enjoyed in September, at Berne, is impressive.

"I lunch", he writes to his mother, "at ten o'clock, with four good dishes and desert, and a small bottle of wine; I always get up at nine. You see what progress I make. From eleven to two or three I smoke while doing my correspondence, or while writing something else, or while reading. I go out walking during fine weather until five, which is the hour for a very good and plentiful dinner. I take my coffee and read my newspapers until seven, or thereabouts, and then I walk about, and when I am tired I return to a café to take my *demi-bouchée* of beer . . .".[1]

But money became increasingly a problem, especially when the parents ran into financial difficulties. The life of a rebel could be very sordid. It was dreadful to Giovanni to have "to enter into material details with which I would never wish to have to occupy myself, preoccupied as I am with moral interests of the loftiest kind".

Despite tiresome material details, the return to Berne was easier for Giovanni than it was for Mazzini, who was immediately detected again – not this time by the police, but by an in-furiated Allier waving bills in his face and upbraiding him for "encouraging" Madame Allier and for captivating the heart of Maddalena. Furious, Mazzini left the digs which Giovanni had found for him and which were comfortable, and moved secretly to others to avoid the enraged Frenchman. But in a few days he decided to move north again, this time to Solothurn, where he stayed in severe isolation until January 8th 1835.

That winter at Solothurn, at the end of 1834, was one of desperate disillusionment. The Central Congregation of Young Italy was no longer meeting and it had not been replaced by any comparably effective Central Committee of Young Europe, possessed, as Young Italy had been, of at least some income of its

[1] Cod. I, 118.

own from subscriptions. So he was left penniless, and therefore powerless to pursue his designs save as he could provide money out of the little sums which his devoted mother stinted herself to send. He made various attempts to raise a loan, through his friend Filippo Bettini, at Genoa, on the security of his "future inheritance" [!]. Occasionally he may have received something from his better off sympathizers, but at least once he refused help from Rosales, for shame at having already lost so much of his friend's money in the Savoy expedition. The influence of his poverty upon his plans was such that he wrote to Melegari, on November 28th, to explain that he could not raise

"the 200 francs necessary for the expenses of a traveller who would establish committees of Young Europe in five French Departments, which only wait for this – the lack of 200 francs makes us ridiculous – all the same, it is a simple fact that I have not got them – patience: I have not yet had news of the loan which I am trying to raise on my future inheritance".

Wretched poverty, separation from the Ruffinis, and a bitter Swiss winter in a dull, foggy, provincial town lowered his morale at Solothurn as disaster never had. Culturally the country seemed to him a desert. The only modern history in the libraries appeared to be books on the Reformation!

"Apart from Geneva, a city where you can find, or quickly obtain from Paris, anything you want, the position is very bad in the matter of books. The further you go north the worse this defect becomes. In Berne there is not a single French journal, literary or scientific; not the *Revue des Deux Mondes*, nor the *Revue Encyclopédique*; nothing – a few political papers, but very few. Go on to Soleure [Solothurn] – to Lucerne – everywhere except Zürich, where there is a little, you will find nothing, absolutely nothing".

It is extraordinary that in the cultural desert of the Jura he managed, in the following year, to do the serious writing that he did. For, besides his own *Faith and the Future*, he contributed articles on contemporary music and drama to the *Italiano* in Paris, a literary paper run by his eccentric dramatist friend Antonio Ghiglione, and he collaborated with Agostino Ruffini in translating Alfred de Vigny's *Chatterton* into Italian, together with part of Victor Hugo's *Angélo*. These translations of plays were intended, with the addition of suitable prefaces, to launch a dramatic library which would bring the contemporary European drama to Italy and would explain there its significance in terms of the aspirations of humanity. But the censorship ruined all, preventing, by a prohibitive duty (as at Naples), or by outright confiscation (as in Piedmont), the effective entry of the *Italiano* into the peninsula, and making it impossible to publish the Dramatic Library, as intended, at Genoa.

However, he had little inclination to study or to write.

"Literature requires peace, if not in the heart at least in the external circumstances, also books, time, and a thousand other things; I have neither books, nor time, nor liberty, nor anything else; I remain almost the whole year shut up in one room living the most monotonous life that is possible for a man".

There was nothing to do but to stare out into the eternal snow and watch the only form of life left in the country, the crows which strutted along in the snow beneath his window. And even that pleasure was qualified for him because, in their seriousness and their blackness, the birds reminded him of the Jesuits! He can joke at times, laugh for a whole minute when a friendly German woman sends him a foot-muff, or enjoy himself luring a cat into his room with sweet biscuits ("the company of a cat is much dearer to me than that of a man – a contradiction which may seem somewhat singular in one who professes to love Humanity, and works for it – nevertheless, I could explain . . .").
But the burden of his letters is dour, indeed:

"I love Italy – not the Italians – Humanity, not men, apart from a few exceptions – I work because I owe it to my conscience, to religion, and to the impulse of my heart . . .". "Men begin to seem unreal to me – perhaps because more and more I am ceasing to care for them, ceasing to care for myself – ceasing to care any more except for Italy – for the idea of her, for certain principles, for my friend [Giuditta] and for my mother".

If at times he was still humorous, and often, in writing to his mother, thoughtful and considerate, he was nevertheless tending to invest himself with a halo of martyrdom, and even with the attributes of Christ, attributes with which others, and especially his mother, were often inclined to invest him, but which came better from them than from himself. "Life for us", he explains to Rosales,

F

"has to be a struggle, a tissue of griefs and disappointments – We feel too much; our spirits are too exposed to love for us to avoid being crossed. We have made our own the cause of the people – spontaneously we have burdened our hearts with the sorrows of a whole generation . . . we have snatched a spark from the eternal, we have placed ourselves between the eternal and the people, we have assumed the part of Christ, the part of the Emancipator – and God has accepted it; now, in the few years that remain to us, we are no more than victims used for expiation . . . ".

It is a revealing letter. Christ was a martyr for humanity. Christ was intercessor between the eternal – God – and humanity. Christ was a victim for the expiation of the sins of mankind. And Mazzini claimed, similarly, to be martyr, intercessor, and victim. And when he has carried out the tremendous mission with which God has entrusted him he will enter – like Christ – into the Kingdom of Heaven.

"I number my sorrows, and I ask myself: how many remain for me to complete my part in the expiation? – There is one thing which they cannot take from us: the final rest – we shall die . . . then, assuredly, having endured the ordeal we shall live the life of love . . .".

So might, so did Puritan enthusiasts of the seventeenth and eighteenth centuries, or Jansenists, write of their sufferings. But with the important difference that they were preoccupied with their own sins, and with their personal need for forgiveness, whereas Mazzini was not. Mazzini, though he was full of sorrow at the distress he had caused to his parents, to the Ruffini family, to Giuditta and other women, treats these tragedies as part of the burden that has been laid by God upon himself, the sacrificial victim. It never even occurs to him that he may have been at fault. He knows that he causes sorrow, but it is a fate that has been imposed upon him; he feels it acutely, but he is not guilty. Sacrificial victims were traditionally pure, and he is pure, always innocent of intent to harm, yet always causing sorrow – God having willed it so.

If the extraordinary power of his personality and the ardour of his apostolate had already given birth to the Mazzini myth, from this winter of 1834 must be dated the beginning of the cult of the Man of Sorrows, of the Martyr of Italy who had taken upon himself the sufferings of the People. And it was in this rôle that he would live in history, as a martyr who had never compromised, never wavered in his faith in an Italy republican and unitary, initiator of a new epoch, embodied in a Third Rome, and the rest; if he had compromised, his religious power would have gone, and his friends – his disciples – would evidently have suffered in vain.

But there was no hypocrisy or pose in his attitude. He believed in himself and in his purpose absolutely save when, like all prophets, he was enduring his one terrible temptation of Doubt, a temptation which only confirmed him in his faith.

It happened partly at this time, partly some eighteen months later; he left a record of it in his Autobiographical Notes:

". . . in those fateful months there grew thick around me such a storm of disasters, delusions, and bitter deceptions, that I suddenly saw, in its naked flesh, the growing old of a solitary soul, and the world deprived of every consolation for me in my battle. It was not only the ruin, for an indefinite period, of every Italian hope, the scattering of our best men, the persecution which, undoing our work in Switzerland, took from us also that base, close to Italy, the exhaustion of our material resources, the accumulation of every kind of difficulty, well-nigh insurmountable, between myself and the work I had begun. It was also the disintegration of that moral edifice of love and faith within which, alone, I could achieve the strength to fight, the scepticism which I saw rising in front of me wherever I looked, the languishing of belief in those who were most closely bound to me on the road which we all knew, even from the first days, would be overgrown with tribulations; and most of all, the mistrust which I saw rising around me in those dearest to me, mistrust of my purposes, of the motives which drove me to so apparently unequal a struggle. It mattered little to me, even then, that most men were opposed to me. But to feel myself suspected of ambition or of other ignoble impulses by the two or three beings upon whom I had concentrated all my powers of affection prostrated my soul with a feeling of deep despair. For this was what was revealed to me in just those months in which, assailed from every side, I felt overwhelmingly the need to recover my strength in communion with those few sister souls who might understand me, although inarticulately; who might intuitively perceive what, having deliberately renounced every joy in life, I was suffering and would suffer, within me. Without going into details, I may say that those souls, at that time, withdrew themselves from me".

Such is his description of his own Gethsemane. For Peter, and James, and John, who slept, or fled, or denied, we must read the Ruffini brothers, their mother, and Melegari. And in the distance stood that unique person, his mother, whose fidelity and love were always unfailing, but who could not understand his purpose or his plans.

"When I felt myself alone in the world – alone, apart from my poor mother, and she far off and unhappy through my fault – I halted, terrified, in front of the void. Then, in that desert, I came face to face with Doubt. Perhaps I was wrong, and the world was right. Perhaps the idea which I pursued was a dream. And perhaps I was not following a *real* idea, but *my* idea, the pride of *my own* invention, the desire for victory rather than the purpose of victory, the egoism of the mind and the cold calculations of an ambitious intellect. . . . The day on which these doubts pierced my soul I felt not only supremely and inexpressibly unhappy, but, like one who is condemned, who is conscious of his fault and incapable of atoning for it. The shootings at Alessandria, at Genoa, at Chambéry, rose in front of me like the phantoms of a crime and a remorse that was yet sterile. I could not make them live again. How many mothers had already wept because of me? How many more would weep if I persisted . . .?.

"I suffered so severely that I reached to the edge of madness. I jumped up at night from my dreams and ran almost mad to my window, called, as I believed, by the voice of Jacopo Ruffini. Or again I felt myself drawn, as though by an invisible force, trembling, to visit the next-door room, with the idea that I would find there some person who was a prisoner, or who was a hundred miles away. The slightest incident, a sound, a sparrow, drove me to tears. Nature, covered with snow as it was around Grenchen, seemed to me covered in the winding-sheet of death, under which she invited me to lie. The faces of those people I had occasion to see seemed to me to assume an expression of pity while they looked at me, or more often of rebuke. I felt every spring of life dry up within me. My spirit died in my body. Had that state of mind been prolonged a little, I would have gone really mad, or have fallen headlong into the egoism of suicide . . .".

But fortunately:

"One day I awoke with my soul at peace and my intellect serene and the feelings of one who has been saved from an extreme danger . . .".[1]

The crisis which concluded this affliction occurred somewhere between Solothurn and Bienne, at the foot of the Jura, in the autumn of 1836. But, though the doubt whether, after all, he might not be wrong, may have been peculiar to that occasion, the sense of isolation, of the reproach of mankind, had been growing upon him since the winter of 1834 and was an outcome of the Savoy expedition. It was not merely a matter of the falling

[1] LXXVII, 248–251.

away of the majority of the Italian exiles, now abandoning the
life of revolution or turning once more to the Carbonaro leadership. More bitter was the scattering of the intimate Marseilles
circle and their loss of contact with him – Nicola Fabrizi going
off to Spain, and later founding a schismatic society of his own,
the *Legion of Italy;* Gustavo Modena and Celeste Menotti going
off to Paris and falling under the influence of Mazzini's now bitter
Carbonaro opponents; Bianco disappearing to Brussels and dying
there by gasing himself; Melegari staying, indeed, in Switzerland,
but growing more and more critical as month succeeded month.
The most faithful were the frail Angelo Usiglio, who would later
go with Mazzini to England, and the stalwart Giuseppe Lamberti
who, from Paris, would set up an "Information Centre" through
which the members of the society could keep in touch, by correspondence. But, though the devotion of Usiglio and Lamberti was
touching to the Chief, neither of them was an intimate of
Mazzini's youth with whom he had dreamed his dreams on the
Acquasola at Genoa. Amongst the exiles only Giovanni Ruffini
had shared those evenings with him, and the days of his adoring
discipleship were now over.

It was natural that some change should take place in the
Ruffini brothers as they grew up. But a decisive event had
hastened the process of change, namely the reception which they
and their "Holy Mother" had been accorded by Mazzini when,
after Jacopo's imprisonment, they had left their home to cross
the sea and join him at Marseilles. On that occasion, it will be remembered, although disaster had been brought upon the family
by its loyalty to Young Italy, Mazzini had merely disappeared
without telling them or anybody else where he was going. That
disappearance, which had stunned Melegari and the other conspirators, had seemed to the Ruffini brothers and to their mother
a personal insult. And although they had all been reunited,
within a fortnight, at the *Hôtel de la Navigation* at Geneva, and
both brothers and their mother had lived with Mazzini at that
hotel until Eleonora had returned to Genoa in November, the
harm done to their intimate relationship was never mended. Had
Mazzini been prepared to explain to Eleonora about Giuditta and
the baby – a subject which he never seems to have mentioned to

anybody – perhaps she and her sons would have understood and forgiven. But he was faithful, always, to some secret pledge Giuditta and he had given to each other, the reasons for his strange behaviour were never properly explained, and the boys were left under the impression that he had deliberately slighted and wronged their mother.

Mazzini, writing in March 1835 to Giuditta, tells her that he only knows Eleonora Ruffini is well by the letters which she sends to Giovanni.

"For the rest, I do not understand how you can ask me whether she still writes to me. I thought you knew or had gathered that all contact, all relationship has been broken between us; that she considered herself and they considered her outraged, spurned by me, and that this belief has made me guilty in their eyes, all the more guilty because the time in question was a grievous one for her. I have done nothing to change this state of things; that it was possible for it to arise suffices to show that it was inevitable it should do so . . .".[1]

Agostino writes to his mother (May 16th 1834) that the episode is one which he cannot contemplate without his blood rising, and which "brings back to us bitter and cruel memories" such as he has just endured in reading her letters to Mazzini of that time.

But Giovanni, closer to Mazzini than was Agostino, was trying, during the summer of 1834, to persuade the Chief to leave the Allier house and to come to live with him at Berne. He writes warmly to his mother about their friend, yet withholds his forgiveness for that fatal episode:

"I can only praise the behaviour of Emily [Mazzini's pseudonym, adopted to deceive the censor, in the Ruffini correspondence, and also in his own correspondence with his mother]. Nobody could be more affectionate, more delicate, more tender than she is towards me. If I could tear out one page from the history of her life I could not have a better friend. But, alas! I cannot, because it treats of an Angel [Eleonora]. She never ceases to concern herself about you, speaks frequently of the trouble in her letters, sees that there is something which grieves me, and says that I do not understand her. She tries by every means to help me; there is nothing she does not do or say for me. And do not imagine that I do nothing for her! I work every day to improve her condition and her spirits and I hope to do so well that she will decide to rejoin me, and will be better off where I am than where she is".[2]

[1] Appendix I, 212.   [2] Cod. I, 106.

And on September 23rd:

"She [Emily] is no longer my ideal, as you know, but I still love her warmly, and even more respect her, for there is in that woman a whole future of happiness, a whole destiny".

He will strive to help "her" "not with the ardour of one who loves, as I once was, but with the calm affection of a brother, such as I am and always shall be to her".

The loss of Eleonora Ruffini's confident love was more shattering to Mazzini than was the growing detachment with which her sons were coming to regard him. It is hard to recapture the mystical awe in which Eleonora was held by all the exiles from the Ligurian coast. She, not Mazzini's own mother, was "The Holy Mother" *par excellence*, and the bust of her which stands so proudly, on its elegant pedestal, at Taggia, today, is a more dignified and dominating monument than any ever erected by a grateful country to Maria Mazzini. She is referred to often, in Mazzini's letters, as his "other mother", and her approval and support, never quite withdrawn, was the approval and support most vital to him.

We are given a strange side-light upon what she meant to him by the lengths he was prepared to go on her behalf at the end of the year 1835. For in that winter Eleonora became bankrupt, after having taken upon herself the debts of that eccentric dramatist and ardent member of Young Italy, Antonio Ghiglione. Her husband would not or could not pay, so she wrote to her sons. They were appalled. How could they pay? – their allowance from their father was insufficient for themselves! So they turned to Mazzini and he concocted a strange scheme to save the situation.

"One morning", writes Agostino to his mother, "Emily [Mazzini] woke up earlier than usual, went to find Agostino, and said to him: we shall get some money. Agostino made a megaphone of his hands and shouted in the direction of Berne, to Francis [Giovanni]: we shall get some money. The Alps echoed back: Money. Two days later a letter was travelling in the direction of Genoa bearing a request for money to an old doctor [Giacomo Mazzini] . . ."[1]

Mazzini's letter was no ordinary request for money. For his

[1] Cod. 2, 99.

father had ceased to subsidise the revolution and was far from sympathetic with Giovanni's view that it was "dreadful to have to enter into material details" and only right to concern oneself with "moral interests of the loftiest kind". He was a conscientious man, disinterested and even heroic in his work (a few months previously he had won the applause of the whole city of Genoa for his attendance upon victims of the cholera epidemic, when others had fled), but he did believe in young men earning an honest competence and establishing their own independence. It was therefore necessary for his son to frame his appeal with these paternal preferences in mind, and very astutely he did so. He described to his father a timber and iron concern in the Alps in which Rosales was interested and whose prospects, he said, were bright, because it had dealings in Germany, where there would soon be railway developments. Shares were 7,000 francs; it would be a fine investment if his father would send him enough to buy one. To Rosales he wrote, warning him of what he had done, so that he could make suitable replies if the doctor should make independent enquiries. The doctor seems to have been delighted by this new and practical turn in Pippo's mind and he forwarded the money forthwith. Pippo, for his part, sent him further news of the company's prospects, this time in the French and British markets, as well.

Part of the 7,000 francs went to the Ruffinis, for the aid of their mother; the rest was used to bolster up the tottering journal *La Jeune Suisse.*

Behaviour of this kind was not congenial to Mazzini and it must be taken as the measure of his regard for Eleonora that he was prepared to engage in such deceptions on her account. Yet still she did not write to him; her thanks for the money was only given in messages to his mother which Maria Mazzini passed on in her letters. Eleonora's sons had seemingly decided that the family honour demanded she should maintain the breach in her direct relations with Mazzini. But as the summer turned to autumn, and his sense of the hostility of even those closest to him became insupportable, Mazzini disclosed to her the state of his mind in a remarkable letter which reveals the extent to which he depended upon her approval.

First, wanting her to understand his treatment of her sons, he draws the parallel between his own followers and the early Christians:

"Fate has placed us in an age of moral disorder and absence of belief; an age the same as that in which Christ died, when corruption and selfishness were, as today, at their height; and the early Christians died, martyrs and derided. But three hundred years later Christianity was ruling, and freed the slaves. We die holding on to our faith. We serve the God we venerate".

But he can only hold on if she will reassure him that his religion is true.

"I want to pour out these ideas of mine and to hear from you – symbol as you are of calm and constant virtue – that they are not illusions; that it is not the mind that leads the heart astray; but that the heart, too, has willed them and given birth to them. Because they have caused harm and persecution to me and to those dear to you, do you love me the less? Am I an egoist? Do I brutally betray my personal duties? Do I love you and my own family any the less? If I were to die a martyr to our faith, to the faith of Jacopo, would I be without sensibility – would I commit a crime? – Do not disclose any thing at all of what I am asking you but if, without violating your conscience, you can give me a word of comfort, give it; if not, be silent, I beg you; I shall know that I am wrong; I shall know that I am pursuing a phantom; that my *religion* – and I call it that because I feel it has all the characteristics of religion – . . . is a false faith to be forgotten; and I would forget it, because I believe in you as in an oracle, as in the most religious, the most virtuous, the purest soul, and the one made most perfect by grief that exists on this earth".[1]

Apparently the brief reply (*biglietto*) which he received from her was consoling – or so he told her on November 5th. But further suspicions and reservations, both her own and her sons', were to follow, leading in a few years to a final separation.

There was one other person whose intimate sympathy and understanding might have alleviated the horror which Mazzini suffered in 1835–36 – Giuditta Sidoli. Desperately he appealed to her to come and rejoin him. Perhaps it was an unreasonable request; certainly she rejected it. Giuditta, after leaving Mazzini's baby with Démosthène Ollivier at Marseilles, had been in Florence for most of the year 1834. At the end of September she

[1] XII, 134.

had left for Naples; by the end of December she was in Rome. Almost the whole of the year 1835 she spent in Rome, trying to find means of settling in the Duchy of Modena once more so as to be with her children. But in this, despite the generous help of Cardinal Bernetti, Pope Gregory XVI's Secretary of State (acknowledged – equally generously – by Mazzini), she was unsuccessful, owing to the profound mistrust which Francis IV of Modena entertained for her. So, after surreptitiously slipping in to Reggio to embrace her children, she was off to Lucca, Leghorn and (by the end of 1836) Genoa, where she threw herself upon the sympathy of Maria Mazzini.

It used to be supposed, as the Florentine police suspected, that Giuditta Sidoli was carrying out political missions for Mazzini during her journeyings. But, if she did some work on behalf of Young Italy, it was only incidentally; Mazzini was always opposed to her arduous travels and always trying to stop them. Others have made of her pilgrimage the occasion to dignify her with the title of *Mater Dolorosa*, another Holy Mother who, in her wanderings and her sufferings, took upon herself, like Mazzini, the sufferings of her country. To the Duke of Modena, however, it seemed that, as a revolutionary, she was likely to prove incorrigible, for her husband had conspired in 1821, she had thrown herself into the revolution of 1831, and since then she had become the intimate of Mazzini and the succour of the brethren of Young Italy. Since it was supposed at the time that her wanderings around Italy were undertaken to enable her to weave Mazzini's web of revolution, it is less surprising that the Duke insisted upon keeping her out of Modena than that Cardinal Bernetti interceded with him on her behalf.

Had Giuditta decided that her place was at the side of Mazzini, her influence might have been incalculable, for month after month and year after year he remained obsessed with her. "You are all my life", he wrote shortly after the Savoy expedition, "the rest is nothing but grief and misery". And a little later:

"I was miserable at Berne, I am miserable at Bienne, I shall be miserable everywhere . . . I would still like to show affection to men, that is do them some good, but I do not any longer want to see them. I am morally ill – I have moral convulsions as another may have

physical convulsions – There are times when I would like to roll on
the ground and bite myself, like a serpent".

To nobody else did he confide so much. During the year 1834
Giuditta's letters, from Florence, brought him some comfort; but
during 1835 her letters from Rome grew steadily cooler; moreover
it seems likely that it was at some time in the spring of that year
that their child, at Marseilles, died. On April 2nd 1835 he wrote to
her:

"Giuditta, my Giuditta,

    "If only I could once tell you in my language, in your language,
that you are dear to me, that I love you desperately, that I love you
every day more, that neither time, nor anything else will ever make
me love you less, that I think of you always, always, that I dream of
you – that I live for you – that I remember you as a prisoner remem-
bers his fatherland, his liberty, that from you alone come joy and
grief for me; that I have loved you, and love you, as I cannot express
to you nor you – forgive me – can understand, nor perhaps would it
be well for you to understand. . . . Do you realize the hours that I
passed as one condemned, the hours of agony, of sacrifice, of expiation
that I passed in a certain part of the country, in a horrible deserted
hovel alone in the midst of the snow, alone for months, living on your
letters, especially those from Naples, do you realize the torments –
laugh if you will – of jealousy, against whom? Why? – I do not know.
Your letters, every syllable, every silence, every change of attitude
from you – I have studied them all and some – why should I not tell
you? – have injected death into me. I know all about you, I have
measured, weighed your love – my poor Giuditta, I have more of it
than I merit from you, more than I would have expected, so anoma-
lous and strange is our position; you love me as your friend, as you
are able, but I have within me a volcano, I love you with love, I have
always loved you with love; I have dreamed, and in my dreams I have
been in Paradise and in Hell . . . my soul is always with you – my
heart beats only for you – if you only knew with what pride and fury
I feel hate towards men! If you could see the satanic smile I have on
my lips for them! – and how they deserve it from me, my fellow
citizens more than all the others – yet my country, our country, I
still love her; indeed I love her more truly, and with more nostalgia,
as the land you now tread, and which can yet be great; and I abomin-
ate even more than I did the tyranny and the foreign domination;
and the fate by which the French are ahead of us in the world of
action, a people, believe it, that is wretched and evil as ourselves, and
worse than ourselves . . . but I do not want here to speak of politics,
nor ever when you do not ask for it. . . . Oh! but this paper will come
into your hands, will be with you, who knows when? – and I shall
not; I cannot throw my arms around your neck, cannot enfold you in

my embrace, and kiss your face, your eyes, your cheeks, your breast –
I cannot feel your arms around me – I cannot feel your lips on mine,
your hands in my hair . . .".[1]

Giuditta replied on April 25th.

"I have received your letter of April 2nd. It does not please me, it
even troubles me in its expression of your love: there is something
about it so uncongenial to my spirit that it causes me a sadness and a
suffering I cannot describe. You must forgive me. Tired and afflicted
as I am, I may perhaps have lost, so to speak, the faculty for understanding certain passions. . . . I would not permit myself to come and
take up my life with you until all the means, however painful, that
are open to me to get back to my children have been closed".

And, even worse, she, like the others, was accusing him of
vanity.

"You need to explain to me", he protested on May 11th, "words like
these: '. . . carrying on the work for the sake of carrying it on, for
vanity' – vanity! The whole world, perhaps, will say the same, but
does it understand aright, that world? Ah! I shall descend into the
tomb with such a smile of scorn for that world, that it will vindicate
me to myself – but to you? A tear squeezed from my dying heart will
then be my only protest . . .".

There is plenty in Giuditta's letters to indicate that, having
generously, but perhaps rashly (in view of her small children) involved herself in the revolution of 1831 at Reggio, and having
indulged her passions a trifle freely at Marseilles, and especially
with Mazzini, she had reached a state of mind, by the year 1835,
when she had had enough both of the political and of the
passionate life and had developed an overwhelming maternal
sense of the need to be with and to look after her family. Mazzini
could understand and sympathize with her desire to see her
children, but he regarded her chosen career as even more important, and he could in no wise endure the doubts which she
expressed from time to time as to whether he and she were not in
some way "guilty". By the precepts of his own religion they were
legitimately married – but then she did not share his religion.

So Mazzini remained alone amidst the aftermath of the Savoy
expedition with mistrust of him extending from Paris, where the
Italian exiles, to a man, were against him, to Naples and Rome,

[1] Appendix I, 221–225.

where even Giuditta was having her after-thoughts. In January 1835 he moved back again from Solothurn to Berne. But the necessity for keeping absolutely hidden at Berne, and the disappointment of his hopes of achieving anything there in the Swiss radical movements, counselled a withdrawal once more to the Jura, this time to Grenchen, on April 27th, in the company of Giovanni Ruffini and Angelo Usiglio.

At Grenchen they were joined in July by Agostino Ruffini, fresh from his mathematical studies in Paris, and at last, so far as the outward circumstances of their lives were concerned, there was, for a year (until the end of May 1836) something better in store for all of them. For at Grenchen they settled with a highly congenial family by the name of Girard, in a large establishment called the Baths, where visitors could take the waters.

Mazzini took pleasure in describing the place.

"There are in the house men and women, a whole family; but they are all the time working and I hardly ever see them. The men think of nothing but productive work and the women do the same; when they do not know what more to do in the house they set to work weeding and tidying up the garden; I see them from my window . . . whenever anybody meets me, whether in the morning or whether after lunch, I am sure to be asked if I have slept well. 'Excellently', I reply, 'and you?' - 'Oh very well' ".

His mother would like to send the Girards some presents, but he explains:

". . . my hosts are not gentlemen, if we are considering their occupations; but they are gentlemen if we are considering money; they have plenty; every weekday the women dress abominably, on Sundays well; don't send sweets, chocolate, etc., they have every kind – as for other things, send if you like, but there is no need because I pay them for their trouble . . .".

But it was not always so peaceful.

". . . On every holiday I am condemned to listen to thirty or forty drunks shouting, singing, quarrelling, dancing and heaven knows what right under my window. Drunkenness is legal in Switzerland; it is not confined just to the people; it includes all the classes; the professors of the University of Berne get drunk regularly, throwing the bottles out of the window; they pass the night under the table, and things like that – the day after they give their lectures perfectly well; nobody finds it odd – *benissimo!*".

The local police were indulgent: "Everybody knows where I am, and amongst others Tavel, who has already sent twice to say

that either I cease from all collaboration on the journal or he will
have me arrested". The collaboration, of course, continued, but
Tavel took no action. Meanwhile, he tells Melegari that if he
wants to come and see him he should: "ask any of the children at
the house, or the men, or anybody you may meet, for Mr *Joseph*,
in room No. 32". There was even a sort of central heating in the
establishment: "Our rooms are heated invisibly by some tubes
which are fixed into the floor and send up heat coming from the
common fire, I think in the kitchen . . .". All the same he liked to
have a fire and was much distressed when there was a fuel
shortage, and only a fire in the living-room, where he found he
could not do his writing. He liked the way in which everybody
was treated as part of the family ("One of our religious-political
beliefs is the abolition of domestic service") and he liked the free
and natural friendship between the sexes. But he had a very
much higher opinion of the women than of the men.

"Women in Switzerland seem to be of a different race from the men;
they have refined minds, and they are capable of delicate feeling; the
men, although kindly and courteous, are rough and gross, and a
hundred thousand of my, of our ideas would seem to them foolish-
ness".

Soon he tells his mother of one of the Girard daughters.

"There is one who is called Francesca and she is the best of them and
the one most full of sympathy for me – I have told her that I have a
sister called Francesca, a most excellent girl, and one who shares almost
all my ideas. She has told me that for so long as I cannot see my sister
she will take her place for me. She is very good and has a refined mind,
but she is without the power to express herself because she has always
worked in the house, learning to read and write, but no more".

She suffered acutely when he left Switzerland, and it was of her
that he spoke in a letter of April 8th 1837, to Melegari, in which
he admitted that there was "another girl morally desolated" on
his account. He corresponded with her almost to the end of his
life, but unfortunately almost all of his letters have been lost; we
know of their frequency in the 'forties from the Young Italy
register kept by Lamberti in Paris, and of his feeling about her
from his letters to his mother.

Francesca had two sisters, Marianna, whom Giovanni considered uncouth, and Maddalena, who fell in love with Agostino,
and pursued him somewhat, and who Giovanni, the connoisseur,

considered was the only one of the three who had the makings of a coquette. As a family the Girards seemed to Giovanni to possess "a consoling atmosphere of patriarchal simplicity", and it was this atmosphere which supplied a needed balm in Mazzini's life. But the arrival of the three attractive young Italians clearly did not assist the daughters to contribute to the patriarchal calm.

One of the joys of life at Grenchen was the proximity of the Lake of Bienne. In the middle of that lake is the island of *Saint Pierre* where Jean-Jacques Rousseau once took refuge. So Mazzini, Agostino Ruffini and a friendly couple, Fritz and Anna Courvoisier, decided to make up a party and go out on a pilgrimage to the island. On October 30th 1835, Mazzini wrote to his mother:

"It was cold; but the crossing, lasting four hours for the journey there and back across the lake, pleased me; and still more so the island, all shrubs and woods, and most of all the room lived in by Rousseau. It is a real Chatterton kind of a room; bare, squalid, with naked walls and three or four crude straw chairs, a wooden floor, and a hiding-place into which he fled from unwelcome visitors. Genius in the grip of wretchedness is imprinted all over that room. And it made a strange impression upon me which I did not disclose because I was not alone and I was with people who might have regarded as affectation what was actually a profound emotion. My cousin [Agostino] and a Swiss lady [Anna Courvoisier] would have understood me; the husband, a good fellow, but a trader, and no more, would have laughed. And that was enough to make me keep what I felt to myself. I would not have expected to receive so strong an impression from Rousseau, a powerful writer, with whom I sympathize, but not strongly, not without reserve, not as I do with Byron, and with one or two others. But the spectacle of Genius and misfortune combined together has always moved me strongly. I would willingly have stayed four or five days in that room, but I cannot plan to do so now. At all costs I must return there one day or other – I will write further about it".

His mother seized at once upon the significance of the occasion and returned to it often in her letters. For here was her Pippo, the persecuted exile and prophet of his age, communing with the spirit of his master, the persecuted prophet of the previous century. And Pippo's, too, was the spirit of Chatterton, that sublime misunderstood genius, driven to suicide in a garret, whose fate, as described by Alfred de Vigny, was even then the furore of

Paris, and would soon be made known in Italy through Agostino's translation of the French poet.

Agostino, too, described to his own mother the little pilgrimage to the island:

". . . Crossing the lake gave me great pleasure. Wrapped up in my coat, like an English captain, I gave myself up to my dreams. Opposite to me was that woman so good, so devoted, so loving, but also so virtuous. . . . After two hours we landed. We walked round the island which, indeed, enchanted us. Emily [Mazzini] was deeply moved and pensive. Anna walked along the paths wholly absorbed in her contemplations. We went to visit Rousseau's room, a room quite bare, with straw chairs, a walnut table, a rough desk, a miserable bed. The walls have names scratched all over them. That room reminded me of Chatterton's room in the play about him which I saw in Paris. Genius always unhappy . . .".[1]

Then the bitter cry of the romanticist: Rousseau "came to seek solitude, he only asked to live by himself, and men tracked him down even there. Then the aristocracy of Berne chased him from that island, as one would chase a criminal . . .". Even so were they chasing himself and Pippo, even so would they chase them right out of Switzerland . . .

But prophetic thoughts never preoccupied Agostino for long. He follows straight on: "We went and had dinner. We cheered ourselves up in front of a good fire by reading the visitors' book".

And Anna Courvoisier, beloved of Agostino? She was not thinking about Rousseau, she was not even thinking about Agostino. She was thinking about Pippo:

"It would be impossible for me to describe to you", she tells her friend, Eugenia du Commun, "the happy moments we passed together, even in the presence of my husband, just speaking to each other and looking at each other. I was on the island against the wishes of F[ritz], who had been obliged to yield to the insistance of Signor M[azzini]. It was cold, but I felt nothing, I was face to face with him, I heard the

---

[1] It is reassuring to turn from these gloomy reflections about Rousseau's life on the island to the great romantic's own account of it. His room was in a large farm house, the home of the agent of the Hospital of Berne, and he enjoyed the company of the agent's family, and especially of Thérèse, with whom he would go round the farm watching the work and sometimes joining in it. On Sunday evenings those who lived on the opposite shore would come across to dance on the terrace which ran the length of the island. "Je comte ces deux mois pour le temps le plus heureux de ma vie, et tellement heureux qu'il m'eût suffi durant toute mon existence, sans laisser naître un seul instant dans mon âme le désir d'un autre état . . .'. (From the *Cinquième promenade* of the *Rêveries du promeneur solitaire*, *Oeuvres*, Paris, 1853, I, 424.)

The Ruffini family, from portraits in Codignola: *I Fratelli Ruffini* and *La Riviera Ligure*. *Above:* Bust of Eleonora Ruffini, "La Madre Santa". *Left:* Jacopo. *Right:* Giovanni. *Below:* Agostino.

Giuditta Sidoli. From a portrait in the Museo del
Risorgimento at Genoa, reproduced in Salucci,
Amori Mazziniani.

voice of Signor Mazz., I drank in the words from his lips as the bee its honey from the rose. . . .

"I was so beside myself that when the gentlemen rejoined me, and the Signor Mazz. asked me why I was so silent, I replied ludicrously: 'I am thinking about my nose, which is cold' – a reply which must have amazed them. Poor Fritz! . . . My friend, what a man this Signor M. is, what a friend! And he, too, wishes me well, he had tears in his eyes when we parted, because he saw how I suffered; he knew how much I love . . .".

In September of the following year poor Anna died of tuberculosis. Mazzini bemoaned the fatality by which disaster always overtook those whose destiny became mingled with his own, and her death accentuated his "tempest of doubt". But if, indeed, her death was due to personal causes, as well as to the disease which had probably been upon her for some time, it was rather Agostino who had cause to reproach himself. For it was Agostino, not Mazzini, who had made love to the poor girl and thereby caused her distress and difficulty. After visiting him at the Baths, at Grenchen, Anna had had some difficulty in tearing herself away.

"You go *too far*", she wrote to him the night before her departure. "We are two children . . . Signor Giuseppe [Mazzini] has properly understood my position; though accustomed to Italian ways he appreciates other conventions and passion does not blind him. . . . Oh my friend, it is providential for me that tomorrow I must leave this house where, I see only too clearly, the chance has been given to us to see each other alone . . . all is over for me, I shall take up again my duties as wife and mother with a clear conscience but with my heart lacerated . . . I may be *forced* to write to you that I renounce your love; do not believe it, never believe it . . .".

In the following year and, as it proved, shortly before Anna's death, Agostino sent her a sharp and sarcastic letter; she had unwisely disclosed in a letter to Agostino that she was aware that he was jealous of her corresponding with Mazzini. When she died Agostino regretted his tart reply. But that did not prevent him from making a characteristic entry, later on, in his diary for the year 1835:

"From Paris I return to Grenchen. Somewhat disillusioned, but still behaving like a romantic. Met Eugenia and Anna. Made love with Anna. Three-quarters pretence and romanticism. Everything romanticized. Meeting with Eugenia and Anna at an inn between Grenchen and Bienne. Expedition to the island of *Saint Pierre*. Separation, due half to virtue half to boredom . . .".

Chapter 9

THE JURA: YOUNG SWITZERLAND

Despite the discouraging reports which he received from Italy after the Savoy fiasco Mazzini had by no means altogether abandoned, as yet, his primary purpose of bringing about a revolution in Italy. Only it would have, now, to be brought about indirectly. Believing, as he did, that revolution was one, and that the enemy was one ("Austria spells despotism in Europe – remove Austria and it is over – Down with Austria! has to be the European cry"), he thought that he could now best serve the Italian cause by rousing Switzerland. This was his purpose in founding Young Switzerland, which was a more promising and effective-looking body than were the other shadowy constituents of Young Europe. His interest in it was immediate and practical, and by no means confined, as he later pretended, to long-term educational objectives.

To Melegari, in September 1834, he tersely made his intentions clear:

"The *political* purpose which informs me in this matter of Young Switzerland is this: to collect together such support as may be necessary; to enable it to organize itself; to preside over that organization; then to cause it to declare itself publicly as a National Association – first objective a Constituent Assembly – to try by every means to time a public demonstration in favour of a Constituent to coincide with a movement in Italy – if it proves possible to launch one there – the one would incite the other – the demonstration in favour of the Swiss Constituent would cause the powers, or anyhow Austria, to intervene diplomatically, or by force – in the midst of this conflict Italy would rise. No need for me to tell you the immense advantage a movement in Switzerland, and a general state of excitement there, would be for Italy at the time of her own movement – Austria put into a terribly embarrassing position – the Swiss movement a connecting link between Italy and Germany – the chance of gaining support, even some men, from Switzerland – the movement gaining a European complexion, dismaying the *masters* and encouraging the *slaves* . . .".

An optimistic programme. There was the special difficulty that the Swiss, with their unique record of maintaining their independence, and of avoiding becoming deeply involved in European conflagrations, might dislike the idea of turning their country into the vortex of this new and dangerous whirlpool. This difficulty Mazzini saw: "These are not things to say openly to the Swiss lest they should fear they are being made use of – which they are not because, in the end, they would win our support".

However, the first steps in Mazzini's programme for Switzerland, namely a National Association, and the summoning of a Constituent Assembly, were in line with those advocated by the more advanced section amongst the Swiss liberals themselves. There was much Swiss advocacy for a stronger federal government, and in particular for one strong enough to stand up against foreign pressure, to which Switzerland's geographical position and her racially and religiously mixed populations made her peculiarly subject. Since the Swiss Pact of 1815 the government of the country had been entrusted to a Diet, whose members were, in effect, "ambassadors" from the different cantons, and which could not even consider matters upon which twelve cantonal legislatures had not previously agreed. The federal executive, called the *Vorort*, was merely the cantonal government of Lucerne, or Berne, or Zürich, acting in a federal capacity. For these three cantons took it in turn, for two years at a time, to add to their own cantonal business the extra and tiresome duty of conducting the business of the federation. During 1835 and 1836, when Mazzini was most concerned with the *Vorort*, it was at Berne.

It was natural enough that a reform of the constitution, designed to strengthen the federal executive, was a first objective amongst Swiss progressives, and a National Association, to work for his end, was being mooted at the very time that Mazzini founded Young Switzerland. But, unfortunately for Mazzini, when this Association came to birth, in the summer of 1835, it did so independently of Young Switzerland and, indeed, in opposition to himself and to much of his programme.

"Some patriots", Mazzini wrote in May of that year, "are announcing that they wish to set up a National Association; we ought not to let them take the initiative now. If a National Association, independent of our influence and not subject to our guidance, could lead to any good that would indeed be something. But convinced, as I am, of the contrary, it is necessary that everything should be done to forstall it, and, when we know the dates they have chosen, we should advertise Young Switzerland simultaneously, and by a published manifesto".

Nevertheless the National Association was formed, and it went ahead while Young Switzerland languished. In January 1836 the Association held a reunion at Aarberg, under the presidency of Enrico Druey, editor of the *Nouvelliste Vaudois* of Lausanne, a man Mazzini courted long and assiduously but failed to win. The reunion was without immediate results, which led Mazzini to observe that "if the association Young Switzerland were not dead, as it is, it would have a fine opportunity, after this assembly at Aarberg, which has been without results and has only shown the impotence of the old gang . . .". But the association he had sponsored was clearly in no position to take any initiative at all. The weakness of Young Switzerland he attributed to its failure to come out into the open and cease to be a secret society. He believed that the degree of political and cultural freedom obtaining in at least some of the Swiss cantons permitted of a society with the objectives of Young Switzerland being conducted openly. He wanted it to establish its headquarters at Bienne, near to where he was living at Grenchen, and a good base for penetration into the German-speaking cantons of the north-east. In these cantons he placed his hope, having seen that the more advanced reformers at French-speaking Geneva and Lausanne were becoming unmistakably antagonistic to him.

But he could effect none of these things owing to the anomaly of his position. Thus, although he had founded Young Switzerland, he did not direct it and he did not sit on its committee; as a foreigner (and as promoter of the Savoy invasion) he would not have been acceptable. And although he had founded, in May 1835, the journal *La Jeune Suisse*, whose first number, in French and Italian, appeared early in July, and sold 700 copies, he did not edit it, nor did he sit upon its editorial board. Soon he limited his share in it to the articles he himself contributed twice weekly. Still more remarkable, the journal did not belong to the Association, whose executive committee complained that *La Jeune Suisse* had been launched under Mazzini's personal auspices, that its articles were much too concerned with European affairs, lying outside the scope of the Association, and that they were too violent and too "lofty" in tone. Mazzini, in reply, dryly noted that his articles were accepted

"because the paper has no other writers, because I don't receive a penny for them whereas other collaborators would expect payment, and because a sense of shame prevents them from repudiating the principles about which I write, and for other reasons".

He was not in a position to see beforehand the other material which the paper proposed to publish and he often disapproved of what it printed. He seems, however, to have had a controlling influence in the appointment of its editor, though it sometimes suited him to conceal this. When, in March 1836, a friend of his, Weingart, was given the post, another candidate had been Allier, that canny Frenchman who had been his landlord and creditor at Berne. Mme Allier pressed her husband's claim, while Melegari accused Mazzini of being prejudiced by personal spite against him. Allier, however, had demanded 1,200 francs, and his keep, to do the job, and Mazzini had been able to reply that, while he would have preferred to have had Allier (which we may doubt), the paper was only being kept alive by the generosity of a few friends and could not possibly pay what he was asking.

The heat and burden of the fight for radical reform in Switzerland were being borne at this time by Fazy in the *Europe Centrale*, at Geneva, and by Druey in the *Nouvelliste Vaudois*, at Lausanne. They were doughty fighters, Fazy being destined to seize power at Geneva, by force, in 1846, and Druey to play a leading part in establishing the new federal constitution of 1848. They had given generous support to Mazzini at the time of the Savoy invasion, and they would give it again after he had withdrawn to England and abandoned his attempt to influence Swiss affairs. But they would not tolerate his attempt, in *La Jeune Suisse*, to lead Swiss radical opinion. At first sight there was not much difference between their political programme and his, for both wanted the creation of an effective and representative federal government, together with the breaking down of oligarchic privilege in the cantons so that cantonal governments, too, might become more representative, especially of the country districts. They were also at one in their pressure for publication of the proceedings of the cantonal assemblies. But the Swiss journalists were not prepared to follow Mazzini in the far-reaching flights of *La Jeune Suisse's* religious fancy and they feared, not without reason, that Mazzini meant to involve Switzerland in some universal disturbance. Their purposes were limited, and strictly Swiss. They wanted a strong federal government because they meant to curtail privilege at home and to withstand pressure from abroad; they did not want a strong federal government so that Switzerland might play a leading part in the emancipation of the European peoples, and they were quite indifferent to the Mazzinian religion which seemed to require something of this sort.

Mazzini has sometimes been credited with having helped to pave the way for the creation of the Swiss constitution of 1848 through his influence upon Druey, who later played so important a part in establishing it. But it is hard to find that influence. The federal movement in Switzerland was older than Mazzini's residence there, and his association with Druey was brief. Druey became president, in 1835, of the National Association formed, as we have seen, in opposition to Young Switzerland, and by June of 1836 he had so far broken with the Italian as to issue a circular to members of the Association specifically directed against Mazzini and reminding them that the Association would have nothing whatever to do with insurrection or with revolution, whether at home or abroad. "Druey's circular", said Mazzini, "is a hateful thing, and the allusions which it contains have, in the present circumstances, something vile about them".[1]

If Mazzini did exercise any important influence in Switzerland it was in the prolonged crusade that he waged against what he regarded as Swiss materialism. He saw materialism lying all around him, in the faces, the behaviour, and the talk of the men he met (as distinct from the women) as well as in the preoccupation of the radical leaders with exclusively Swiss political

---

[1] It was printed in the *Nouvelliste Vaudois* for June 21 1836 and is reprinted as a note to XI, 405–407.

interests. But his *bête noire*, in this matter, was Fazy of the *Europe Centrale*. Mazzini's articles in *La Jeune Suisse* became, as he admitted, a steady crusade against the tenets of the *Europe Centrale*, and the Genevan paper replied in kind. Fazy accused him of mysticism, he accused Fazy of socialism. Fazy could not abide his talk of God, of Duty, of Principles; he could not abide Fazy's preoccupation with the interests as opposed to the duties of the workers. Much of what Mazzini said in these articles he had already said in criticism of the Carbonari and of the Saint-Simonians, though it was a point his critics loved to make that he was "tainted with Saint-Simonian mysticism". And much of it, on the economic side, anticipates his later quarrel with Louis Blanc, with Karl Marx, and with Bakunin.

Tirelessly, in the face of the mounting irritation, he went on repeating in his articles:[1]

"Every revolution is the work of a *principle* which has been accepted as a basis of faith. Whether it invoke Nationality, Liberty, Equality, or Religion it always fulfils itself in the name of a Principle . . . we recognize no other meaning in revolutions . . . without this purpose there may be riots, and at times victorious insurrections, but no revolutions".

Revolutions are sacred whereas insurrections are immoral. The uprising of 1830 in France and those conducted by the Carbonari in 1820–21 and 1831 in Italy appeared to him to have been made in the name of no intelligible general principle. They were thus merely insurrections and, as such, they were both ineffective and immoral.

It is easy to see why Mazzini's argument made him few friends and many enemies amongst the revolutionary exiles in Switzerland or amongst the Swiss themselves. It went hard with the exiles to be told that the revolutions in which they had sacrificed themselves had been immoral, nor was it evident to them that Mazzini's own revolution had been any more effective. As for the Swiss journalists, it was quite true that they were much pre-occupied with the problem of economic privilege and that they hoped, like the British Chartists, to cure what they regarded as its evils by political means. But they could not understand why this made them materialists or wanting in principle.

[1] His crusade against Fazy is mostly to be found in VII, 237–265 and 281–317.

Mazzini, for his part, would not admit that he ignored the economic factor.

"Do we, then, preach principles for their own sake, faith for its own sake, as the romantic school of literature today preaches art for art's sake? God forbid! We do not ignore the economic factor . . . but we subordinate it to the moral factor because, if withdrawn from the controlling influence of morality . . . it would result in a brutal egotism . . .".

What follows shows that Mazzini had, in fact, very sweeping views about social and economic change:

"If, by your example, you can root in the heart of a nation the principle which the French revolution proclaimed but never carried out that the State owes every one of its members the means of existence or the chance to work for it, and then you define existence justly, you have prepared the triumph of right over privilege".

But it was by a moral rather than a political revolution that he sought to end pauperism so that the poor need no longer be dependent upon "Christian charity" or be abandoned to "cold brutal maxims like those of the English school of political economists". He regards it as a moral problem because the necessary change can only come about "when the gospel of the brotherhood of all the men of a nation has made the soul a sanctuary of virtue and love". It cannot be had from "sophists who would found a godless Nationality" or from a political party which succeeds in capturing power. "Nationality is belief in a common origin and a common end" and a true conception of it, a conception which embraces a really religious idea of fraternity, can only grow

"when the mother repeats this pure and holy doctrine to the child at her knee at those hours of morn and even when woman, grown to be an angel, teaches her offspring heavenly truths uttered as immutable axioms and principles . . .".

This sort of language was altogether too much for Fazy, who countered it with a straight appeal to rights and interests. But, though Fazy, not Mazzini, won the ear of the radical movement in Switzerland, it would be rash to deny any effect, amongst individuals, arising from Mazzini's moral crusade, especially when we come to encounter the popular enthusiasm for him at the time of his withdrawal to London.

Warfare makes strange bedfellows. Mazzini's hostility to the "materialist" outlook of the Swiss radicals led him into expressing some sympathy with the particular object of their aversion, namely the Catholic priests and the cause of the Catholic cantons. For this was the period when the quarrel was developing apace between the seven Catholic cantons, which sought to defend the traditional rights of the Church, and with them the cause of cantonal independence, and the remaining fifteen cantons, which stood either for a stronger federal state or at least for the extension of anti-clerical laws to all cantons. It was a quarrel which would lead, in the year 1847, to the civil war of the *Sonderbund*, the crushing of the Catholic cantons by the Protestant majority, and the emergence of the stronger federal state, with an anti-clerical outlook, invoked by Druey and Fazy.

The early stages of this quarrel are interestingly reflected in Mazzini's letters. On the one hand, his aspirations for Italy as well as his religion of humanity and progress had made him irrevocably anti-Papal and anti-Jesuit so that, in so far as the Catholic cause in Switzerland was bound up with the matter of permitting the Jesuits to teach there, or with the maintenance of the rights of Rome, he was on the side of the anti-clerical majority. But in as much as he hated the kind of secular state which he saw Fazy and his friends trying to make, and in as much as he was prepared to recognize a real concern for the fundamentals of religion amongst some of the priests, he was sometimes inclined to espouse their cause. He disliked both sides – "I stand between the intolerance of the Socialists and that of the neo-Christians". He was really looking, in Switzerland (as in Italy and in France), for a progressive element amongst the priests which was prepared to embrace his own faith. But this, of course, he found it hard to discover.

In the early spring of the year 1836 the Swiss religious quarrel reached Mazzini's own neighbourhood, near the Girards' establishment at Grenchen. For the Canton of Berne had adopted various measures modifying, amongst other things, the marriage laws, in a manner unacceptable to the Catholic population. In the Jura mountains there was a protest against these measures, and the cantonal government sent troops to check the demonstrations; later, after a note had been received from the French government, both the troops and the measures were withdrawn. To this little episode, on his own doorstep, Mazzini reacted sharply. Although it was a case of a religious minority standing out for a principle in which it believed, he poured scorn upon the peasants in question who were "ignorant", he noted that they were "mostly women" (a curious commentary upon his belief in the superior religious sensibility of women), he blamed the priests, and, although he was sufficiently accustomed to the habit of planting trees of liberty, he was very unfavourably impressed when these peasants planted trees in honour of the Madonna. Clearly, while Mazzini detested the spirit of secularism, the religion he considered necessary was his own.

Such, indeed, is the burden of the articles in *La Jeune Suisse* in which he treats of this religious quarrel. What he seeks to defend is not any existing religions, as such, but what he calls the religious sentiment, which he hopes and believes will turn towards his own faith. He tells Fazy and his friends to "remember that religion is a desire, a need for the People; that no change of form that has taken place in the world has ever succeeded in extinguishing the religious sentiment", that to preach political reform whilst denying or neglecting the religious sentiment is to "will the end without the means, the construction without the necessary instruments".

Not, then, the faith of the Jesuits, who were striving to rekindle a livelier devotion to the ancient religion, nor the faith of the radicals, who left no room in their programme for any religion, but a new faith, Mazzini's faith, was the message Mazzini preached to the Swiss, knowing that many would remain "cold and impervious" but hopeful that "in some corner of our Switzerland" – as *La Jeune Suisse* told its readers –

"in the recesses of our mountains, or maybe on some shore of our blue and tranquil lakes, will be found the white and virgin soil of some virtuous youth who will draw his inspiration from our faith, some mother who loves in all holiness, and who will receive our words and whisper them softly in her children's ears".

Perhaps some such there was. But we only know that mothers went on planting trees to the Madonna, and that Fazy and Druey were largely successful in achieving their purposes.

Chapter 10

THE JURA: THE LAST STAND

Abruptly, at the end of May 1836, the peaceful life at Grenchen was shattered.

The expulsion came in dramatic circumstances. The government of the Canton of Solothurn, in which Grenchen is situated, claimed to have information that Young Germany was planning the invasion of the Grand Duchy of Baden – an invasion of the same kind as Mazzini's invasion of Savoy – and that a meeting between members of Young Germany and Young Switzerland, to draw up the plans, was to take place at Grenchen. Mazzini denied his own or Young Switzerland's complicity in such a plot, which seems to have been one of the many hair-brained schemes of Harro-Harring's friend "General" Rauschenplatt, of whom Mazzini had much occasion to complain ("If Rauschenplatt had not insisted upon planning expeditions which he had neither the means nor the determination to carry through we should all be undisturbed"). But the cantonal government determined to take the opportunity to be rid of Mazzini.

"Imagine it", he told his mother, "troops and gendarmes on the march – two hundred men; the house where I live invested as though it were an enemy fortress; all this parade of strength brought out, you must realize, from the city (Solothurn), necessitating a march of four or five hours; rifles loaded, munitions distributed, etc. – and the result the arrest of two people, whom you know well, an arrest made, remember, with their consent and the free disclosure of their names, etc. – these two people taken and put in a carriage and conveyed in great pomp to the city . . .".

Clearly Mazzini appreciated the humour of the situation, which grew more pronounced when no incriminating evidence could be found upon him, or upon Agostino Ruffini who was arrested with him, and when the gendarmes demanded, in the evening, to be allowed to serenade their prisoners. The next day they were released and escorted back to Grenchen, but they were also ordered to leave the Canton within twenty-four hours, on the grounds that their papers were not in order. Their return was marked by

"scenes of joy and congratulation never to be forgotten in those parts – peasants dancing, music, shouting, greetings, a regular ovation – everybody in the village drunk – the two of them having to kiss and shake hands with everybody -- and pay for wine for most of them, in recognition of it all . . . I don't need to tell you that the whole family of which I have often spoken to you [the Girards] showed its love for me more than ever, their grief, their joy, their threats of rebellion, the crying of the children, in short the demonstrations of real love were such that a man's own family could have done no more".

The importance of the occasion was that the crowd, both at Grenchen and at Solothurn, had shown its feelings so clearly that government could not but take notice, especially when the Commune of Grenchen followed it up by offering them citizenship. This offer, however, required to be approved by the cantonal government, where there was much opposition to it, and the confirmation had not, in fact, been given before Mazzini decided to depart with the Ruffini brothers for England.

The occasion had been heart-warming, but it had deprived Mazzini of his happy home at Grenchen and had made him a wanderer once more. We know little of where he lodged except that, after two days nearby, at Langenau, in the house of a Protestant pastor ("a family of angels"), he moved to Solothurn; that he remained secretly at Solothurn until early in September; and that for the rest of the year he was living hidden in the vicinity at the foot of the Jura mountains. For some days, at least, at the end of October, he was at the inn between Grenchen and Bienne where he and Agostino had been wont to meet Anna Courvoisier and Eugenia duCommun in the happier months of the previous year. Anna had died in September, but her husband Fritz entertained the Italians with great kindness. Agostino's diary tells us of a month at an inn run by a certain Widmer at Solothurn, and of two months at the house of an old man called Biehli: "A miserable, crazy life with continual arguments. Very natural, being shut up like that, with no comfort, no hope, nothing to look forward to".[1]

[1] Cod. 1, 445.

Mazzini, too, found this period of confinement a strain, but his idea of the best kind of existence for a revolutionary differed somewhat from the ideas of the Ruffini brothers:

"I could very well live all my life shut up in one room provided that I had all my books with me; but without books, without my guitar, without sight of the sky, it is too much. The two brothers, on the other hand, need to be able to move about; I don't know what I wouldn't give if I could only secure citizenship for them, or at least freedom for them to move about within one canton. . . . Citizenship would only be harmful to me because it would deprive me of the chance to live as a recluse, without seeing a soul in the world. My idea of perfection would be for myself to be hidden in that way while they were free, and while the few whom I love were safe for a year, at least, from the cholera (then raging in Italy) and from all other danger . . .".

It was difficult for Mazzini to find the *juste milieu*. Life at Grenchen had been the best that he had found in Switzerland, but it had always been liable to be spoilt by visitors. One day a colonel had come to see him there. This colonel, he told his mother,

"for fifty years has never ceased to serve, travel, suffer, see things, feel things, and tells the whole of it, beginning again at the beginning as soon as he has finished. He kept me pinned, for a whole day, against a window, so that I had to listen to him like a victim – you will realize that if I were quite free to follow my inclination I shouldn't speak four words in twenty-four hours. He has a daughter and has put it into her head that she plays the guitar well: 'ask her to play to you', he said to me: 'then you'll see'; so I asked her, she accepted, everybody silent, expectant, recollected – O God! not one note correct – I remained still, petrified, unable, in conscience, to compliment her, yet obliged to say something. I turned to the music from which she was playing, muttering: 'This looks like difficult music, who wrote it?' . . . The good girl, convinced by her father that she played well, clung to me: 'Yes indeed, it is difficult, but listen to this, and this . . .'. When Jesus was willing she stopped. Oh what a day! . . . I could have screamed . . . yet I could recognize goodness of heart and friendliness and I forced myself to be polite and to smile though within me I was blaspheming . . .".

The Ruffini brothers were readier than Mazzini to be rude, but they also found it less of a strain to be sociable.

The expulsion from Grenchen was followed in July by the arrest of those at Bienne who were in charge of the production of *La Jeune Suisse;* the paper appeared no more after the end of that month. And on August 11th the Diet voted the *Conclusum*, a general sentence of expulsion passed upon certain classes of the exiles, namely those who had been involved in the Savoy invasion, those who were implicated in the plot for a Baden invasion, and those who were accused of interference in the internal affairs of Switzerland. This *Conclusum* required to be confirmed by the Grand Councils of the cantons, but the large majority, including Solothurn and Berne, did confirm it. Vaud and Geneva were amongst the few which refused to do so and Druey attacked the measure vigorously. It was generally felt that this new pressure put upon the exiles was due to the threatening notes which the Swiss *Vorort* was receiving from the foreign ambassadors, and this foreign intervention rallied to Mazzini's support even some of his enemies.

The pressure came mainly from France. When Mazzini had first come to Switzerland the Austrian ambassador, Bombelles, had complained most. After the Savoy invasion much had been heard, naturally enough, from the Sardinian ambassador, Pralormo. In those earlier days the French ambassador, Rumigny, had tried to exercise a moderating influence and even to protect the Swiss government from being coerced. But events since had hardened the French attitude. There had been the revolts at Lyons and Paris in April 1834. And in July 1835 there had been the bomb thrown at the French king by Fieschi and his friends. The Baden plot was a new reminder that no territory bordering upon Switzerland could regard itself as immune from attack. So Mazzini had to suffer for the indiscretions of others, and bitterly he complained of their follies. Yet his complaints were not without their ironical aspect. Fieschi was no longer alive to remind him of how he had once backed Procida or "a certain Pole"; but Rauschenplatt was still there to recall to the Chief how he had obeyed a summons to a Savoy invasion, chasing along the western shore of the Lake of Geneva, with Harro-Harring, in a char-a-banc. Mazzini it was who had taught them to risk themselves: "action breeds action", "the tree of liberty grows stronger when watered by the blood of martyrs", "the dagger of the assassin is never so deadly as when sharpened on the tombstone of a martyr".

The new French ambassador, representing a government now

determined to secure Mazzini's expulsion, was the Duc de Montebello. He found the Swiss government in a submissive mood on the subject of the exiles, and on June 22nd 1836 he received a note from the *Vorort*, still frightened by the discovery of the Baden project, in which it expressed its intention of rounding up the undesirable aliens and requested that the French government should receive them at the frontier. To this note Montebello replied, on July 18th, with some *hauteur*, that the measures thus far adopted by the *Vorort* in the matter of the exiles had proved inadequate because they had been left for their enforcement to the cantons, and that the federal government must now see to it that it took more effective steps. If it failed to do so the French government would itself be forced to intervene. But more remarkable is the expedient he adopted, on the same day, to ensnare Mazzini, the Ruffini brothers, Rauschenplatt and one or two others. For he presented another note to the *Vorort* warning them to beware a certain dangerous character called Conseil, who had been mixed up in the Fieschi affair in Paris, and who was now in Switzerland. Yet this Conseil was none other than a French spy, paid and despatched by the French government, with instructions to ingratiate himself with the Italian exiles (he was a native of Ancona in the Papal State), and particularly to find out the secrets of those listed; and Montebello's warning, which was naturally given publicity, was designed to encourage Mazzini and his friends to believe in the impostor and to take him into their confidence.

What Montebello, however, did not know was that Conseil had already arrived in Switzerland, where his story and his passport had been so unimpressive that the immigration authorities had already expelled him. The unfortunate spy had retreated to Montaubon and had there procured another French passport, this time in the name of Corelli. Determined to fulfil his mission he returned to Switzerland, and went straight to Berne and saw Montebello. The ambassador gave him further instructions and some cash for immediate purposes and off he went again to make contact with Italian exiles. He soon found one who chose to call himself the Conte de Giorgi-Bertola (a remarkable fraud whose imprisonment Mazzini later on helped to secure in England) but the "Conte" was a more experienced deceiver than was Conseil and it did not take him long to discover that the new immigrant had not in fact been an associate of Fieschi, and that in other respects he was not what he pretended to be. However, having satisfied himself that Conseil was a spy, the Conte saw no reason why he should not turn his knowledge to advantage, so he agreed to keep quiet in return for a share of the ambassador's gold. Conseil returned to Montebello, pointed out the defects in his new passport which had been made clear to him by Giorgi-Bertola, and obtained yet a third one, this time in the name of Hermann, and some further money and instructions. But, when one of Giorgi-Bertola's friends also discovered the fraud, the game was up, the police were informed, and Conseil was arrested at Nidau. He had not managed to see Mazzini, who had mistrusted what he had heard about him and had prudently declined a first overture. The facts were carefully sifted by a committee of the Diet[1] and, as a result, a rather natural indignation with Montebello and with the French government was given voice in public demonstrations. Mazzini found himself something of a hero. It was too late for the disclosures to affect the attitude of the Diet, which had already voted the *Conclusum*, but it was not too late for them to affect the General Councils of Vaud and Geneva, which were still considering that measure, and which rejected it.

Nevertheless the pressure upon Mazzini was intensified. On September 1st he wrote to his mother:

"I had hoped to be able to tell you of the rejection of that *Conclusum* by the majority of the cantons, but, instead, it has been approved by most. As a result, not only are the difficulties greatly increased in that matter of giving us citizenship [the Grenchen proposal] but the state of things whereby we are immobilized and have to stay in hiding lasts indefinitely. This is a great handicap; it can be supported for a time, but not indefinitely. We shall see. Meanwhile Angelo [Usiglio, their frail and faithful companion, who had been suddenly expelled], who I had hoped could stay, has suddenly been compelled to go without even having time to give us news of how, or why, or where. We shall hear soon. I grieve for us and for him. We lose a most faithful friend; he will be alone, separated from us whom he loved, and thus wretched . . .".

---

[1] Its report, together with a quantity of other papers concerning the case, is printed in the appendix to Vol. XII.

The arrest of the editor of *La Jeune Suisse*, Weingart, had followed that of the staff of his paper; there was no longer any prospect of publishing it again. And the society was as dead as the paper. Mazzini was, in fact, without effective support, even though popular elements at Geneva or at Lausanne might cheer for him, and though Fazy and Druey might support him in his struggle with the ambassadors. Those two powerful journalists still disapproved as strongly as ever of what he was preaching, and it is probably to their ascendancy in the liberal movement in Vaud and Geneva that we must attribute the rather curious fact that Mazzini never seems to have considered moving to Lausanne (where Melegari lived, comparatively untroubled) or to Geneva.

Reluctant to face the inevitable, he would grasp at the most wispy of straws. The Conseil affair, it occurred to him, might provoke war between Switzerland and France, and that would induce Italy to "rise". But it was not the policy of the Swiss government to press home any charges against the government of France. Its policy was to squeeze Mazzini out of the country.

In his final decision to withdraw Mazzini was influenced by his concern for the Ruffini brothers. "I shall depart", he told Rosales early in September, "if things go on like this, because my two friends cannot stand this life . . . if I cannot secure that my two companions can move about freely in some city I shall go". And later in life he recollected:

"I remained, hunted for futilely everywhere, until December of that year and I would have remained indefinitely if the way of living to which we were compelled by the circumstances had not seriously threatened the health of the two friends who shared the persecution with me".

When we remember that this was the time when he was writing that desperate letter to Eleonora, their mother, for confirmation in his faith, we shall not lightly dismiss the influence of the Ruffini family upon his decision. And his concern for the brothers was now the greater because they had lost their own faith: "The Ruffinis are now my *idée fixe*. Their principles no longer give them any cause for their sacrifice". Had there been any hope of effective action no doubt he would have stayed, but there was not, so how should he allow his preference for solitude, and a view of the

G

soaring Alps, to override the Ruffini preference for a life of freedom in London?

There were, however, certain practical difficulties about removing to England. Could he obtain an effective passport? Would he be free from arrest during his passage through France? If a Tory government came into power would he be welcome in England? These were the questions which he now asked himself.

The means by which he could ingratiate himself with English opinion were made plain by the British Minister at Berne, David Morier, a pious man who wrote a book on religion and politics. Morier had a long conversation with Mazzini's friend Filippo Ugoni, who told Mazzini that the ambassador insisted

"that we Italians, in order to better our lot, should give our cause a religious character and propagate the Bible amongst the people; I replied to him that, although Bible Societies might have done good in savage countries, in those that were civilized they could do as much harm as good, and then I held forth against the Anglican religion whose ministers, so far as I know them, are all hypocrites, in love only with money. He professed himself very much attached to that faith, while admitting that twenty years ago what I said was true . . . and he added: 'I would like to see Mazzini, I would very much like to know him, I realize that he has very noble and religious principles; I would like to say to him what I have said to you . . .'".[1]

Here was an early sign of that strange British endeavour, to which Mazzini himself never lent much encouragement, to work a Protestant Reformation in Italy through his ideas. But the necessary British visas were promised by the ambassador without an interview on the matter of Bible Societies, and it only remained for Mazzini to secure a passport which would guarantee him a safe conduct through France. On this matter Morier consulted with Montebello, who proved only too ready to oblige, and a correspondence started between the French ambassador and the exile upon whose head, at the instance of the ambassador, the Swiss government had by now set a price of twenty-five *louis-d'or*! The correspondence is dignified, but ironical. Mazzini refuses to come to Berne to see Montebello, even under safe-conduct, because of the insults to which the *Vorort* there has subjected him; his objections, he tells the ambassador, "reposent

[1] XII, 216, Note.

sur des sentiments honorables que vous, monsieur le Duc, comme Français, êtes sans doute en même de déviner et d'apprécier". Montebello concedes the point and promises to despatch the passports provided that the three of them undertake to leave immediately after receiving them and not to linger in France on the way. Mazzini promises to leave within fifteen days of hearing from Montebello, this little delay being imposed by

"the multitude of financial and other arrangements which have to be carried out when one is making a complete change of home, and having regard to the state of our linen, and of our personal belongings, etc., which arises from the way in which we have had to live for some time".

Amongst his final dispositions was the selling off of the store of arms still hidden in the mountains near Nyon. The money realized from this, and from Fritz Courvoisier's sale of a stock of copies of *Faith and the Future* was to go to the cause. The cost of his journey to England was defrayed by his mother.

For the last day or two before their departure they were free to stay once more at the Baths at Grenchen. Mazzini wrote a last letter, on December 31st, to Eleonora Ruffini:

"I pray for you, on my knees, a better year, and one which may end for the three of you more happily".

To his mother, on the same day:

"With the new year begins a new life for me . . . may it be less sad . . . for you who so want my good, for my father whom I love so, for my sisters, for the holy mother of my friends, and for my poor Giuditta, for she too certainly thinks of me with love and trembling . . .".

And a last one, too, to Melegari, who must keep the faith alive:

"I send a few papers which belong to Young Europe . . . as a society Young Europe is dead . . . not as a faith . . . but its effects cannot show themselves until an upheaval has taken place . . . there is need for a new religious synthesis . . . the French mission of initiation is exhausted . . . the social epoch dawns . . . the three peoples, the Germans, the Poles and the Italians are the initiators of that epoch . . . I will give you an address to which to write to me in London, but, if you have need to write anything important use concealment; starch is the most handy material . . .".

Then Montebello's chief secretary, Belleval, appeared in person at the Baths with the passports, there were songs and tears and toasts until four in the morning, and they were off, escorted on the first stage of their journey by three carriages bearing members of the Communal Council of Grenchen, with whom they had dined the night before and who now carried a banner.

From Troyes, on their journey, Mazzini wrote again to his mother. All had gone smoothly and they were enjoying travelling freely, with normal passports, and not with the humiliating papers of refugees. In the French city they had picked up Angelo Usiglio and they were taking him with them to England. There had also been time to visit the cathedral and one or two churches, and to send a line of warning to the devout Melegari: ". . . The churches are empty; a few women who look like statues in a sepulchre – there you have the Christian religion in France".

Finally, a stormy crossing of eleven hours from Calais to London, much sea-sickness for all four of them until they got into the Thames estuary, and then the first views of free England and the "incredible sight" of the shipping in the Thames.

Ashore, at last, in London, and through the customs:

"The sky is rainy, cloudy; the atmosphere of the city is filled with something which seems like a light smoke. The piazzas are huge, from one end you cannot see the other through this atmosphere. A very tall column, seen through the fog, appeared to me like a giant. The whole city, with its houses of sooty, blackened brick seemed like a phantom; to most people it is unpleasing, but it pleases me. I feel I am in a city which puts me in mind of Ossian and his poems . . .".

And there, in freedom but in fog, with a few cigars he could ill afford, smoked on an empty stomach, he would explain his faith to a small but gradually growing group of friends, while Agostino moved on to Edinburgh to practise as a lawyer and Giovanni to Paris to practise as a writer. For eleven years he would await that upheaval in Europe which he had told Melegari, in his last letter, must come before they could usefully emerge once more. Not until the governments of the continent were being shattered by the convulsions of the year 1848 did he return to Italy. But his myth there he had already made.

Chapter 11

MAZZINI'S THEOLOGY

The welcome extended by Mazzini to the London fog is in keeping with his character. It is of a piece with his romanticism, his
preference for the suggestive. Soon he extended a similar welcome to the English temperament, and even to some important
elements in the English religious outlook. No doubt, as Mr.
Griffith in a recent essay insists, "he had no affinity with
Protestantism in any form . . . his thought was dominated by
Catholic collectivism and universalism",[1] but he is also right
when he insists that Mazzini's upbringing, all that he had heard
and thought about "the Elect" and "Duty" had "mediated"
Calvinism to him through the filter of Jansenism. To the early
influence of his mother and of a Jansenist tutor must, in fact, be
attributed the presenting of Christianity to him in a manner
which cannot have been without its influence upon the way he
developed his own religious thought. It led him to embrace
certain elements of puritanism which met with an answering
echo more readily in England than they had encountered from
his revolutionary friends of Modena or Reggio. It was observed
long ago by Gaetano Salvemini that Mazzini's religious influence
was exercised in England rather than in Italy, and, most of all,
amongst English women; almost the only Italians, in fact, who
embraced it fully were those whom these English women
married. Salvemini attributed this to the classical tradition in
Italy:

"There is very little romanticism in the tradition of our culture, which
is almost entirely classical. Mazzini's mysticism is an outlook which
does not seem suited to our mental climate, or at least has not hitherto
succeeded in establishing itself in it".[2]

[1] *Mazzini Yesterday and To-morrow, Associazione Mazziniana Italiana*, 1954,
p. 10.
[2] *Mazzini*, Catania, 1915, p. 112.

These words were written in the year 1915. Since that date the Mazzinian religion has made headway in Italy. Mussolini, concerned to propagate ideas of duty and mission amongst the Italians, made much of Mazzini; but, more important, a new Mazzinian movement arose in Italy out of the war-time resistance and is now organized in the *Associazione Mazziniana Italiana*, which has published studies of considerable interest. There is also, for example, a Mazzinian review, the *Idealismo Realistico*; a recent article in this journal states: "It is clear enough" that, with the decay of Christianity, "the new religion is that of Giuseppe Mazzini".[1]

It goes without saying that this is an extreme standpoint and that the author arranges a somewhat premature burial for the Church in Italy. But it is useful to notice that Mazzini himself did exactly the same thing. Throughout his life, from his early preaching at Marseilles to his last important writing, which was an attack upon the Vatican Council of 1870, he was announcing that the Papacy was dead and that Christianity was dying. And it was precisely his view of the condition of Catholicism in his day that prompted his invocation of the "new religious synthesis", convincing him that humanity was in the very act of bringing forth from her womb the faith of the future. Since, also, it was his rooted belief that religions always emerge from humanity, his diagnosis of the religious conditions of his times was the necessary foundation of his own faith, and this lends a deep significance to the fact that he proved to be wrong about what was happening to Christianity in his own century. For the nadir of the Papacy was not in the nineteenth but in the eighteenth century. Many other observers, besides Mazzini, thought the Papacy was moribund; but actually it was just entering upon a period when it would grow greatly in spiritual (though not in temporal) influence while Christianity, whether Catholic or Protestant, was also about to enjoy a very notable revival, and to be spread all over the world.

The peculiar *animus* with which Mazzini attacked the Church, which helped to drive him on to construct his own theology, was part of his opposition to the ruling political powers of his day in

[1] Anno 21, Fascicolo 20, article by Maria Marchi.

Italy and of his anger at finding the Church generally supporting them. This led him, in the words of the Principessa di Belgioioso, to characterize Christianity as "a stupid and treacherous superstition, thrown in the eyes of the people to blind them and make them obedient to the clergy who had made themselves the chief instrument of the tyranny of the kings". The Saint-Simonians then convinced him that the people were capable of producing a new religion of their own, while the fate of Lamennais, who had tried to invert Catholic Authority, so that it derived from the People, and had been duly condemned by Pope Gregory XVI for doing so, finally persuaded him that the kind of religion for which he was looking could never be found within Christianity. This view was much strengthened in him by what he chose to call the "resignation" of Silvio Pellico, Manzoni, and a host of other Catholic patriots in Italy who seemed to him (as many Protestants later seemed to him in England) to place the salvation of their own souls before the emancipation of Italy.

On the other hand he sharply criticized the French revolutionaries for being anti-religious, and the secularism of many of the radicals of his own day, such as Guerrazzi, or Fazy, or Louis Blanc disgusted him. Religion, he was sure, was necessary; on this point he was at one with the Pope. But while the Papacy, impressed by the sufferings of Pius VI and Pius VII at the hands of the French Revolution, drew the deduction that, since the spirit of revolution was mostly secularist, it was wisest, for the sake of security for the Church's work for souls, to follow Saint Paul in supporting what was called legitimate authority, Mazzini drew the deduction that something new was alive in humanity which needed to be consecrated in a new religion. And because, throughout his lifetime, the Church continued generally to support the rulers in Italy (though taking a different line in Ireland, Belgium and Poland) Mazzini hardened in his opinion that it was not only blind to the times but also moribund. He may have been right in the former deduction – it is a matter for argument – but he was proved wrong in the latter.

As we turn to the theology he constructed we should notice, in passing, that he was more successful in his political than in his

religious forecasts, and this is not without bearing upon his
religious teaching because politics, with him, were only a branch
of religion. It seemed to many, just after the First World War,
that he had rightly understood his times, for the Treaty of
Versailles was supposed to create a Europe of free peoples, and
many of these peoples, especially those in central and eastern
Europe, were those to whose aspirations he had particularly
drawn attention. President Wilson, when he was still a professor
of history at Princeton, had lectured on him, and it was said that
the President's League of Nations had been foreshadowed by
Mazzini's Young Europe. Lloyd George, at Genoa in 1922, had
exclaimed "How right he was!". And if it is true that today much
of Europe – though perhaps not Italy – looks less Mazzinian than
it did in 1919 it is still something notable in politics to have been
proved right, a hundred years later, even if what has been fore-
seen does not last. In religion, however, anyhow as Mazzini
conceived it, something deeper and more lasting is to be expected
of prophecy, and it is not yet clear that the modern European
nations bear more than a superficial resemblance to Mazzini's
vision. It would rather appear, in fact, as though they were a long
way from being his "sacred peoples". They emerged, as he foresaw they would, from out of the ashes of the Austrian Empire,
but their relations with Heaven and with each other were not
what he intended. They were not free peoples, unravelling, in
harmony, the letters of God's law. It may be said that he had
warned of the the danger of a narrow nationalism, and also of
the danger of materialism, communism, and other things. But
the present nations can hardly rightly be seen as imperfect or
blighted Mazzinian peoples if only because the faith which he had
intended should bless their birth and bring them to fruition has
itself not yet emerged. "Not explicitly", some may say, "but
perhaps implicitly". But then Mazzini was quite explicit about
it, and even dogmatic.

And what was his dogma?
It had all been defined by the year 1836, before he left
Switzerland; his English friends, though they often tried, never
succeeded in modifying it.

First there is God, a separate, personal God, distinct from His creation. Mazzini clings to this theism, in the face of the pantheists as well as the materialists, and he reaffirms it, in answer to some vision, on his death-bed at Pisa, in March 1872 (*Si, si, credo in Dio!*). Yet Mazzini's God is a distant figure. He has set His universe in motion, giving it a Law of Progress which it must discern for itself and which will ultimately bring it to its own perfection. He does not interfere much in the painful processes of earth; He lives in heaven, where the virtuous, the *buoni*, will ultimately join Him; what happens to the bad, the *tristi*, is left uncertain. Too much a child of the Enlightenment to believe in hell, Mazzini yet does not relish the idea of meeting people like Louis Philippe in heaven.

God despatches to mankind, to guide her, Men of Genius – Hildebrand, Dante, Luther, Descartes, Newton, Napoleon, or Byron; these men point the way to the revelation of "the next letter of the Law". But, for Himself, God remains shadowy, a very pale reflection of the Christian God about whom Mazzini had been taught as a boy. Once He has given to Humanity the Law of Progress He leaves it to unravel that Law, for the most part unaided.

After God, His fundamental law, namely Progress.

Mazzini first learnt about Progress from Condorcet, whose book on the progress of the human spirit he was wont to read during Mass. But he learnt it again from the Saint-Simonians, in their paper the *Globe*, edited by Pierre Leroux, as well as from Herder, Victor Cousin, Comte, and no doubt others. It was the great discovery of the eighteenth century and the faith of the nineteenth. The idea of the progress of humanity provided the mainspring of his whole system, and had he been more severely logical in his theology he might have become, like his mentor Pierre Leroux, a pantheist, and a believer in reincarnation here on earth. Leroux felt that belief in inevitable progress really invited belief in reincarnation because only by reincarnation could the benefits won by progress be enjoyed by the generations which had gained them. God, and a distinct heaven, seemed to lie outside such a system and only to make the whole picture rather untidy. Mazzini felt the force of the argument and admitted to pantheism "in a certain sense". But he nevertheless clung to God and to heaven, and much that he has to say about Men of Genius and about the efficacy of martyrdom really confuses what he had been taught, as a child, about the Christian saints and what he learnt a little later about progress.

With an assurance which, even in the age of the romantics, was remarkable, Mazzini was ready to show how the law of progress had actually worked in history. So we hear much about the "immobile East" (the successor, in the age of the nineteenth century progressives, to the "civilized East" admired by the eighteenth century) and about the idea of liberty being introduced by the Greeks. Christianity had discerned and added a new letter of the law, namely equality, the equality of all men before God, and the Catholic Church of the middle ages had provided a "synthesis" for mankind which, at its best, recognized the liberty, the equality and the essential unity of mankind. Then, in a curious way, the cycle seems somehow to be repeated, for liberty is reintroduced by Luther and Descartes, and equality by the French Revolution. The synthesis, too, has somehow disappeared, and it is the peculiar mission of the nineteenth century to reassert this necessary idea. For the achievement of the eighteenth century and of the French Revolution has been to provide the apotheosis of the free individual – Napoleon, Byron and Goethe are the trio selected by Mazzini to illustrate his teaching that the individual has now attained to the highest point which he can reach in isolation. But the age of individuality is now over, and in future there will be no "great individuals" because the coming age will be the age of association, and especially of the nations. That is as far into the future as Genius (Mazzini) can penetrate, for the time being. But the probability is that the age of the nations will be followed by that of humanity.

Arbitrary and dogmatic as Mazzini was, the development of nationalism since his day has partly justified him, as the development of socialism has partly justified his Saint-Simonian mentors. The Saint-Simonians were chiefly interested in what we should now call the "planning" aspect of the matter, and in the vital rôle which scientists would play in the new civilization. Mazzini was chiefly interested in the nationalist aspect of it, and

in the religious justification with which the belief provided him
for preaching the moral unity of Italy and, until Italy should be
formed, of Young Italy. The Saint-Simonians, as good Frenchmen whose country had been united for some centuries, were not
so interested as was Mazzini in nationalism. Mazzini's tutors in
nationalism were Herder and Schlegel, whose country, like
Mazzini's, was yet to be born; it was from them that he learnt
about the missions of the different peoples and about the peculiar
contributions which the fatherlands of the future would bring to
the common stock of humanity. What seems, today, strangest
about these notions is that it does not seem to have occurred to
any of the romantics, and least of all to Mazzini, that the age of
the fatherlands would be other than an age of peace. "Cabinets
may cheat one another", wrote Herder in his *Ideen*, but "Fatherlands do not move against each other: they lie side by side in
peace and, like families, assist one another".[1] The romantics had,
however, no reason to envisage any difficulties because they had
abolished evil as something extraneous and artificial, introduced,
for their own ends, by the corrupt powers ruling societies, and
shortly to be removed by their own revolutionary efforts.
Humanity would be virtuous as well as free once she had shaken
off the shackles of the outmoded priesthoods, aristocracies and
princes. The people were good. They could be misled, but not for
long – the great task (as Rousseau had explained in the *Contrat
Social*) was to prevent their being deceived.

When he came to read Lamennais (who had himself read
Rousseau, and had tried to graft him on to Catholicism) Mazzini
found, in the Breton priest's *Paroles d'un Croyant* (1834), the
doctrine of an emergent humanity, a *peuple* which was pure and
good, and which contained hidden within itself the Truth; a
peuple which was the true interpreter of Christianity and which
might be deceived by rulers and aristocracies but could never be
finally corrupted. Lamennais "perfected Rousseau". Mazzini
had already taken from Rousseau that prophet's famous doctrine
of the General Will, the notion that the popular will "by virtue
of what it is is always what it ought to be", and the belief that
this Will periodically expresses itself by laying down the consti-

[1] Werke, Vol. 17, p. 319.

tutional principles of the State. From Lamennais he proceeded to take even more mystical notions about the People – the notion, for instance, that the Word of God was planted like a seed in Humanity, which was destined to bring it, through infinite suffering, to fruition. The *Paroles d'un Croyant* inspired Mazzini's *Faith and the Future*, published in the following year, in which, as we saw in Chapter 7, he wrapped his belief about with optimistic aspirations in words which would be echoed by romantic progressivists, on both sides of the Atlantic, in poetry and in prose, throughout the century:

"Forms change and are broken. Religions die out. The human spirit deserts them like the voyager the fire at which he warmed himself during the night. He enlightens his way by other suns; but religion remains . . . it disengages itself from the coating which analysis has pierced; it shines pure and brilliant, a new star in the sky of Humanity. But this again is only one beacon the more; and how many must be lighted by faith that the whole of the path of the future may be illumined? How many stars, unravelled concepts of each epoch, must be raised in the sky of intelligence that Man, complete embodiment of the earthly Word, may say to himself: *I have faith in myself; my destiny is accomplished?*".

The effect of Mazzini's writing on religion was to encompass the notion of Italy about with fleecy clouds which seemed to bear it upwards towards celestial heights and helped to give to nationalist impulses a heavenly halo and a place in the scheme of things ordained by the Creator. But, reiterated in every article and essay, and in a large proportion of his ten thousand published letters, his concepts, Progress, Humanity, Association, and the rest, naturally tend to pall, and it is hard to agree with the verdict of Bolton King, who said that the loss, somewhere in the Alps, of the manuscript in which Mazzini brought together his religious ideas is a loss more grievous to mankind than that of the manuscript of any unknown Greek tragedy. It is permissible, today, to sigh rather for the tragedy, if only because we have been left in little doubt about Mazzini's religious beliefs.

Beneath the superstructure of Mazzini's dogmatic theology lay its implications in the ordinary life of the individual – his moral theology.

"Life is a Mission. Virtue is sacrifice. Without these two principles I understand nothing".[1] "Every fact has two laws permanently superior to it. . . . One is the general law of the epoch . . . the other is the universal law of humanity".[2]

Mazzini thought that the general law of his own epoch was that a man must work for the association of the peoples into Nations; he must subordinate every aspect of his individual life to this purpose. Even the most intimate aspects of his family life should be dominated by this duty. He is much preoccupied with the rôle of women in inspiring and educating the young and he unhesitatingly prefers second-rate Italian poets or dramatists, in whom he can find a call to struggle for the national idea, to Manzoni, or Silvio Pellico, or Leopardi.

Since the new religion would be concerned with collectives, its initiator would be a people rather than a person, a people that for long had lain buried, silent, oppressed, ignored. Not the French people; they had more than fulfilled their mission to humanity by their gift of the Enlightenment and of the French Revolution. The new revelation might come from the struggling, heroic Poles, with their passionate patriotism. It might even come from the divided Germans, now awakening to a sense of Fatherland. But Mazzini did not much like or understand the Germans. There was, however, one supremely gifted people, from amongst whom had already, twice, gone forth the word of unity to the world, but who, for long, had lain dormant, and who had never been united into a nation. Surely the Italians had the opportunity, if they would only take it, not merely to unite their country, but to become the initiator-people of the new religion, so that their capital, Rome, city of the Caesars and city of the Popes, might for a third time give forth the word of unity to the world.

With the doctrine of the Third Rome we reach the point where the Mazzinian religion and Mazzini's practical political purposes for Italy become identified. In his prison-cell at Savona he had dreamt, as he stared out upon the sky and the sea, of an Italy one, united, and free, which had thrown out the Austrians,

[1] X, 323.   [2] I, 306.

thrown over the princes and the aristocracies, and made of herself a people who could set the example to the new Europe. Was this practical objective, then, the prime reality in his mind, the reality around which his whole religious synthesis shaped itself, merely to provide his politics with a good moral sanction?

We cannot so easily dismiss his religion to a secondary place, if only because most of his religious-political reading, and the framework of his faith, preceded the vision of the future Italy which he saw at Savona. Moreover his religion determined the kind of Italy that he preached. It was precisely because of his religious notions that he wanted to create an Italy with a sense of mission, and that he so detested the kind of Italy conceived by many of the Carbonari and by the later "Moderates". The notion of a nation with a mission is the most distinctive notion in his teaching and it is also what gives a dangerous edge to it. His "Italy" is a very highly charged concept and his attempts to preserve over against it the personal liberties which centre around the family were ineffective by comparison with his main theme, and it is not for them that he is remembered today.

Amongst the consequences of his idea of a messianic Italy were his teaching on National Education, which will instil patriotic precept into the young, and his determination that Italy shall be a large and centralized state and no mere federation. On this latter point he differs fundamentally from Rousseau, who wanted small city states like Geneva. Such states were no use to Mazzini because they were too weak to fulfil missions. It was for their smallness, and their consequent ineffectiveness *vis-à-vis* Europe, that he criticized the Swiss cantons even though they had preserved their republican liberties for five hundred years. The driving force of Mazzini's message is contained in this insistence upon purpose, what we may call his teleology. The individual and the family exist *for* the nation and the nation exists *for* humanity. And since humanity was, in his system, the interpreter of the will of God, its demands were, naturally enough, compelling. For the Christian concept of a soul responsible to God, its maker, and of a political and social order only ordained to safeguard the life of the free soul, he substituted a religion of humanity in which the soul was ultimately responsible to a law progressively discovered by humanity, whose progress its first duty was to foster, through the nation. All his attempts, alongside this collectivism, to preserve freedom for the soul, represented little more than a clinging to the Christian concepts in which he had been nurtured and which, despite himself, he still tried to preserve.

This antithesis becomes most clear when he treats of the supreme test of any faith, namely martyrdom. It is martyrdom that proves to him that progress and humanity are real, for he feels that martyrdom is man's highest act, yet it seems to him a senseless act unless humanity, in its progress, is going to enjoy the fruits. "Can you say 'in the name of thy own advantage sacrifice thyself! In the name of thy well-being die'?" A provocative question, and one which he was entitled to put to the Benthamites, or even to some of the Carbonari. But the martyrs of the centuries of Christendom could have replied:

"We did not suffer martyrdom primarily to win progress for posterity here on earth. We suffered for love of God, and of His truth, for the salvation of our own souls and in the hope of propitiation for the sins of others".

Martyrdom preoccupies Mazzini because he is certain that Italians will never win their liberty until they have learnt to die for it. And he believes that the revolutions of the Carbonari failed because their ideals were insufficiently lofty; they were only trying to win their personal and local rights. The revolutionaries will achieve nothing until they have learnt to think in terms of duty and mission. And Italy will not be made until she, too, is thought of as an instrument for the service of humanity, as possessed, herself, of a mission. All this is, in an important sense, impressive, because it is so infused with the notions of duty and sacrifice. But it is hard to see why Mazzini should deny the equal efficacy of self-sacrifice for purposes other than that of assisting the (inevitable) progress of mankind on earth; why a man might not die for what he called the "negative" right of individual liberty, for which the Carbonari, at their best, had shown themselves ready to die, or, likewise, for the sake of Christian devotion of the kind that sublimated the spirit of Silvio Pellico.

One is compelled to the conclusion that Mazzini's theology was important only to himself and to one or two converts later on, not as a force in history, or intrinsically, or on the merits of its logic, its profundity, or its appreciation of human nature. "For all his love of Dante he lacked Dante's sense of sin", says Mr. Griffith, and who has ever yet constructed a convincing theology while leaving out sin? When Italians won freedom to write and to argue more freely about such matters after the year 1846 they did not concern themselves with Mazzini's God, or with his Progress, Humanity, Duty, Thought-and-Action and the rest; but they did derive inspiration from what he had said about *Italia*, *Libertà*, and *Il Popolo* and still more from what he had suffered for them. The glow with which he had lit those words might for him be only a reflection of the light within him, but it was the reflection that men saw. The light itself escaped them, and has escaped most people since.

"Oh if the few intelligent Italians did but understand! If they could only feel, as I feel it, the hidden movement which pulses in the world. . . . If they but understood that either one must resign oneself to perish, blaspheming, in the void, or one must give oneself up to live or to die for the planting of the new faith, the new Gospel which will arise! . . .".[1]

Italians have neither blasphemed in the void nor have they planted the new faith. They have tried, for better or for worse, with success and with disaster, like the rest of mankind, to make their country; and in doing so, despite a sharp quarrel with Rome, they have mostly retained their traditional faith. But in their hard task they have been much strengthened and sustained by Mazzini, and chiefly by the example of his devotion. That devotion was even more obvious at the end of his life than it was when he withdrew from Switzerland; yet his decisive impact had been made before that date. His influence may have been less widespread than she supposed, but it must have been much what that singular lady said who knew him both at Genoa and at Marseilles, and whose remarkable beauty should not be allowed to obscure the fact that she was also intelligent – the Principessa di Belgioioso:

[1] XI, 313.

"Mazzini, as soon as he made his appearance [at Marseilles], sought to make himself an ally of God; but his God was the God of French revolutionaries, not the God whom the people of Italy adore; He was a God without forms of worship, without ministers, without churches, almost without laws . . . there was much talk about Giuseppe Mazzini, and the most widely opposed and exaggerated opinions were held about him . . . I believe that Giuseppe Mazzini's intentions were straight and pure, especially in those early days of what he called his apostolate . . . he succeeded, in the course of a very few years, in transforming the Italian people, and in inspiring them with hate of the foreign domination, and with the love of liberty and of independence, and of the freedom of their country".[1]

[1] R. Barbiera *Passioni del Risorgimento*, Milan, 1903, pp. 21, 122.

BIBLIOGRAPHICAL NOTE
PRIMARY SOURCES

A. *The Mazzini Papers.*

The original letters of Mazzini belonging to this earlier period of his life are mostly now either at the Museo del Risorgimento at Genoa which possesses, e.g., the Melegari correspondence, or at the Giunta Centrale di Storia Moderna in Rome, which possesses his correspondence with his mother. Nobody who has tried to decipher the originals will be inclined to minimize the labours of the National Commission, and the first thirteen volumes of their *Scritti editi ed inediti di Giuseppe Mazzini* (Imola, 1905–12) to which I have referred by volume and page only, provide the basic text for the subject, even though the explanatory annotation in these volumes and the dating of the letters sometimes today require correction. Volumes I and VIII contain Mazzini's youthful literary writings, II, III, IV, VI, VII and XIII his political articles, mostly taken from the *Giovine Italia* or *La Jeune Suisse*, and V, IX, X, XI and XII his letters. To these writings should be added his Autobiographical Notes, written between 1860 and 1865 as editorial explanation to the first collected edition of his works which was made during those years by GINO DAELLI. These notes were collated and published in Volume LXXVII of the National Edition and also in a small independent volume (Florence, *Le Monnier*, 2nd Ed., 1944) to which MARIO MENGHINI, the indefatigable secretary of the National Commission, supplied a valuable preface.

Thanks to the efforts of the National Commission it is unlikely that much more remains to be discovered which will throw light upon the first phase of Mazzini's life. Some precious collections of his letters were destroyed by their recipients for security reasons, as his mother destroyed those in her possession in the summer of 1832. Others, such as those written to Elia Benza in 1823–24 or to Démosthène Ollivier in 1833–35, have not been found but might yet conceivably come to light. The policy of the Commission is to publish, in Appendix volumes, whatever is found. Hitherto, most of the letters belonging to this period thus published late appeared in Appendix, Volume I (1938) which contained, amongst others, the earliest known letter of Mazzini – written to Elia Benza in 1825 – two letters to the historian Sismondi, two to the Polish leader, Stolzman, of February 1834 (both about the Savoy fiasco) and the whole collection of Mazzini's correspondence with Giuditta Sidoli of 1834–35, copies of which had been found by Fr. I. Rinieri amongst the secret police papers at the Vatican and published by him in *Il Risorgimento Italiano*, Volumes VIII–XII. An interesting letter of May 1834 to Paolo Pallia, surveying the prospects of Young Italy at that date, appeared in Appendix, Volume VI (1943). The only papers which the Commission is at present in course of publishing are miscellaneous personal notes of Mazzini's such as sketches for articles or fragments from his note-books. Some can be seen at the Istituto per la Storia del Risorgimento Italiano in Rome, others at the Museo del Risorgimento at Genoa. They mostly belong, like the interesting note-book published in 1954 by the Domus Mazziniana at Pisa, to later periods of Mazzini's life, but there are at Genoa a few note-books belonging to his youth, discovered and discussed long ago by Gaetano Salvemini and F. L. Mannucci.

B. *The Ruffini Papers*.

After Mazzini's own correspondence and articles the most important to our purpose are the papers of his friends of the Ruffini family. The letters of the two brothers Giovanni and Agostino to their mother during the period November 1833 to December 1836 have been published by Arturo Codignola in the two volumes entitled *I Fratelli Ruffini* (Genoa, 1925 and 1931). In quoting these volumes I have given the reference *Cod*. The originals of the letters, together with other papers of interest such as the brothers' correspondence with their friends, account books and diaries are available in the Archivio Ruffini of the Museo del Risorgimento at Genoa.

C. *Miscellaneous*.

A number of important documents bearing upon this phase of Mazzini's life were published by ALESSANDRO LUZIO. In *La Madre di Giuseppe Mazzini* (Turin, Bocca, 1919) he published Maria Mazzini's letters to her son of 1834–39 from police copies which he discovered at Turin. In *Mazzini Carbonaro* (Turin, Bocca, 1920) he printed extracts from the evidence given by Albinola, Doria, and others at Metternich's Milan Enquiry of 1831–33 into the activities of the secret societies. In his *Carlo Alberto e Giuseppe Mazzini* (Turin, Bocca, 1923) he printed extracts from the judicial proceedings of 1833 which resulted from the arrest of members of Young Italy. Luzio's method has been followed by later Italian historians, and most notably by ARTURO CODIGNOLA (*La Giovinezza di G. Mazzini*, Florence, 1925), in which appeared documents from the archives of the University of Genoa, and by E. PASSAMONTI (*Nuova luce sui processi del 1833 in Piemonte*, Florence, 1930).

We catch glimpses of Mazzini in the eighteen-thirties through the letters or memoirs of a variety of his friends or visitors at Marseilles or in Switzerland, such as the Principessa di Belgioioso, G. La Cecilia, Enrico Mayer or Niccolò Tommaseo; but much the most important evidence is that given by his treacherous associate Michele Accursi. In Volumes XVI–XXI of *Il Risorgimento Italiano* (1923–28) Fr. I RINIERI published a series of articles entitled *Le cospirazioni mazziniane nel carteggio di un transfuga* in which he brought to light the remarkable series of letters sent by Accursi to Pope Gregory XVI. The writer was a member of Young Italy who had been imprisoned in the Sant' Angelo in Rome in November 1832 for revolutionary activities but who had secured his release in March 1833 on the understanding that he would spy upon Mazzini and the revolutionary societies and keep Rome informed. This he proceeded to do, with remarkable effect, being trusted implicitly by Mazzini until October 1836 when the Chief first showed signs of suspecting him. Until the end of August 1833 Accursi was in Paris whereas Mazzini, until June of that year, was at Marseilles; the fact, therefore, that Accursi's accounts of what was being planned correspond closely with Mazzini's own accounts in his letters suggests that, if the plans did not always, in fact, originate in Paris, Mazzini must at least have been closely in touch with the revolutionary committees there. Thus the projected Neapolitan uprising, which is the theme of Mazzini's letters in July and August 1833, is outlined by Accursi from Paris as early as the beginning of July. On August 19th Accursi reports the despatch of 50,000 francs from Paris to Mazzini. From September 15th until after the Savoy invasion of the following January Accursi was with Mazzini at Geneva. Whether Mazzini ever appreciated the full extent of Accursi's treachery may be doubted. At all events Accursi sat alongside Mazzini in the revolutionary Roman Assembly of 1849 and appears to have enjoyed his confidence!

One other group of contemporary documents requires special mention: those which relate to the Savoy invasion of January 1834. The most important of those not printed in the National Edition are contained in (i) *Précis des derniers événements de Savoie, par le Général Ramorino* (Paris, Dupont, 1834) which is Ramorino's apologia; (ii) "Une relation inédite de l'expédition mazzinienne de Savoie en 1834" (*Rassegna Storica del Risorgimento Italiano*, Vol. 35, p. 229) which is a contemporary account by the Vice-Intendant of Faucigny; and (iii) *Mémoires sur La Jeune Italie et sur les derniers événements de Savoie* by HARRO-HARRING (Paris, 1834) which is the first-hand account of a participant in the exploit.

SECONDARY SOURCES

A. *Some selected studies bearing upon Mazzini's life before the year 1837.*

U. LIMENTANI, *L'attività letteraria di Giuseppe Mazzini* (Turin, 1950). Contains some interesting reflections upon the inner necessity which drove Mazzini to eschew a literary career.

A. SALUCCI, *Amori Mazziniani* (Florence, Vallechi, 1928). Despite its title this is a scholarly book and discusses much that is relevant, on the personal side, to the understanding of Mazzini's early life.

A. CUTOLO, *Gaspare Rosales, vita romantica di un mazziniano* (Milan, Hoepli, 1938). An eloquent exposition of Mazzini's debt to Rosales' generosity. But wherever Mazzini did go when he left Marseilles with Giuditta Sidoli in June 1833 it seems impossible that he should have gone to stay with Rosales at Lugano (cf. p. 74).

C. VIDAL, *Louis-Philippe, Mazzini, et la Jeune Italie (1832–34)* (Paris, Presses Modernes, 1934). Based upon the French diplomatic papers, this study shows (p. 114) that Mazzini was in touch with Louis Napoleon in the middle of the year 1834 through the agency of La

Cecilia and Colonel Vaudrey. But it is improbable that he was a party to schemes for reviving the Napoleonic Kingdom of Italy.

L. RAVENNA, *Il giornalismo mazziniano* (Florence, Le Monnier, 1939).

G. FERRETTI, *Mazzini e l'Europe Centrale* (Rassegna . . . 1939).

L. BALESTRERI, *Dati sulla tiratura e diffusione dei giornali mazziniani* (Rassegna . . . 1950).
Three studies of the vicissitudes of Mazzinian journalism.

E. ARTOM, *Un compagno di Menotti e di Mazzini, Angelo Usiglio* (Modena, 1949). Much of this is based upon Usiglio's letters to Melegari, which throw some light upon Mazzini's motives.

A. G. GARRONE, *Filippo Buonarroti e i rivoluzionari dell' Ottocento, 1828–37* (Florence, Einaudi, 1951). This is an important original study with a chapter entitled "Buonarroti e Mazzini". Garrone stresses the close contact between Mazzini and Buonarroti in the vital year 1831, a contact maintained partly by a correspondence now lost and partly through their mutual friend Bianco and the society of the Apofasimeni. To Buonarroti's influence he attributes the extreme social and economic egalitarianism – the *babeuvism* – of Mazzini's revolutionary propaganda during his first year at Marseilles. Later, in 1832–33, Mazzini came under the influence of the Saint-Simonians, then active in the city, and his viewpoint tended to veer away from the "suffering, blood, terror" of the class war when he became more preoccupied with his new mentors' more humane notion of Association. His intimate friend became Démosthène Ollivier and he began to share the viewpoint, amongst the French radicals, rather of Carrel of the National or of Cavaignac of the Tribune than the extreme position occupied by Buonarroti.
Moreover, their national prejudices helped to separate the two leaders. To Buonarroti Paris remained the focal centre; he looked back to the year 1793 and his ideal was a Europe of egalitarian republics loosely federated with France. Mazzini looked to an Italian initiative and to emancipation from the French ascendancy. The quarrel was aggravated by the progress of Buonarroti's Veri Italiani and became irreparable as a result of his opposition to Mazzini's Savoy invasion.
Much of this was already deducible from the National Edition, but Garrone has shown the picture from the other side illustrating, for example, from his circulars to his own secret societies Buonarroti's growing mistrust of Mazzini.

B. *A few of the better general books on Mazzini.*

JESSIE WHITE MARIO, *Della vita di Giuseppe Mazzini* (Milan, Sonzogno, 1886). Written by a disciple, but even its extraneous material and its undisguised hero-worship are valuable as bearing witness to what the Mazzini myth meant to those who had known the master.

BOLTON KING, *Life of Mazzini* (Dent, 1902). The first serious attempt to make a balanced estimate of Mazzini's significance, but rather arbitrary in its judgments and standing in greater need of correction than its author anticipated was likely.

G. SALVEMINI, *Mazzini* (Catania, 1915). The great Italian scholar had already made important discoveries concerning Mazzini's student days. In this book he made a critical, even harsh analysis of Mazzini's thought, which he separated from his life.

F. DE SANCTIS, *Mazzini* (Bari, Laterza, 1920). Contains much penetrating criticism by the well-known Italian literary critic.

G. GENTILE, *I profeti del Risorgimento Italiano* (Florence, Vallechi, 1924). A study of Mazzini's and Gioberti's politico-religious idealism by a pupil of Benedetto Croce who became Mussolini's Minister of Education.

G. O. GRIFFITH, *Mazzini, Prophet of Modern Europe* (Hodder and Stoughton, 1932). A brilliantly written book, the best in English, it recaptures the spirit of Mazzini but is unashamedly uncritical of its subject.

A. CODIGNOLA, *Mazzini* (Turin, E.T.E.T., 1946). A balanced recent life by a distinguished Mazzinian scholar.

E. MORELLI, *Giuseppe Mazzini, saggi e ricerche* (Rome, Ateneo, 1950). Some penetrating essays by the present secretary of the National Commission. It includes a balanced survey of the more important historical writing on Mazzini.

A. LEVI, *Mazzini* (Florence, Barbera, 1955). The most recent study, and one which takes into account, though in a relatively brief compass, the whole range of Mazzinian studies.

APPENDIX

The Problem of Mazzini's Child by Giuditta Sidoli

As I have suggested earlier, the importance to our subject of the birth and brief life of Mazzini's and Giuditta's child consists in the crisis it caused in Mazzini's life in the summer of the year 1833 and in his preoccupation with it for some months afterwards.

For long, despite the compelling evidence produced by Fr. Rinieri when he published the Mazzini-Giuditta correspondence of 1834–35, and despite the explicit testimony (which Bolton King refused to accept) of the French Premier Émile Ollivier, son of Démosthène, who remembered the "beautiful Italian from Reggio" and her baby by Mazzini left in his father's house, the child's very existence was denied by Mazzinian *dévotes* who regarded it as inconsistent with their hero's purity of soul. Today it is common ground that the child existed. The problems are: When was it born? When did it die? And why did the parents fly so abruptly from Marseilles in the middle of June 1833?

Until comparatively recently, from the time, that is, when Arturo Salucci published his suggestive but scholarly *Amori Mazziniani* in 1928 until the appearance in *Il Ponte*, in May 1951, of a disturbing article by Alessandro Garrone, it seemed fairly certain that the baby was born at Montpellier in July 1833 and that Mazzini's departure with Giuditta from Marseilles the month before had been due to his desire to stand by her, in her confinement, away from the other revolutionaries. How else were to be interpreted their secrecy, Mazzini's references to the claims of delicacy, Usiglio's appeals to Melegari's honour and delicacy, or Giuditta's "I cannot justify myself; appearances are too much against me . . ."? The police reports had shown that Giuditta arrived at Marseilles in February of 1832; by October of that year Mazzini was staying hidden, for a brief spell, at her house. The evidence seemed to point to a birthday in the high summer of 1833.

However, in his article in the *Ponte* Garrone disclosed that he had found what looked like the child's birth certificate in the city archives at Marseilles and the date of birth was not 1833 but August 11th 1832. The names of the child on the certificate were Josèphe, Démosthène, Adolphe, Aristide, and it was described as "of parents unknown". Josèphe was Mazzini's name, Démosthène that of the foster-father, and Aristide that of Démosthène's brother who was friendly with them all. The witnesses were Démosthène Ollivier and a certain J. Reymonet, a Marseilles doctor, later mentioned in Mazzini's letter to Giuditta of April 17th 1835 as treating their anonymous "A" (the symbol by which they normally referred to their baby). Moreover, Garrone also found the same child's death certificate which notified decease at the age of two and a half on February 21st 1835, Démosthène again being one of the witnesses.

This discovery is, to say the least, very suggestive. But if the certificate does indeed relate to Mazzini's child we must abandon various suppositions held hitherto. Thus Giuditta must have come to Marseilles in 1831, not in February 1832, or must, at least, have visited Marseilles in the earlier year. Much more difficult, Mazzini's references to the child in his letters to Giuditta during most of the year 1835 are hard to explain if the child had, in fact, died in February. Either Démosthène Ollivier deliberately kept him in the dark about the child's death or else Mazzini was deliberately concealing the fact from Giuditta. Either explanation is possible, given the almost suicidal state of mind of the parents at that time. And finally, the crisis of the summer of 1833, with the hurried departure of both parents from Marseilles, must have been due to some other cause than the child's impending birth, because it was already born. Possibly the baby was already with Giuditta's friends at Montpellier and had fallen gravely ill – we know that it was constantly ailing afterwards.

One very odd piece of evidence seems to support Garrone's theory. In a letter of October 6th 1832 to Accursi, in Rome, Mazzini, as was often his practice, prefaced a serious instruction, written in invisible ink, with a pretence letter, written in ordinary ink, and intended to throw the police off the scent. In this pretence letter, which is concerned with fictitious business matters, occurs the surprising sentence: "How are your boys? The elder is at school? I have placed mine at Montpellier, and they tell me that he makes good progress".[1] Though this sentence is part of a "pretence" it seems very odd that it should have been a pretence which, in the following year, became a truth. But, if Garrone is right, then their child, having been born nearly two months earlier, probably was, indeed, already at Montpellier when this was written. Mazzini was fond of amusing himself by inserting bits of the truth into his deceptions of the police and it would seem he may have been doing so here. At all events such a supposition is easier than the supposition that the statement was wholly fictitious and yet – by a coincidence – a child of his *was* at Montpellier in the following year, which is the coincidence required by the earlier theory.

Despite the difficulties, it would seem likely that the certificates at Marseilles do, indeed, refer to the child of Mazzini and Giuditta.

[1] V. 145, 146.

INDEX